Other Books by Linda West Eckhardt

America Loves Hamburgers

America Loves Chicken

Feed Your Family on Ten Dollars a Day

Barbecue Indoors and Out

The Only Texas Cookbook

Linda Eckhardt's Great Food Catalog

Books by Linda West Eckhardt and Diana Collingwood Butts

Rustic European Breads

Bread in Half the Time

Dessert in Half the Time

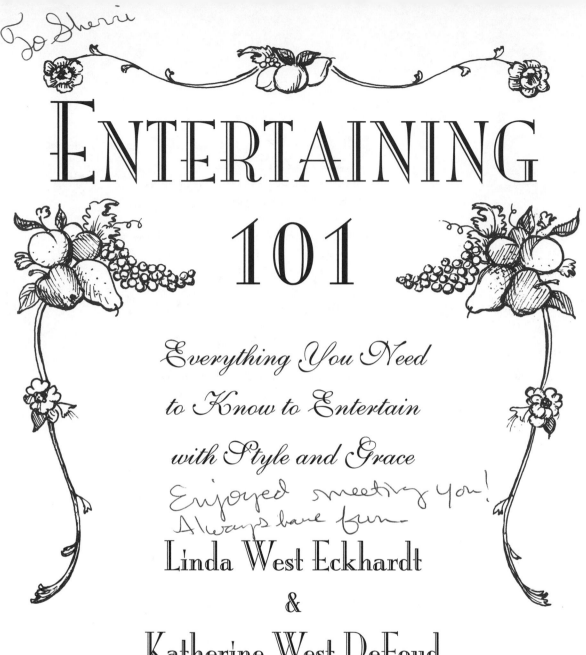

To Sherie

ENTERTAINING 101

*Everything You Need
to Know to Entertain
with Style and Grace*

*Enjoyed meeting you!
Always have fun*

Linda West Eckhardt

&

Katherine West DeFoyd

Kathein West DeFoyd

Doubleday

NEW YORK LONDON TORONTO SYDNEY AUCKLAND

Published by Doubleday

a division of Bantam Doubleday Dell Publishing Group, Inc.

1540 Broadway, New York, New York 10036

Doubleday and the portrayal of an anchor with a dolphin are
trademarks of Doubleday, a division of Bantam Doubleday Dell
Publishing Group, Inc.

Book design by Jennifer Ann Daddio

Library of Congress Cataloging-in-Publication Data
Eckhardt, Linda West, 1939–
Entertaining 101 : everything you need to know to entertain with
style and grace / Linda West Eckhardt and Katherine West DeFoyd.
—1st ed.
p.   cm.
Includes index.
1. Entertaining. 2. Menus. 3. Cookery.   I. DeFoyd, Katherine West.
II. Title.
TX731.E25   1997
642—dc21   97-10623
CIP

ISBN 0-385-48542-5

1 3 5 7 9 10 8 6 4 2

This book is dedicated to
Gordon Murray,
Great Cook and Enthusiastic Taster,
with love and devotion

ACKNOWLEDGMENTS

This book is the result of generosity. A group of friends, their elbows on the table, got together and said, yes, you can do this. You can put all our best ideas on paper, in one place, so that the next time we want to have a dinner party, we can pull this book down off the shelf and find answers. Never mind that we're all overworked, overcommitted, and barely have a chance to catch our breath, we want to entertain—and here are our best contributions.

First of all, we want to acknowledge the commitment our editor, Judy Kern, at Doubleday, has made to this project. She believed in the concept, she believed in our ability to throw this shindig. Her good cheer and great wisdom are notable. We are grateful.

We are also grateful to the people who made this book happen. To Martie Holmer, who illustrated the text, to Amy King, who designed the book jacket, and to Jennifer Daddio, who designed the book. The fact that you "got it" when you only had an intermediate draft to work from makes us feel humble and proud.

Thanks also to Jill Melton at *Cooking Light* magazine, for the thoughtful instruction that has made us better cooks and recipe testers. Many recipes in this book got their start by passing through the *Cooking Light* test kitchen; and for Becky Pate and the excellent test kitchen staff, we appreciate your educated appraisal of both recipes and menus.

We also thank the Center for Reproductive Medicine and Infertility at Cornell Medical Center for giving us the impetus to start this project, and we thank them for coming through—just at the right moment. We're shopping for more chairs to pull up around our dinner tables as this book goes to print, high chairs that is, and are we happy about that!

To Gordon Murray, Katherine's husband and soulmate, we thank you for your unflagging attention to detail, for editing, and cooking, and thinking, and supporting us in the making and marketing of this book. You're the best husband a woman could have, and the best son-in-law on the planet.

We had a lot of help from food purveyors. First of all, Mr. McFadden, who owns Staubitz Meats in Brooklyn, and who taught us how to treat a good piece of beef. To Jim and Andy, whose fruits and vegetables were simply perfect, and to the spice and herb gurus at El Asmar for providing us not only with product, but also with ancient wisdom about how best to use these little fillips that make a meal memorable. Thanks to Wendy Burrell of the Burrell Group, who provided us with terrific Norseland cheeses and filo dough for testing. These are the real party foods.

LeCreuset, and Nadine at the Phoenix Mall in particular, provided us with great cookware and advice on how to get the most out of it. We thank you.

To the three experts who generously gave us their time for the interchapters about pairing wines with foods, creating a cheese course, and borrowing caterers' techniques, we really thank you. Our hats are off to Paul Bolles-Beaven, co-owner and wine master of the Union Square Café, New York; Lea Batzold, day manager of Chanterelle Restaurant, New York; and Suzanne Tinker McCray, Celebrations Catering and Lexmark International, Lexington, Kentucky. We are grateful to you for sharing your wisdom.

To Lizette Reyes Cain, Katherine's Phi Beta Kappa friend from San Francisco State University days, who edited this book from the get-go (Lizette would never let us say get-go in the book. Too colloquial, she'd frown), many thanks.

We particularly wish to acknowledge the generous support of Marlys Bielunski and the National Cattlemen's Beef Association, who made promotion of this book possible.

To all those friends who gathered 'round our table to offer recipe suggestions, menus that had worked for them, and ideas galore—Diana Collingwood Butts, Alicia Villamarin, Debra Pucci, Melissa Schenker, Meredith Pollack, Sylvia Kristal, Barbara Askins, Sandra Mounier, and Andrew Jack in Paris—we say thanks.

Thanks to Jeanne Voltz for organizing our trip to France. Your knowledge of food and enthusiasm for cooking are an inspiration to us. Thanks to Anne Willan for offering La Varenne to us for cooking and testing. Thanks to Karen Haram for recommending the Northern Ireland trip, and thanks to the Northern Ireland Tourist Board and the Bushmills Whiskey people for making it happen.

Thanks to all the Eckhardt clan for gathering at our house for testing and tasting: the doctors Laurel Eckhardt Young, Michael Young, and Natalie and Arissa Eckhardt Young. Thanks to Eric Schmidt, who proved that fourteen-year-old boys can learn to make perfect two-crust fruit pies—day in and day out for weeks on end, and love doing it. Thanks to Jay Eckhardt and Cara Roberts for enthusiastic participation at meals. We're grateful to Joe Eckhardt, who ate his way through yet another book project with good cheer.

We believe Auntie Mame was right when she said that life is a banquet. We're grateful so many people showed up for this affair. Thanks to you all.

Linda West Eckhardt
Katherine West DeFoyd

Ashland, Oregon, and South Orange, New Jersey
July 1997

Contents

SPRING: A NEW BEGINNING

THE BOUNTY OF AUTUMN

ENTERTAINING
101

Introduction

Entertaining at home goes in and out of fashion. Once the go-go eighties had receded into memory, Americans began, once again, to think of throwing parties at home. The Boomers began families and found it wasn't as easy as it had been to get out to restaurants. The Generation X-ers found that, indeed, apartments do come with kitchens. We all began to long for the safety of Ward and June Cleaver, the "Brady Bunch," those sitcoms that served as baby-sitters for a generation of cooks and diners who now turn the key in the lock and order the meals. Dinner parties are back. Cocktail parties are back. Cigars are back. Good grief, before you know it, pill box hats will be back.

But some things have changed—irrevocably.

There was a time when a celebration meant days of planning and days of cooking. It also meant days for recuperation. After all, there were dirty dishes from one end of the kitchen to the other. There were wine-stained linens. Crumbs on the carpet. Occasionally, olive pits in the potted plants. There were painful moments of truth. Can I ever do this again?

Life in the last gasp of the twentieth century has become one interminable New York minute, and the thought of preparing another of those sumptuous multicourse fiestas has become nothing more than a fleeting hope/nightmare.

The truth is that our lives are so harried, most of us don't do any real cooking for midweek dinners. After work, we may never use recipes or menus at all. We just make do and get something together to feed ourselves. But for special events, nothing is quite so welcome as a home-cooked meal.

This book gives you all the information you need to throw a terrific party at home—and is suitable for both beginning cooks and those with more experience. It is, indeed, our basic course in entertaining. Glance over the menus and you may say to yourself, they sound too ambitious for beginners. But we not only tested them ourselves, we turned them over to some less experienced cooks who have given these menus their enthusiastic seal of approval.

Truth be told, *none of us*, experienced or not, has a lot of time to devote to entertaining, even on the most special holidays. If we can give a couple hours to preparation for Thanksgiving dinner, say, we're lucky. Sure, the turkey cooks for hours and hours, but we're talking time in the kitchen getting everything else ready.

We have simplified all these recipes, eliminating unnecessary steps. And we have worked out the timing for each menu. We realize that learning how to time a meal so that all of the dishes are ready at the same time comes only with experience. We have worked with these menus, and we have worked out the kinks.

We're the first to admit the powerful attraction to tradition. We want to gather friends and family around us to mark the special moments in our lives. We still do want to entertain. What's changed is the *way* we entertain.

We've finally let go of the make-everything-from-scratch-mantra that enslaved us and made entertaining more an endurance contest than a pleasure. Now, we'll add our own touches to a box cake, buy a loaf of bread from the bakery, choose ready-washed greens for the salad, and commercially prepared pasta sauces and salsas to pump up the dinner party flavors.

We believe there is no one *right* way to do anything. Want to serve dinner from a black pot at the kitchen table? Why not? If the stew is well made and the kitchen warm and toasty, nothing will please your friends and family more. Want to do your entertaining in the morning? Brunches are a great way to kick off the weekend. Don't have a lot of fancy dishes and table-setting stuff? So what? Let the food be the star at your table.

As French chef Marc Meneau, in the Burgundy four-star restaurant à l'Espérance, told us, much of what makes a stylish feast is nothing more than careful shopping. With the proliferation of exotic ingredients and the mainstreaming of first-quality prepared specialty foods, fixing a memorable feast for family and friends is eminently doable. Many dishes are naturally beautiful. Roasted red peppers, shiny and bright; endive, cool and green; golden polenta; red strawberries; curry. Really, you don't have to be a food stylist to make food look gorgeous.

We're mother and daughter and have been preparing family feasts together for more than thirty years. Now that we're separated by career moves and time zones, we've continued to share our entertaining secrets across the country, from Oregon to New York and back, via fax, phone, and e-mail. Daughter, Katherine, is Director of Development for Media Workshop New York, a project of the Bertelsmann Foundation. Over the years, working in City Hall for New York City mayor, David Dinkins, then for Manhattan borough president, Ruth Messinger, she's picked up time- and labor-saving tips from caterers, florists, and banquet managers.

Mom, Linda, award-winning cookbook author of a baker's dozen books, contributing editor to *Cooking Light,* and contributor to the Chicago Tribune Media Services, has learned valuable lessons from readers who have been telling her how they do it for more than twenty years. Linda put Katherine in the kitchen before she put her into school, stirring together cakes, setting the table, entertaining the company. This book represents a collection of the ideas the two have worked out through years of experience both together and separately.

To prepare for this book, we spent time together, cooking and shopping and interviewing on both coasts, at Martha's Vineyard, Dutchess County, New York, Philadelphia, Ashland, Oregon, and in Burgundy, Alsace, and the Provence regions of France. Katherine took a couple of brush-up courses at Peter Kump's Manhattan Cooking School and Linda did some workshops at International Association of Culinary Professionals (IACP). But mainly, we just did what we've always done—lived to cook and to eat, loved to entertain and share ideas and the wealth of our larders with each other and with friends and family.

We both threw a lot of parties to test recipes and ideas for this book. The summer of '96 will always be remembered in our family for the three weeks in Oregon when one of Linda's other daughters, Laurel Eckhardt, and her husband, Michael Young, also came from New York with their two daughters, Natalie, nine, and Arissa, seven, and Houston cousin Eric Schmidt, fifteen. In a whirlwind three-week period, we held family celebrations and retested the menus in the manuscript for all the major holidays.

We celebrated Thanksgiving, Christmas, St. Patrick's Day, The Fourth of July, and Halloween. The kids helped with the cooking, the decorating, and the cleanup. We put up a mini-Christmas tree one night. Wore Halloween costumes another. We had skits. We went for picnics in the woods.

For his part, Eric made a double-crust fruit pie every night for two weeks. At the end of that period he could have gotten a job as a pastry chef. The little girls learned to use knives properly and to set the table. By telescoping the entire year into one short period, we were able to feel—just for a moment—what it was like to have a traditional family, where the generations live in the same neighborhood. Quite unlike the actuality of our family, where three generations are scattered from coast to coast and professional demands for all are intense.

We wouldn't want you to get the idea that writing this book together was all roses and champagne. We found we had some rather opinionated differences. (Imagine—two generations of opinionated women. What a shock. How could that have happened?) When asked the question, "When should you make the party potluck?" Linda replies *any time you can* and Katherine says *never.* But that simply represents the difference in our age, temperament, and locale.

In Oregon, among the semirural people of a certain age, potlucks are the rule. We've even been to a potluck wedding—a second wedding, the mother of the bride informed us, but potluck and proud of it, nevertheless. Katherine is rather scandalized at the whole idea.

But then again, she lives in South Orange, New Jersey. Her friends must come to visit on the train or in a car. It's not too practical to think of lugging along a vast salad or a crockpot of stew when you're confined by transportation. So, as we say again and again, you should do what works for you.

We actually have a third partner in this project, Katherine's husband, Gordon, who never let his day job on Wall Street get in the way of fine-tuning the text of this book, acting as syntax taskmaster and recipe tester extraordinaire. Gordon does a lot of writing in his job at Standard and Poors, and he made us as careful as accountants, whether we liked it or not.

And Katherine's friend from college, Lizette Reyes Cain, exercised her Phi Beta Kappa standards on the logic and grammar of the book. We are grateful for her patience, intelligence, and good taste.

Katherine and Gordon worked on this book weeknights and every weekend for more than a year. Linda worked on it while keeping up a busy magazine and newspaper writing schedule combined with cooking school and seminar duties all over this country. Not to mention, taking care of Joe and the dogs. We cooked and tested and cross-tested for each other and through it all remained friends.

So that now, together, bridging the regional, work, and generation gaps, we offer you a way out of the nineties' dilemma and tackle the question, can you still entertain with style and grace while your life is racing by? We think so.

What You'll Find in This Book

We've suggested fifty-two seasonal menus, each with three or four recipes and suggestions for things to buy to fill in. The menus developed here take into consideration the taste, color, and texture of the foods we recommend. They also include timing suggestions, so that all the food is ready at once. Finally, every meal will look good without hours of elaborate garnishing tricks. After all, nature made most of the foods we recommend beautiful; you just have to compose them attractively on the plate.

What You Won't Find in This Book

You won't find overly ambitious faux Martha Stewart efforts at big shindigs like home weddings where you do everything but make the dirt for the floor of the tent. No, not here. You see, the ugly secret is that Katherine and I did her wedding that way. We fed 150 people a sit-down dinner we had cooked ourselves with the help of a New York Peter Kump Cooking School graduate chef and a couple of college kid waiters. It was *way* too much work. Everyone had a marvelous time—except us. Never again. We took the vow. And it is our oath to you. If you need to feed and water a large group of people, call a caterer. Life is too short. Believe us. We speak from experience.

How to Use This Book

Each menu has a list of preparation steps to help you with the timing. "All the Trimmings" tells you how to serve the meal and offers suggestions for arranging the food and decorating the table. Wine suggestions are also included. Each recipe lists the preparation time and the cooking time and how far in advance you can make the dish. A roast chicken, for example, may take only five minutes of preparation time but must cook for one hour. Of course, during that hour you can shower, have a glass of wine, whatever.

Soon, you'll probably be mixing and matching the recipes, as we do. At the back of the book, we've given you a collection of our own secret weapons, including our suggestions for a basic 101 pantry, including both the hardware and software we find essential, as well as an appendix of good mixed drinks.

Whatever you do, don't ignore the interchapters. We've interviewed some of the nation's best-known talents about their specialties: Wine expert, Paul Bolles-Beaven, managing partner at Union Square Café in New York, offers a short course in pairing wines and foods and has suggested appropriate wines for all our menus. The manager of another New York four-star restaurant, Chanterelle, Lea Batzold, who is responsible for buying and planning that restaurant's famous cheese course, tells us how to make a terrific cheese course at home. Experienced caterer and giver of fabulous parties, Suzy Tinker McCray, of Lexington, Kentucky, former owner of Celebrations by Suzanne Catering, shares her secrets for a successful party. The suggestions of all these experts will make entertaining *easy* for you.

Entertaining is about comfort, about making people feel safe in the lap of tradition. Just remember that in order for your guests to be relaxed, *you* must be relaxed. For you to be relaxed, everything must be under control *before* the guests step over the threshold. This book will help you get control of your kitchen and pantry. Think of it as your first course in entertaining. Who knows? We believe you'll find yourself entertaining more often. After all, feeding people is lots of fun.

How to Set the Table

Sometimes we set the table days before the party. Sometimes, only moments. You should do what suits your time and temperament. Do you want a formal setting or a more informal one?

Whether you use a tablecloth, place mats, or simply a gleaming bare table, the first step is preparing the tabletop to suit your taste. Add lots of candles for evening—all over the house—and the centerpiece of your choice.

Make sure you choose a centerpiece that people can see over and around. Nothing is more annoying than a tabletop extravaganza that makes you feel like Tarzan and Jane in the jungle, trying to see through the bush to locate the other guests.

Fold or roll the napkins and place them in napkin rings if you wish. Napkins can be placed to the left of the dinner plate, on the dinner plate, or at the head of the dinner plate. Your choice. For special events, you could make decorative bows to tie around the napkins. If you're using place markers to assign seating for a formal dinner, write them out in your neatest handwriting and place them at the head of each dinner plate.

Actually, with rare exceptions, we think you're better off skipping place markers. An attentive host or hostess will pay attention to the conversations that begin during cocktails and let guests group-up according to their own desires. You can, of course, use a more formal approach, placing a guest of honor to the right of the host, with that guest's escort to the right of the hostess, then placing people in a sequence that keeps the men and women alternating around the table. But for most home parties, this seems a bit too formal to suit our tastes. Since our aim is to make our guests feel comfortable, we'd rather let them choose for themselves.

Now, as to the actual table settings—think about English movies you've seen where the white-gloved butler is walking around the dining table with a ruler measuring to make sure the downstairs maid has placed the silverware exactly one inch away from the table's edge and that each place setting is exactly twenty-four inches from plate center to the next plate center.

We never use a ruler, but we do make an effort to allow each diner sufficient elbow room and to make the silverware look nice around the dinner plates. Where to put the silver is easy. Place the knife and spoon(s) on the right side, and the fork(s) on the left, arranging the silver in the order it will be used from the outside in. In other words, if you're using a salad fork for a salad you're serving before the main dish, the salad fork goes on the outside to the left of the dinner fork on the left side of the plate. However, if you're using the salad fork for dessert, or for salad served *after* the main dish, the salad fork is placed

Formal Table Setting

Informal Table Setting

beside the plate, inside the dinner fork. Boy, this does begin to sound as complicated as a computer manual. But lay it out and you'll see it's easier to do than to say.

Turn the blade of the dinner knife toward the plate, then lay the spoon(s) beside the knife, so that you now have a dinner plate placed in the center, and at least one inch from the edge of the table, with a knife and spoon(s) to the right, and fork(s) to the left.

Place the water goblet above the blade tip of the dinner knife. Add wineglasses to the right of the water goblet. You may choose an all-purpose wineglass, or specialized glass-ware—a straight-sided white wineglass, a rounded glass for reds, an oversized balloon for either—as well as for a lot of desserts—a brandy snifter, a champagne flute, and a dessert wineglass.

Salt and pepper shakers should be arranged between every two places.

How to Fold Napkins

We like no-iron cotton or linen napkins that are about eighteen to twenty inches square. No matter which way you fold napkins, keep the hemmed edges folded inside, and place the folded napkin with the four corners folded nearest the diner's left hand so it will be easy to unfold in the lap.

If you wish to do the simplest presentation of a napkin, suitable for formal and in-formal dinners, fold the napkin into a classic rectangle, folding the napkin first into quarters, then folding that square into a rectangle about $4^1/2 \times 9^1/2$ inches. Place the napkin to

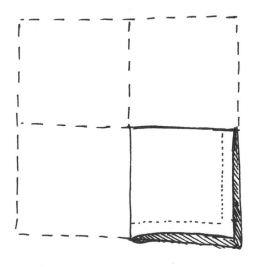
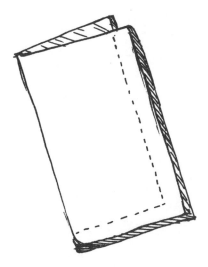

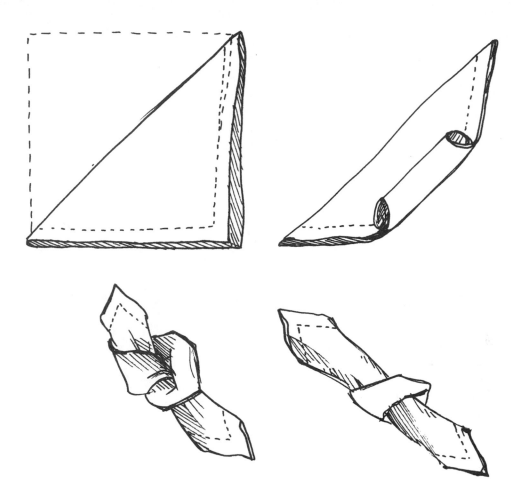

the left of the plate, with the four points placed on the inside beside the dinner plate, with or without a ring, nearest the table's edge.

Our favorite way to handle napkins is with a napkin ring. We each have several sets, of pewter, wood, and ceramic. We sometimes mix and match them. At other times, we use only the more formal pewter. To place a napkin in a ring, fold it into quarters, making about a nine-inch square. Holding the napkin by the folded corner, pull it halfway through the napkin ring. Even simpler, pinch up the center of an unfolded napkin and stuff it through the ring, creating a ruffled "skirt" look. You may simply roll the folded napkin. Place this to the left of the plate, on the plate, or at the head of the plate.

Another simple way to fold a napkin is known as a Bow Tie. Fold the napkin into a triangle, then, beginning with two points, roll it to form a cylinder. Tie a loose knot at the

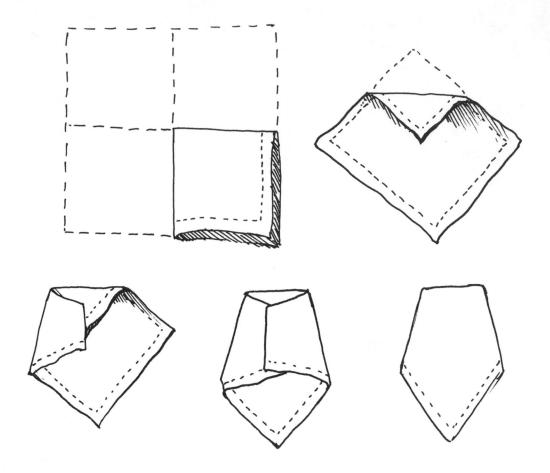

center and adjust the ends to form a V shape. If you wish, tuck little flowers, decorations, or favors your guests can take home into the knot. Last year at Thanksgiving, we used this method and tied a sprig of dried herbs into each knot.

A graceful, more formal fold is called the Astoria. Fold the napkin into quarters with the points facing away from you. Fold the top points down to the center. Now fold the left corner so that its point reaches just past the center. Cross the right corner over the left. Turn the napkin over and place it on the plate or to the left of the plate.

For buffet service you can make one of several choices. Stack folded napkins beside the silverware at one end of the buffet table or in a basket. We like to place forks and spoons in glasses or sturdy vases, tines and spoon bowls *up*, for easy pick up by guests. If you have more time, sit down and make individual place settings by folding napkins into what's known as the Buffet Server. This napkin fold holds the silverware and looks attractive grouped on a buffet sideboard. Fold a napkin into quarters with the cut points away from you. Fold the point of the top layer down to meet the bottom corner, forming a pocket. Fold the left and right corners under, then tuck cutlery into the pocket.

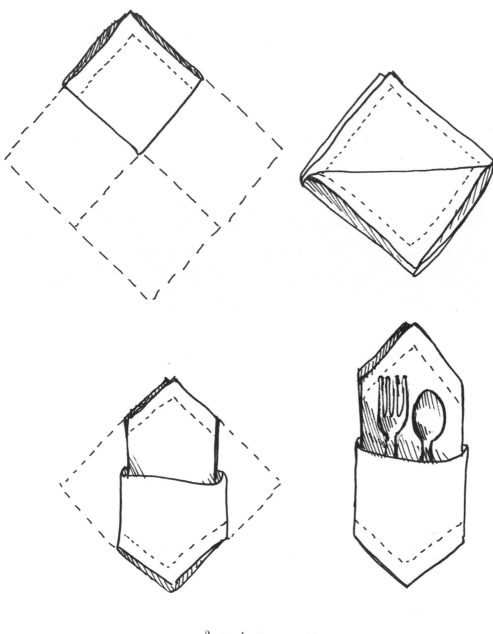

Four Styles of Food Service

In this book, in the "All the Trimmings" sections we recommend one of four types of food service: buffet, family, formal family-style, or plate service. Because *formal* service calls for servants, we only call for formal *family* service. Our recommendation depends on many factors. How formal is the party? How many guests are invited? What is on the menu? and What is the occasion? Below is a description of each type of service and the elements involved.

BUFFET SERVICE

- *Accommodates as many diners as your house can comfortably hold.*

- *May be laid out on a sideboard, on a dining room table, or in the kitchen. The table need not be against the wall. Katherine has an oval table she puts in the center of the room so you can walk completely around it.*

- *Stack dinner plates at the beginning of the line, then cold foods, then hot, with any carved meat at the end of the line with the silverware so your guests don't have to balance too many items as they serve themselves.*

- *Use warming trays or candles under dishes or chafing dishes to keep the hot food hot.*

- *Set up drinks, dessert, and condiments at separate stations.*

- *Make decorative additions organic to the arrangement, using edible fruits and nuts in a centerpiece, and scattering them along the buffet table to unify the theme.*

FAMILY SERVICE

- *Suitable for casual meals.*

- *Serves as many as your table(s) will comfortably hold.*

- *Salads, the appetizer course, or the soup course may be preset before the guests sit down.*

- *Guests seat themselves according to their wishes or the host or hostess's direction.*

- *All food is passed around the table in bowls and platters and the guests help themselves.*

- *If a platter is awkward, hold it for the person on your left to serve from.*

- *Desserts can be plated ahead of time and held in the kitchen or placed on the table, if you wish.*

- *Never scrape or stack plates at the dinner table. This is kitchen work and should be invisible to the guests.*

- *Keep centerpieces low and informal.*

- *Use lots of candles.*

MORE FORMAL FAMILY SERVICE

- *Suitable for more formal or ceremonial dinners.*

- *Serves as many as your dining table(s) will comfortably seat.*

- *Plates are stacked at the hostess's place and she serves the entrée, then passes the plate to the host, who serves the primary side dishes. Guests help themselves to condiments and other side dishes.*

- *Salads, the appetizer course, or the soup course may be preset before the guests are seated.*

- *The guest of honor is seated to the host's right, with that guest's escort to the right of the hostess.*

- *Never scrape or stack plates at the dinner table. This is kitchen work and should be invisible to the guests.*

- *The centerpiece may be fairly formal, but should be low enough to see over.*

- *Lots of candles.*

PLATE SERVICE

- *To be used for no more than six guests, unless you have back of the house help.*

- *Plate the salad and place it on the table first, or hold it in the kitchen until serving time.*

- *The appetizer course, or the soup course may be preset before the guests are seated.*

- *After the soup course, the bowls are removed and the hostess plates the main course in the kitchen, paying attention to the pattern on the plate so that any design (say a bird) is properly situated.*

- *Wipe up any spills on the edges of plates or bowls in the kitchen, then bring each plate of food to the table, serving each guest from the left. Carry no more than two plates at a time to and from the kitchen.*

- *If you're using this service, it's always a good idea to enlist the help of your partner or a willing friend to help you transfer dishes to and from the kitchen.*

- *Keep the centerpiece low and use lots of candles.*

- *Never scrape or stack plates at the dinner table. This is kitchen work and should be invisible to the guests.*

Warm Winter Celebrations

Holiday Southwestern Pasta Dinner

With all the holiday parties you give and go to, don't you just get sick and tired of all that traditional holiday food? This year we decided to take back our Texas roots and throw a quasi-traditional, new age, old-fashioned party for friends during the busy holiday season. We didn't invite everybody to whom we owed an obligation. We just called up four of our very best friends, told them to come casual, dug up some salsa music, and set a table decorated with the red and green of Mexican curios left over from trips to the border, not the red and green of St. Nick. By making the flan ahead of time and marinating ready-to-eat shrimp two hours to overnight, this party went together faster than a Mexican Hat Dance—which we still had the time and energy to do, once the dinner was over.

The Menu

MARGARITA SORBET

SALSA SHRIMP COCKTAILS WITH HOT FLOUR TORTILLA WEDGES

MANGO COLESLAW

SOUTHWEST TEXAS ROTEL TOMATO PASTA

FLAN ALMENDRA (SEE PAGE 262)

Cooking Tip

An easy way to heat flour tortillas is to place an entire package in the microwave on high (100 percent power) for a couple minutes. Remove the heated tortillas from the package, cut them into wedges while still hot and steamy, then wrap them in a clean white cloth inside a basket.

All the Trimmings

Preset the table with the shrimp cocktails. When you clear the cocktail dishes, serve individual bowls of the Rotel Tomato Pasta, and pass the Mango Coleslaw to be served on a side salad plate. Mexico's artisans produce some of the most beautiful Christmas ornaments anywhere. If you can get your hands on these ornaments at a Christmas fair, or have them from a trip to Mexico or the Southwest, combine them with red Christmas cacti to make a beautiful centerpiece. Other options include a red tablecloth and napkins.

MARGARITA SORBET

2 limes, 1 cut in half and squeezed, 1 cut in 6 thin rings

Margarita salt (or kosher salt if margarita salt is not available)

1 (6-ounce) container frozen limeade concentrate

1 (6-ounce) container frozen pineapple juice concentrate

2 cups Tequila Gold

1 cup triple sec or other orange liqueur

4 trays of ice cubes

If you have ever been to Texas, or to some good/bad imitation of a Texas cantina, you've probably had what some people know as margarita slushes. Congressman brother Bob Eckhardt taught us how to make them right. All you need is a great bottle of Tequila Gold, plenty of ice, great limes, and a blender with the heart of a lion. Lay in a good supply. You may find yourself making more than one batch.

PREPARATION TIME: 5 MINUTES

MAKES 12 COCKTAILS

Best if made and served immediately. You can dip the rim of the margarita glasses in salt and set them aside at least 1 hour in advance.

Wipe six balloon wineglass rims with lime juice, then dip them in margarita salt. Hang a lime ring over the edge and set the glasses aside until party time.

In a blender, combine the limeade, pineapple juice concentrate, and half the tequila, and pulse to mix. Fill the blender to the top with ice cubes and blend on high until thick and slushy, holding the lid down firmly. Transfer to a large pitcher. Add remaining ingredients to the blender and blend until thick and slushy. Pour into the pitcher with the fruit juices. Stir to mix. Pour immediately into the glasses. Refrigerate the remaining margarita mix for second helpings.

SALSA SHRIMP COCKTAILS WITH
HOT FLOUR TORTILLA WEDGES

1 1/2 pounds shrimp, cooked and shelled*

1 cup fresh hot salsa

2 green onions with tops, minced

1/2 cup chopped cilantro leaves

Salt and freshly ground black pepper, to taste

3 cups shredded romaine lettuce

2 ripe avocados, pitted, peeled, and cut into thin slices

Mexican restaurants in Texas serve these in ice-cream parlor coupes, but we like them in balloon wineglasses. Texans prefer Gulf Coast medium shrimp that they boil, shell, and devein before they begin. With no back of the house help, we find that cooked, shelled, and chilled bay shrimp work admirably. Either way, they're colorful, almost too-easy-to-believe to put together, and hotcha hot to keep everybody alert.

PREPARATION TIME:	10 MINUTES
MARINATING TIME:	30 MINUTES TO 1 DAY, COVERED, IN THE REFRIGERATOR
MAKES 6 SERVINGS	

You may marinate the shrimp overnight. The flavor deepens and improves with overnight refrigeration.

In a medium bowl, combine shrimp with the salsa. Cover and refrigerate for at least 30 minutes or up to 1 day. Just before serving, stir in the green onions and cilantro. Taste and adjust the seasonings with salt and pepper.

To serve, divide the lettuce among six footed coupes or balloon wineglasses. Spoon the shrimp mixture atop the lettuce and garnish with slices of avocado. Serve immediately.

* We suggest buying precooked and shelled shrimp for this recipe.

Mango Coleslaw

1 small head green cabbage, shredded (6 cups)

2 ripe mangoes, peeled, seeded, and chopped

¹/₂ cup chopped green onions with tops

Sauce:

3/4 cup mayonnaise

1 (8-ounce) container plain yogurt

4 pickled jalapeños, stemmed, seeded, and minced (1/3 cup)

2 tablespoons Dijon mustard

3 tablespoons sugar

Juice and zest of 1/2 lemon (about 2 tablespoons of each)

Salt and freshly ground black pepper, to taste

PREPARATION TIME: 10 MINUTES

REFRIGERATION TIME: 1 HOUR

MAKES 6 SERVINGS

May be prepared from 1 day to 1 hour in advance.

In a large bowl, toss together the cabbage, mangoes, and onions. In a small bowl, whisk together the mayonnaise, yogurt, jalapeños, mustard, sugar, lemon juice, zest, and salt and pepper. Pour over the cabbage mixture and toss to mix. Cover and refrigerate at least an hour. Serve from a colorful Mexican-style bowl.

Southwest Texas Rotel Tomato Pasta

6 quarts water

2 tablespoons sea salt

1¹/₄ pounds linguine

Sauce:

¹/₄ cup (¹/₂ stick) butter

¹/₄ cup extra virgin olive oil

¹/₂ teaspoon hot red pepper flakes

³/₄ cup vodka

1 (10-ounce) can Rotel tomatoes and green chilies *

1 cup heavy cream

Salt and freshly ground pepper, to taste

1 cup freshly grated Parmesan cheese

Mysterious, smoky flavors that come from the cupboard . . . what could be more desirable during the busy holiday season? This recipe originated in Rome with intermediate stops in Turkey for vodka and Mexico for chilies. You can't be too tired to make this. Trust us. We speak from experience.

PREPARATION TIME: 10 MINUTES

COOKING TIME: 20 MINUTES

MAKES 6 SERVINGS

Best if made and eaten at once.

Pour the water and salt into a large stockpot and bring to a boil over high heat. Add the linguine to start cooking. Place a large ovenproof serving bowl in the oven set on "low" to warm it.

While you wait for water to boil, make the sauce. Melt butter and oil in a large skillet over medium heat. Add the red pepper flakes and cook 30 seconds, then add the vodka and boil 2 to 3 minutes. Add the Rotel tomatoes and chilies and the cream and bring it to a boil. Cook gently for fifteen minutes, whisking from time to time. Taste and adjust the seasonings with salt and pepper.

When the pasta is cooked *al dente* (see instructions on the pasta package), reserve I cup of the cooking water, then drain the pasta and return it to the pot. Add back the reserved cooking water a little at a time until the pasta stops absorbing it, then stir the pasta so the strands won't stick together. Turn the heat to low, and pour in the sauce. Add the Parmesan and mix thoroughly. Pour into the heated serving bowl and serve.

* If Rotel products are unavailable, use two thirds of a 10-ounce can of tomatoes combined with three quarters of a 4-ounce can of mild green chilies.

Christmas Day Dinner: Beef Tenderloin with Peppercorn and Mustard Seed Crust

A fine Christmas feast can be made even finer if the primary cook doesn't carry all the responsibility. We try not to even *think* the word potluck when it comes to this traditional winter celebration, but, in fact, all of our lives are so hectic at this time of year that assigning different dishes to different guests is the only thing that makes sense. If we've invited ten guests and we ask one to bring the wine, another the dessert, another the bread; if we ask somebody to make the gratin, another the scones, and another to whip up the hot salad; somebody else to bring flowers, and someone to make the hors d'oeuvre, before you know it, about all the host has to do is drag out the best china, shine up the table, and cook the roast. That is what we call a real Christmas gift. Got more people on your list? Add dishwashing and cleanup to your assignments.

The Menu

WHITE BEAN AND ROSEMARY SPREAD WITH SLICES OF
SOURDOUGH BREAD

HOT SALAD OF MUSTARD GREENS WITH MINT AND PANCETTA

BEEF TENDERLOIN WITH PEPPERCORN AND MUSTARD SEED CRUST

CRANBERRY HORSERADISH SAUCE

BEETS IN AN ORANGE VINAIGRETTE ON A BED OF BABY GREENS
(SEE PAGE 344)

TURNIP POTATO GRATIN

CRANBERRY SCONES (SEE PAGE 174) AND SWEET BUTTER

BÛCHE DE NOËL (FROM THE BAKERY)

Wine Suggestions

Appetizer—A bubbly sets the tone for this festive meal. Try a Prosecco from the Veneto region of Italy. This fun, creamy-mouth-feel bubbly will go well with the Italian-inspired appetizer.

Main Course—Try a mature French Bordeaux from the Pauillac. The tannins in the wine will be a great complement for the meat. Be sure to decant the wine and let it breathe for at least 20 minutes before serving. This will allow the flavors to really open up. You will probably have to spend from $20 to $40, but what better time to enjoy a great wine than Christmas? Besides, a tenderloin will really show off a good Bordeaux! You could also try a California Merlot for a similar effect.

Dessert—Try a dessert muscat from Greece, California, or Australia. It will be sweet enough to stand up to dessert, and it's so good you will want to pour it on your pancakes.

Cooking Tip

Make friends with a butcher. Order the tenderloin in advance. Consult with the butcher for length of cooking time. Our butcher said to cook it precisely $30^1/_2$ minutes at 425° for medium rare. We laughed, but we did what he said and our tenderloin came out perfectly. You can buy a whole or half tenderloin, depending upon the size of your party. A whole beef tenderloin will weigh 4 to 6 pounds and will serve ten to twelve people generously. If buying a whole piece, ask for an untrimmed tenderloin, which will have the tapered end that includes the best-tasting meat on the animal. Cut this off and save it for yourselves later. With this small precious end piece, you can make Chateaubriand, filet mignon, or beef tenders with peppercorn sauce for two.

Tradition determines expectations for Christmas table decorations. In 1959 grandmother decided she'd like to be "modern"; she put away all the old hand-blown glass ornaments and did up the house and table in a uniform "blue" look, with all blue bulbs on a phony white tree, blue decorations on the Christmas table, and even blue lights in every socket she could find. The result was, in a certain ten-year-old's mind, a disaster, though it might be considered cool right now in Soho. So our advice to you is, don't meddle with tradition!

All the Trimmings

This one day a year we love red-and-green plaid cloth napkins tucked into brass napkin rings; evergreen boughs from the yard, laid on the table and sprinkled with red glass bulbs; and fat red candles. Linda has a big holly bush in front of the house, so adds some holly to the mix. But mainly, we let the food, served family-style, be the star. The term "groaning board" is not an empty phrase on Christmas at our house. Our table is bountiful, colorful, and aromatic. We expect the guests, when they are called to the table, to gasp at the sheer beauty of it all before they even take a chair. All the hubbub of passing dishes is very exciting!

Serve the tenderloin on a large platter surrounded by sprigs of rosemary and pickled beets. Carve it at the table and top each serving with a jot of Cranberry Horseradish Sauce. Pass the other items and allow your guests to serve themselves.

You're Invited!

Being invited to a "cooperative" Christmas includes a responsibility for the guest to bring something. So a phone call to discuss the venture is best. Talk over the menu and see what each guest is willing to bring or cook. Mark up your master menu, then send a quick note to confirm the arrangement, noting the time of the dinner, and the agreed-upon contribution. People enjoy participating in this Christmas gift to one another. What a fine thing to give to each other. A day of pleasure and plenty at table.

White Bean and Rosemary Spread
with Slices of Sourdough Bread

2 (16-ounce) cans cannellini or great northern beans, rinsed and drained

2 cloves garlic, chopped (1 teaspoon)

1/4 cup extra virgin olive oil

Juice and zest of 1 lemon

2 teaspoons chopped fresh rosemary leaves

1/2 cup chopped flat-leaf parsley, plus sprigs for garnish

Salt and hot pepper sauce, to taste

1 loaf sourdough bread, cut into thick chunks

If you can work a can opener, you can make a true appetizer that will leave your guests lunging for the dinner table. Cannellini beans seem to come in a variety of can sizes. And in some parts of the country, not at all. Not to worry. Use navy beans or Great Northerns. You're looking for white beans in a can that weighs roughly 1 pound. Use what you can find and go forth. Measurements are not critical here.

PREPARATION TIME: 10 MINUTES

REFRIGERATION TIME: 30 MINUTES TO 2 DAYS

MAKES 3 CUPS TO SERVE 10 TO 12

A definite do-ahead. Find 10 minutes somewhere in your busy schedule and whip this together as much as 2 days in advance.

Combine all the ingredients except salt, hot sauce, bread, and garnish in the food processor bowl fitted with the steel blade. Process until smooth, about 30 seconds, then season to taste with salt and hot sauce. Transfer to a bowl or jar and refrigerate until 20 minutes before serving time.

To serve, place the bean spread in a bowl and garnish it with parsley sprigs. Set the bowl on a platter and surround it with the bread chunks. Let your guests serve themselves.

Hot Salad of Mustard Greens with Mint and Pancetta

2 tablespoons extra virgin olive oil

6 slices pancetta or bacon, chopped

1 large yellow onion, cut into quarters and segments separated

6 cloves garlic, chopped (3 teaspoons)

2 pounds fresh mustard greens, well washed and stemmed

1/4 cup sherry vinegar

Salt and freshly ground black pepper, to taste

1/2 cup fresh mint, coarsely chopped

Here's a great beginning to your Christmas dinner. Serve a small, smoking serving to each guest at the dinner table to whet his or her appetite. Got an eager assistant in the kitchen? Assign that cook the job of making the hot salad. It's simple, but it needs tending. Substitute kale, spinach, or other sweet hot winter greens if you wish. Choose your largest skillet or stew pot to hold all the greens.

PREPARATION TIME: 15 MINUTES

COOKING TIME: 20 MINUTES

MAKES 10 TO 12 SERVINGS

For a bright colored salad, sauté the greens just before serving.

Heat the oil in a large skillet over medium-high heat and fry the pancetta or bacon until translucent, about 5 minutes. Pour off all but 2 tablespoons of fat. Add the onion, turn the heat down to medium, and cook and stir until the onion is soft and golden, about 8 minutes. Add the garlic and continue to cook 2 to 3 minutes more.

Chop the mustard greens and discard the stems. Add the vinegar and greens to the skillet, cover, and cook just until the greens are wilted, about 3 to 4 minutes. Season the cooked greens with salt and pepper, then toss with the mint. Transfer to a bowl and serve.

Beef Roasting Chart

Roast type	Oven temperature (preheated)	Weight in pounds	Approximate total cooking time (based on meat removed directly from the refrigerator)		Remove roast from oven when meat temperature reaches:
Eye Round Roast yields 4 (3oz) servings of cooked, trimmed beef per pound	325° F	2-3	medium rare: 1½ - 1¾ hours		135° F
Rib Eye Roast small end	350° F	3-4	medium rare: 1½ - 1¾ hours medium: 1¾ - 2 hours		135° F 150° F
Yields 3 - 3½ (3oz) servings of cooked, trimmed beef per pound		4-6	medium rare: 1¾ - 2 hours medium: 2 - 2½ hours		135° F 150° F
Rib Roast Chine bone removed	350° F	4-6 (2 ribs)	medium rare: 1¾ - 2¼ hours medium: 2¼ - 2¾ hours		135° F 150° F
Yields 2½ - 3 (3oz) servings of cooked, trimmed beef per pound		6-8 (2-4 ribs)	medium rare: 2¼ - 2½ hours medium: 2¾ - 3 hours		135° F 150° F
Round Tip Roast Yields 3½ - 4 (3oz) servings of cooked, trimmed beef per pound	325° F	3-4	medium rare: 1¾ - 2 hours medium: 2¼ - 2½ hours		140° F 155° F
		4-6	medium rare: 2 - 2½ hours medium: 2½ - 3 hours		140° F 155° F
Tenderloin Roast Yields 3½ - 4 (3oz) servings of cooked, trimmed beef per pound	425° F	2-3	medium rare: 35 - 40 minutes medium: 45 - 60 minutes		135° F 150° F
		4-5	medium rare: 50 - 60 minutes medium: 60 - 70 minutes		135° F 150° F
Tri-Tip Roast bottom sirloin Yields 4 (3oz) servings of cooked, trimmed beef per pound	425° F	1½-2	medium rare: 30-40 minutes medium: 40-45 minutes		135° F 150° F

- Medium rare doneness = 145° F final meat temperature after 10-15 minutes standing time

- Medium doneness = 160° F final meat temperature after 10-15 minutes standing time

Beef Tenderloin with
Peppercorn and Mustard Seed Crust

1 tablespoon black peppercorns

1 tablespoon white peppercorns

1 tablespoon coriander seeds

1 tablespoon mustard seeds

2 teaspoons salt

1 tablespoon Dijon mustard

1 (4- to 6-pound) whole beef tenderloin

6 to 8 sprigs of fresh rosemary, for garnish

1 (16-ounce) jar cold pickled beets, for garnish

The sight of a whole beef tenderloin on a bed of rosemary studded with cold pickled beets will say "Merry Christmas" before your guests even take the first bite. Buy the beef from the best butcher you know. Nothing could be easier to prepare, and, done right, it has a buttery soft interior with a crisp, pungent crust. All you need is a meat thermometer, a roasting pan with low sides, and a rack. Serve it with a jot of Cranberry Horseradish Sauce. "God Rest Ye Merry Gentlemen" . . . and remember there'll be plenty of beef for sandwiches the next day.

PREPARATION TIME: 15 MINUTES

ROASTING TIME: 25 TO 45 MINUTES

RESTING TIME: 10 TO 15 MINUTES

MAKES 10 TO 12 SERVINGS

Best if made and eaten at once.

Preheat the oven to 425° and spray both the rack and the shallow roasting pan with cooking spray. Place the roast straight from the refrigerator, fat side up, on the rack. Don't add water or cover the pan.

Combine the peppercorns, coriander seeds, and mustard seeds in a Ziploc bag. Close the bag and crush the seeds with a rolling pin or mallet. Add the salt and stir to combine. Rub the outside of the meat with Dijon mustard, then press the spice mixture into the surface. Transfer to the rack and roast until done to your taste.

Don't overcook the roast! Because the meat temperature will rise 5° to 10° *after* it's removed from the oven, remove it when the thermometer reads about 130° for medium-rare, 140° for medium, 150° for well done.

Stick a meat thermometer into the thickest part of the meat to test it. Roast about 40 to 50 minutes, to achieve 130° for medium-rare; about 50 to 60 minutes, to rise to 140°

for medium; or up to 70 minutes, or to rise to 160° for well-done. Transfer the meat to a warmed platter, garnish it with the rosemary sprigs and beets, cover it with foil, and set it aside for about 10 to 15 minutes before carving so the juices will settle down and the meat will firm up for easy slicing.

Other Classic Roasts for Holiday Meals

Beef rib roast, beef rib eye roast, or beef eye round roast will all work well with this recipe for a peppercorn and mustard seed crust. Follow the chart below for cooking times and temperatures. Here's a tip. Ask the butcher for the small end of the rib or rib eye roast for best flavor and tenderness.

When choosing meat from the counter, beef roasts should be a bright cherry red color. If vacuum-packed, the meat may look darker, but it will redden as it's exposed to the air. Store roasts, unopened, in the refrigerator for 3 to 4 days, or frozen in the store packaging for up to 2 weeks. To defrost properly, transfer the meat to the refrigerator and allow from 4 to 7 hours per pound for thawing.

CRANBERRY HORSERADISH SAUCE

1/2 cup sour cream

1/2 cup mayonnaise

2 tablespoons prepared white horseradish
(or to taste)

1/2 cup dried cranberries

PREPARATION TIME: 5 MINUTES

MAKES 1 1/2 CUPS TO SERVE 10

May be made as much as a day in advance, covered, and refrigerated until serving time.

Stir the sauce ingredients together, place in a bowl, cover, and refrigerate.

TURNIP POTATO GRATIN

Sauce:

3 cups half-and-half

2 teaspoons chopped garlic (4 cloves)

1/2 teaspoon nutmeg

1 1/2 teaspoons salt

Freshly ground black pepper, to taste

Vegetables:

6 medium turnips (about 1 1/2 pounds)

6 large russet potatoes (about 3 pounds)

1 large yellow onion (about 3/4 pound)

Salt and freshly ground pepper, to taste

1/2 cup seasoned bread crumbs

Parsley leaves, for garnish

PREPARATION TIME: 15 MINUTES

BAKING TIME: 55 TO 70 MINUTES

MAKES 10 TO 12 SERVINGS

May be made a day in advance and reheated in the oven or microwave just before serving time.

Preheat oven to 425°. Combine the half-and-half with the garlic, nutmeg, salt, and pepper in a saucepan, and boil about 10 minutes.

Spritz a large (4-quart) gratin or baking dish with cooking spray. Peel and slice the turnips, potatoes, and onion into $^1/_4$-inch-thick slices and overlap them, alternating the vegetables in the baking dish and making concentric circles. Season generously with salt and freshly ground black pepper to taste.

Pour the hot cream sauce over the vegetables, sprinkle with bread crumbs, cover the dish with foil, and bake the gratin 30 minutes. Remove the foil and continue baking until the vegetables are tender but still hold their shape, about 25 to 40 minutes more. Garnish with the parsley leaves and serve hot.

Winter Solstice
Formal Sage Chicken Dinner for Eight

Once a year, you'd like to invite your very special friends over for a formal dinner. A dinner where the hostess can wear a terrific-looking dress, your men friends can test the fit of their tuxedos, and your table can be dressed up too. This means the dinner needs to be a "do-ahead." With most of the work taken care of the day before, the only cooking you'll do on party day is to roast one chicken or capon—just enough cooking to fill the house with the heavenly aroma of roast bird.

Fill in with the best-quality commercial products you can find, including dinner rolls from the finest bakery in your neighborhood, great cheese, Italian amaretti cookies for dessert, and a couple of bottles of great dinner wine, plus a Sauternes to accompany the mousse.

The Menu

WINE-POACHED PEARS WITH EXPLORATEUR

ROAST SAGE CHICKEN IN A NEST

COMPANY DINNER ROLLS AND SWEET BUTTER

BLACK-EYED PEA AND SPINACH SALAD

DARK CHOCOLATE MOUSSE WITH AMARETTI

ESPRESSO

Wine Suggestions

First Course—French Languedoc, Jurançon. The pear and apple tones of this wine will complement the pear and marry beautifully with the cheese.

Main course—French Maconnais Chardonnay. The buttery rich Chardonnay (non-oaked, of course) will nicely complement this rich chicken dish. Forget about heavily oaked California Chardonnays. The oak flavor clashes and overwhelms nearly all flavors.

To Follow Dessert—Amaretto liqueur of course!

Cooking Tip

Pears for poaching need to be ripe, but pears are sold green and must be allowed several days in your warm kitchen to come to perfection. To ripen the fruit, buy it several days ahead and put the pears in a brown paper bag. Add a banana if you're really in a hurry— the gas given off by the banana will ripen many fruits. Then close the bag. To test, hold a pear in the palm of your hand and press gently at the stem end with your thumb. When the pear yields slightly to your touch, it's ready.

A poached pear is quite beautiful in and of itself, but to avoid making your guests deal with the core while spooning up the delicious wine sauce, you can core a pear in seconds with a melon ball scoop. With the melon baller, simply excavate the pear from the bottom center, creating a cylindrical cavity. As you work your way upward into the pear, you will end up removing the core and seeds. The cylindrical cavity also allows steam inside to cook the pear faster.

All the Trimmings

Now is the moment to use your whitest tablecloth. Have it washed, starched, and ironed if it's been stored too long, then let it billow over a table and decorate from there. Katherine solved the problem of not having a large enough dining table by purchasing a 4 × 6-foot sheet of plywood, then gluing a white felt covering onto both sides. Now, whenever she wants to host eight or ten people, she simply places the plywood tabletop over her smaller antique gateleg table, tops it with grandmother's white cutwork cloth, and it's a formal dinner.

Roses make a lovely and elegant trouble-free centerpiece. We think those white dripless candles in clear glass or crystal candlesticks are elegant all through the house. To finish the look, place groups of four votive candles on plates in key places and turn off most of the lights. Always put a candle in the bathroom! Elegant and inviting. There is something about candlelight—it whets the appetite. Can you ever have enough candles? We don't think so.

The pear and cheese first course should be preset at each place before seating your guests. Serve the chicken on a bed of romaine lettuce, surrounded by the beets. Compose the salad according to the instructions and pass it. Serve the bread in a basket or on individual bread plates. Of course, the mousse is served in a pots de crème cup, small wine glass, or demitasse. Take them out of the refrigerator just as you sit down so they will warm up and be more flavorful.

You're Invited!

Holidays are a busy time, so if you want to have a full table, you'd be well advised to send out written invitations about 2 weeks ahead of party time. Ask for an RSVP. Pick up a premade holiday party invitation or make your own. Handwrite the invitations on white 4- × 6-inch cards, slip them in an envelope, and pop them in the mail. Nothing could be nicer.

WINE-POACHED PEARS WITH EXPLORATEUR

3 cups Merlot, or the wine you are serving for the first course

2 cups water

1/2 cup packed light or dark brown sugar

1 cinnamon stick

12 peppercorns

2 tablespoons mild honey

Juice and zest of 1 lemon (about 1/2 cup juice)

4 firm but ripe Bartlett, Comice, or Bosc pears

4 ounces Explorateur (or other white triple-cream) cheese

Fresh mint sprigs, for garnish

Zip up the gentle taste of pears with peppercorns and cinnamon, serve them with a piece of creamy cheese, and they become a perfect opener. Explorateur, the French triple-cream cheese, has just the right tartness to balance the subtle perfume of the pears.

PREPARATION TIME: 20 MINUTES

COOKING TIME: 5 TO 10 MINUTES

REFRIGERATION TIME: 30 MINUTES TO CHILL

MAKES 8 SERVINGS

Make these pears a day or two before and refrigerate them until serving time. The seasonings soak into the fruit so that every bite is a thrill.

Pour the wine, water, brown sugar, cinnamon, peppercorns, honey, and lemon juice and zest into a large microwave-safe dish.

    Leaving the stems intact, core the pears from the bottom (see Cooking Tip, page 33) with a small melon baller. Peel the pears and cut a thin slice off the bottom of each one. Stand them upright in the poaching liquid and cover. Microwave on high (100 percent power) for 5 minutes. (Or simmer in a large saucepan, covered, for 10 minutes or until tender.) The pears are done when a fork easily slips into them. Refrigerate at least 30 minutes or until serving time.

    To serve, arrange the pears on individual plates with a wedge of cheese, and garnish each serving with a fresh mint sprig. Offer a sharp knife and a salad fork to each diner for this course.

ROAST SAGE CHICKEN IN A NEST

1 (5- to 6-pound) roasting chicken or capon

Salt and freshly ground black pepper, to taste

1 bunch fresh sage leaves (about 1 cup)

1 cup Chardonnay, or other dry white wine.

1 head romaine lettuce, washed, drained, and sliced into 2-inch pieces

1 large carrot, scraped and shredded

$^1/_4$ cup cold water

$^1/_2$ teaspoon cornstarch

1 tablespoon Dijon mustard

2 tablespoons butter

$^1/_3$ cup half-and-half

1 (16-ounce) jar pickled beets, drained

A golden roasted bird nestled on a bed of braised, bright green lettuce sparkling with shards of carrot and ruby red beets makes a centerpiece that tastes as good as it looks.

PREPARATION TIME:	20 MINUTES
COOKING TIME:	1 HOUR 20 MINUTES TO ROAST BIRD, 10 MINUTES TO REST BEFORE CARVING, WHILE YOU MAKE THE SAUCE.
MAKES 6 TO 8 SERVINGS	

While the bird is roasting, you can make the salad, set the table, and light the candles.

Preheat the oven to 425°. Oil a rack and place it in a roasting pan large enough to hold the bird.

Generously salt and pepper the inside of the bird, then the skin. Lift the skin over the breast meat and arrange a few of the sage leaves in an artful pattern. Stuff the cavity with the rest of the sage leaves. Tie the legs and tail together and place the bird on the rack.

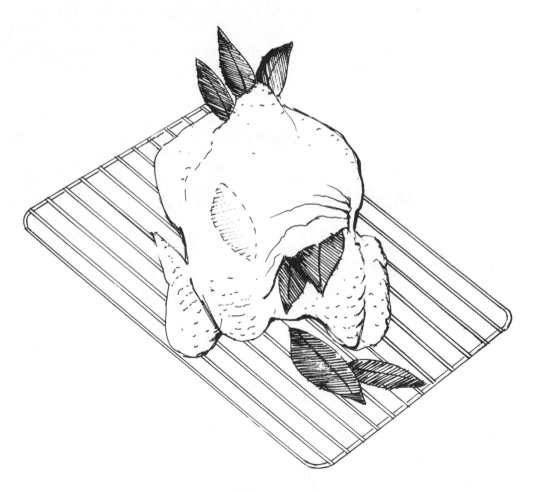

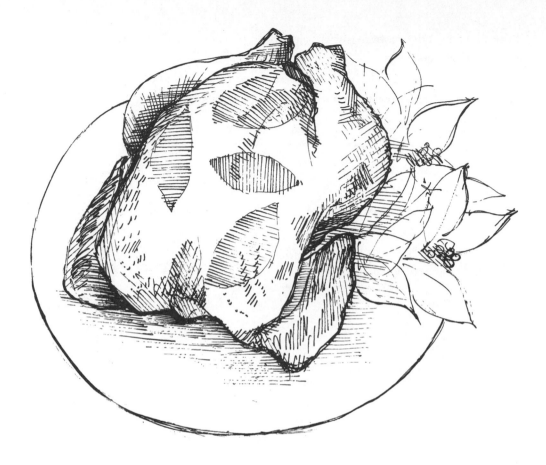

Roast until the skin is crisp, and the juices run clear, about 1 hour and 20 minutes. A thermometer inserted into the thickest part of the meat—not touching a bone—should read 170°.

Place the roasted bird on a large ovenproof platter, remove and discard the sage from the cavity, cover the bird with foil, and set it aside to rest for 10 minutes. Meanwhile, degrease (see page 38) the roasting pan, then place it on the stovetop, and bring the pan juices to a boil. Scrape up any browned bits clinging to the pan, and add the wine, a little at a time, continuing to scrape. Boil hard, then drop the lettuce and carrot into the boiling pan juices, cover, and braise the vegetables for 4 to 5 minutes. Now lift the vegetables to a colander to drain, then nestle them around the bird on the platter. Hold the platter in a warm oven while you finish the sauce.

Boil the pan juices over high heat until reduced by half, about 5 minutes. Meanwhile, dissolve the cornstarch in $^1/_4$ cup cold water, then stir it into the boiling pan juices. Cook and stir until the sauce is thick up to 10 minutes. Swirl in the mustard, butter, and cream.

Taste, and adjust the seasonings with salt and pepper. Pour the sauce into a sauceboat and pass it with the chicken.

To serve, nestle the cold beets in threes around the bird, and carve the chicken at the table, offering slices of meat along with the braised vegetables and cold beets to each diner.

Degreasing is simplest if you buy one of those degreasing measures. All you have to do is pour the pan juices into the measure. The fat will rise to the top. The lip of this measure starts at the bottom, so carefully pour the pan juices back into the pan, leaving the fat in the measure. Discard the fat.

BLACK-EYED PEA AND SPINACH SALAD

4 cups cooked black-eyed peas, 2 (16-ounce) cans or 2 boxes frozen, or 2 cups dried, cooked as directed above

4 thick slices bacon

2 large yellow onions, thinly sliced

$^1\!/_2$ cup malt vinegar

$^1\!/_4$ cup vegetable oil

$^1\!/_4$ cup water

$^1\!/_4$ cup packed light or dark brown sugar

$^1\!/_8$ teaspoon Tabasco (or to taste)

Salt and freshly ground black pepper, to taste

$^1\!/_2$ pound fresh spinach (or one 10-ounce bag), washed and spun dry

1 large European cucumber, scored and thinly sliced

Black-eyed peas made their way to the American South from Africa, where they were a dietary staple. The notion that black-eyed peas bring good luck originated in Africa as well. You may use canned or frozen peas. If you prefer dried peas, cook the legumes in barely salted water to cover just until tender, about 1 hour, then drain and proceed.

PREPARATION TIME: 25 MINUTES

REFRIGERATION TIME: MARINATE 30 MINUTES TO OVERNIGHT

MAKES 6 TO 8 SERVINGS

This salad tastes good chilled or at room temperature. The peas may be marinated the day before, then composed at serving time on a bed of fresh spinach.

Drain the cooked or canned peas in a colander, then transfer them to a large bowl. Lay the slices of bacon in a roasting pan and bake them for 15 minutes in the oven at 450° or until crisp. Drain on paper towels. Crumble and set aside, covered, until serving time. Add the onions to the hot bacon fat and sauté on top of the stove over medium-high heat until they begin to turn golden. Pour in the vinegar, oil, water, sugar, Tabasco, and salt and pepper, and bring to a boil, scraping up any browned bits from the bottom of the pan. Reduce the sauce to about half its original volume, about 10 minutes, add it to the peas, cover, and marinate in the refrigerator until serving time.

    To serve, arrange the fresh spinach leaves on a large, deep platter. Drain the peas and mound them over the spinach. Garnish with the crumbled bacon and the cucumber slices, and serve.

Dark Chocolate Mousse with Amaretti

2 (4-ounce) bars German's sweet chocolate

2 tablespoons sugar

1 cup heavy cream

4 large egg yolks

1 teaspoon vanilla extract

Dense with chocolate perfume, the smallest serving of this dessert will do. If you have half-cup "pots de crème," use them. Otherwise, use small wineglasses or demitasse cups.

Amaretti are luscious Italian cookies sold in Italian delis or by mail. Call 1-800-472-5264, Mangaharo's of New York.

PREPARATION TIME: 5 TO 10 MINUTES

REFRIGERATION TIME: 1 HOUR

MAKES 8 SERVINGS

The mousse can be made up to 2 or 3 days in advance, covered, and refrigerated.

Break the chocolate into chunks and place it in a microwave-safe bowl. Heat, uncovered, for 2 to $2^1/_2$ minutes at high (100 percent power). Remove from the microwave and stir until the chocolate is completely melted. Alternatively, heat in double boiler over barely simmering water, about 5 minutes.

In a medium bowl, whisk together the sugar, cream, and egg yolks until foamy. Stir this mixture into the melted chocolate, combining it thoroughly.

Cook the mousse, uncovered, for 2 minutes at high (100 percent) power. Remove from the microwave and stir in the vanilla. Alternatively, cook in double boiler until the mousse firms up, about 5 minutes. Divide mousse among eight serving dishes, cover, and refrigerate at least 30 minutes until serving time. Serve with Amaretti.

Home for New Year's Eve Cold Poached Salmon Formal Dinner for Six

After many years of being at crowded parties or bars on New Year's Eve, constantly looking at our watches in anticipation of the evening's climax—which is so often anticlimactic anyway—we have decided that we'd rather stay home with a few close friends. The food and champagne are better, and, with enough of the bubbly, you will be dancing on the tables. Katherine's birthday is on New Year's Eve, so we always celebrate.

The beauty of this colorful and brightly flavored menu is that much of it can be made in advance. The host can enjoy the guests, and drink as much champagne as he or she can manage. The dessert is a dazzling finish to an elegant meal.

The Menu

NEW POTATOES WITH SOUR CREAM AND FRESH SALMON CAVIAR

ENDIVE TIPS WITH CREAM CHEESE, BLUE CHEESE, AND A RED GRAPE
(SEE PAGE 147)

MINT, PEA, AND SPINACH SOUP

COLD POACHED SALMON WITH ESSENCE OF CLOVE
ON A BED OF GREENS

FRENCH BREAD

CHEESE COURSE (SEE PAGE 287)

POACHED PEARS IN PHYLLO IN A POOL OF CHOCOLATE SAUCE

Wine Suggestions

Appetizer and Dessert—Champagne. When buying champagne, stay away from the five or six champagnes that control the American market. Most of them are cheaply made, mass-produced wastes of money. We like Krug, Pommery, Pol Roger, and Bollinger. Otherwise look for the tiny letters R.M. at the bottom of the label. That stands for *Recoltant Manipulant,* which means that the grower is also the producer. Though this champagne is rare, and most always found on labels you won't recognize, it is usually outstanding. Ask for it at your bottle store. If the liquor store owner gives you a blank stare, don't trust his champagne stock. Find a better source.

Judging a good champagne is really simple. Mouth feel and texture are everything. Plus, it should plain taste good. Champagne that foams up in your mouth like hydrogen peroxide just won't cut it. Champagne should taste clean and refreshing, with tiny bubbles that feel creamy in the mouth. If you get that mad dog feeling and find your champagne bitter or harsh, it's bad. Use it to lift the spots off your sweater. Drink only the good stuff.

Main Course—Oregon Pinot Noirs are always wonderful with salmon. Try to get a Pinot Noir that has a low alcohol content (12.5 percent or lower). Because salmon is a fatty fish and because the spices called for in this recipe create a punched-up flavor, a Pinot, with its soft tannins and fruity/acidic quality is lovely. If you want to serve a white wine, try a sauvignon blanc, a dry, bracing wine, to achieve that lovely *opposites* effect with the rich salmon, or a French or California Chardonnay (non-oaked) for the *similars* rule—buttery Chardonnay and fatty fish.

All the Trimmings:

Set the table with a white tablecloth, sprinkle foil confetti everywhere, and place uncoiled streamers (the ones that people throw for bon voyage) all over. We usually decorate the ceiling fan and even the plants with streamers. The candles should be lit, the hors d'oeuvre out, the table set, and champagne on ice when the guests arrive. And what better night than New Year's Eve to wear funny hats and make noise with the noisemakers. We like to place hats and noisemakers at each place. Place cards will tell your guests where to sit and what hat to wear. Give the princesses in the room (there is at least one in every crowd) tiaras. Set up the New Potatoes with Sour Cream and Fresh Salmon Caviar along with the Endive Tips . . . on a tray in the living room for an extended cocktail hour. Don't rush. Let the appetites grow. Arrange the salmon on the greens on individual plates. Put out the cheese course and the dessert plates, and hold everything in the kitchen to be brought in at the appropriate time. Have the soup served at each place when the guests sit down at the table. Get volunteers to help clear the table and bring in the next course.

Champagne Tip

It is best if you chill the champagne the night before, but if you forget, a bottle of champagne can be chilled in a bucket of water and ice in 15 minutes. Champagne bottles each hold six glasses of bubbly. Think like a caterer and figure on about four glasses per person over the course of the night. You might want to have an extra bottle just in case. You can ask your guests to bring the champagne. It is a good value to buy a magnum and there is nothing more festive than the giant bottle. For a more in-depth discussion of the best champagnes, see page 97.

You're Invited!

This is the moment to pick up some beautiful stationery and handwrite the invitations. You might want to include the menu. We like to put a pinch of confetti in the envelope to set the mood. This is definitely a night for fun, and the invitation should convey that feeling.

New Potatoes with
Sour Cream and Fresh Salmon Caviar

15 small new potatoes	¹/₄ ounce fresh salmon caviar*
¹/₂ cup sour cream	

PREPARATION TIME: 10 MINUTES

COOKING TIME: 15 MINUTES

COOLING TIME: 10 MINUTES

MAKES 6 SERVINGS

The potatoes can be boiled up to 1 day in advance, filled up to 1 hour in advance, and stored in the refrigerator.

Place the potatoes in a large saucepan and cover them with cold water. Bring to a boil and cook for 15 minutes, or until they are easily pierced with a fork. Remove from heat and drain. Refill the pot with cold water, add the drained potatoes, and let them sit for 10 minutes. Drain and dry. May be made ahead to this point then refrigerated.

Cut potatoes in half, and using a melon baller (see below), scoop out a little bit of potato from each half, leaving a cavity for the filling. Reserve the potato centers for another use, such as fried potatoes for New Year's Day breakfast. Fill each potato with a scant teaspoon of sour cream and about a jot of fresh salmon caviar. Cover and refrigerate until ready to serve.

A melon baller is a handy tool to keep with your other utensils. Without a melon baller, scooping the potato flesh becomes a very frustrating procedure—this task is almost impossible using a knife or a spoon. Melon ballers are available at any houseware or kitchenware shop and are part of our secret weapons in the kitchen arsenal.

* Fresh salmon caviar is available at most gourmet shops. It is much less expensive than beluga, is orange in color, and not too salty. You can buy it in advance and freeze it. It is also available by mail order from many stores, including Zabars, in New York City (212) 496-1234.

MINT, PEA, AND SPINACH SOUP

2 medium onions, chopped

4 tablespoons butter

1 (10-ounce) box frozen spinach (1^1/$_4$ cups)

1 (10-ounce) box frozen peas (1^1/$_4$ cups)

^{1}/$_2$ bunch fresh mint, leaves removed from
stems, chopped (about 2 cups), reserving 4 to 6
leaves for garnish

2 (13-ounce) cans chicken broth

1 cup heavy cream

Freshly ground black pepper to taste

PREPARATION TIME:	10 MINUTES
COOKING TIME:	20 MINUTES
MAKES 4 TO 6 SERVINGS	

Can be made up to 1 day in advance. Store covered in the refrigerator and reheat in the microwave or stovetop if you wish.

In a medium saucepan, sauté the onions in the butter until they are translucent, over medium heat about 5 minutes. Add the spinach, peas, mint, and chicken broth and bring to a boil. Boil 2 minutes. Remove the pan from the heat. When cool enough to handle, pour into a food processor or blender in batches and puree. Return the pureed soup to the saucepan, add the cream and freshly ground pepper, and bring back to a boil. If you'd like a thinner soup, just add additional chicken broth. Serve in individual bowls and garnish each serving with a mint leaf. Serve hot or cold.

Cold Poached Salmon with Essence of Clove on a Bed of Greens

6 cups water (1¹/₂ quarts)

12 peppercorns

6 juniper berries

6 whole cloves

¹/₂ teaspoon salt

¹/₂ cup cider vinegar

4 Chinook salmon fillets (1¹/₂ pounds), about 1¹/₂ inches thick

³/₄ pound mixed baby greens (Mesclun)

Three-Citrus Dressing (see page 93)

PREPARATION TIME: 5 MINUTES

COOKING TIME: 5 MINUTES

REFRIGERATION TIME: 30 MINUTES TO 1 DAY

MAKES 4 TO 6 SERVINGS

The salmon can be poached up to 1 day in advance. The plates should be composed just before serving.

In a 12-inch skillet or flameproof gratin pan, combine the water, peppercorns, juniper berries, cloves, salt, and cider vinegar. Bring to a boil. Gently place the fillets in the pan and simmer over medium-low heat for 5 minutes. Carefully remove the salmon fillets from the poaching liquid and place them on a plate to cool for about 5 minutes. Cover and refrigerate until ready to serve. Cut large fillets into pieces.

Toss the greens with the vinaigrette, divide the mixture among the plates. Top with the salmon pieces, and serve immediately.

Poached Pears in Phyllo
in a Pool of Chocolate Sauce

3 cups water

1 cup fruity white wine

¹/₄ cup sugar

6 ripe Comice or Bosc pears, cored and peeled, stems intact (see page 33)

1 pound phyllo, about 16 sheets, thawed if frozen

¹/₄ pound (1 stick) butter, melted

Chocolate syrup

This is such an elegant dessert. Very simple, yet guaranteed to get a few oohs and ahs!

We can't think of an easier initiation into phyllo usage than this recipe. It's almost too easy. Thaw the phyllo laid out onto a damp towel. Butter your hands, then pick up a piece, slather it in butter, and fold. If you tear a

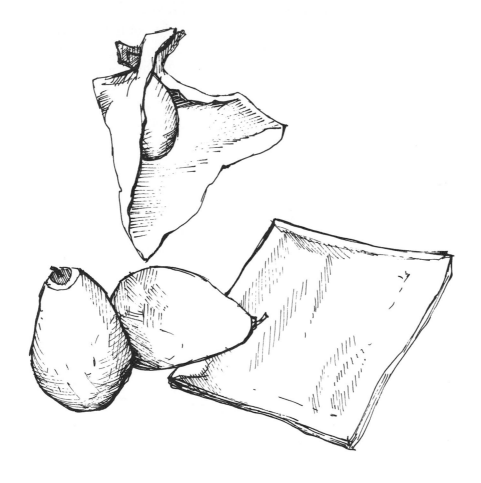

sheet or two, don't panic. By the time you've baked it, the result will be a dazzling, golden package of flaky, aromatic pastry with a luscious surprise in the middle, and no one will even notice whether or not your phyllo technique is perfect. To order excellent fresh phyllo, call The Fillo Factory, 1-800-OK-FILLO, 56 Cortland Avenue, Dumont, New Jersey, 07628.

PREPARATION TIME: 25 MINUTES

COOKING TIME: 10 MINUTES

BAKING TIME: 20 MINUTES

MAKES 6 SERVINGS

Pears may be poached the day before. May be made up the morning before.

Preheat the oven to 400°. In a medium saucepan, bring the water, wine, and sugar to a boil. Carefully place pears upright in the water-wine-sugar mixture and boil gently, covered, for 10 minutes. Remove from the liquid and set aside. Fold a sheet of phyllo to make a square. Brush it with butter and add two more layers of phyllo in the same shape and brush again with butter. Place a cooked pear in the center of the phyllo. Butter your hands and gather

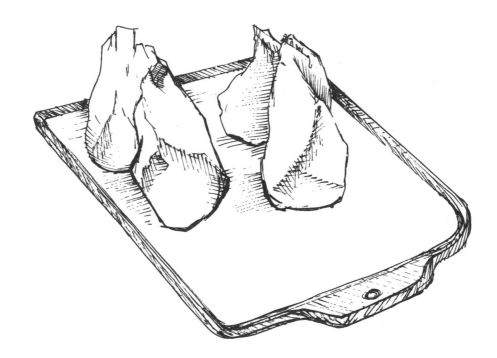

the phyllo up around the pear. The butter will act like glue and hold the phyllo together. Carefully place the pear packets on a cookie sheet sides not touching and continue with the remaining phyllo and pears.

Bake for 20 minutes, then set aside in the refrigerator until serving time. Just before serving, pour a pool of chocolate syrup slightly off center on each dessert plate and carefully place a pear in the center of each plate, overlapping the sauce.

TGI-Friday Night Fish Supper
with Friends

We reserve Friday nights for friends and relaxation. We want something simple so we can gather together to watch a ball game on television, or celebrate a birthday so casually that the honoree forgets he's a year older. We want our friends. We want no trouble. This is the menu that works. This shellfish stew over rice is easy. Down to the wine and dessert, this is comfort food. A little entertainment, a great wine, close friends, and satisfying food is what we need after a hard week's work.

The Menu

SAVORY CHÈVRE CHEESECAKE

CAJUN SHELLFISH STEW

RICE

BREAD AND BUTTER PUDDING

Wine Suggestions

Main Course—A low alcohol (12.5 percent or lower) German Riesling, Auslese or Spätlese. Don't be intimidated by the Gothic names of German Rieslings. The Germans are obsessed with labeling each variation. Riesling is feel-good wine and it is one of the best-kept secrets of the food geeks of this world or the next.

Dessert—This is an Australian recipe for bread pudding, so we thought it would be fun to serve an Australian Sweet Muscat. The honey, buttery flavor of the wine will marry well with the bread pudding.

All the Trimmings

Friday nights are reserved for close friends and have no trimmings. By definition, our friendship is all the decoration we need. We usually serve this meal buffet-style, right out of the kitchen, and sit in the living room with paper napkins!

SAVORY CHÈVRE CHEESECAKE

10 rye crisp crackers (about ²/₃ cup), crushed

2 tablespoons soft unsalted butter

1 cup 2 percent fat whipped cream cheese

8 ounces chèvre (goat cheese)

2 large eggs

2 tablespoons all-purpose flour

2 cloves garlic, peeled

¹/₂ teaspoon freshly ground black pepper

¹/₄ teaspoon cayenne

¹/₂ teaspoon herbes de Provence*

1 cup heavy cream

Cilantro leaves and edible flowers, for garnish (optional)

Thin wedges of this puckery hors d'oeuvre decorated with fresh herbs and winter flowers will start your celebration in style. You may make the cheesecake the day before. If you use the food processor to whiz up the rye cracker crust, then to blend the goat cheese and seasonings, it'll be in the oven in 10 minutes. After baking, cool on a rack, then cover and refrigerate until 30 minutes before party time. Bring to room temperature to serve.

PREPARATION TIME: 10 MINUTES

COOKING TIME: 30 MINUTES, THEN 30 MINUTES TO COOL

MAKES 12 SERVINGS

This hors d'oeuvre can be made the day prior to the party.

Preheat the oven to 325°. Coat an 8-inch quiche or cake pan with the soft butter, then sprinkle evenly with the crumbs. Wipe out the food processor bowl, then add all remaining

* Available at fine food stores.

ingredients except the cream and process until smooth. Add the cream and pulse to mix. Pour the cream mixture into the pan. Bake for 30 minutes, or until the center is set. Test by wiggling pan. Cool on a rack for 30 minutes, then cover and refrigerate until party time.

To serve, cut into thin wedges and place on salad plates. If you wish, garnish the top with cilantro leaves and edible flowers (borage, lavender, violets).

CAJUN SHELLFISH STEW

3 tablespoons extra virgin olive oil

4 large leeks, quartered and washed thoroughly to remove all sand, white and green parts chopped

6 cloves garlic, peeled and chopped (3 teaspoons)

2 medium carrots, peeled and diced

1 tablespoon chili powder

$1/2$ teaspoon cayenne

$1/2$ teaspoon ground cinnamon

2 teaspoons salt, or to taste

2 (16-ounce) containers (cardboard box preferred, or canned) Italian-style tomatoes with their juice

2 cups dry white wine

1 cup water

$1^1/2$ pounds medium shrimp, shelled, tail section left on

$1^1/2$ pounds sea scallops

12 mussels in the shell

12 small clams in the shell

6 oysters in the shell

$1/2$ cup freshly chopped cilantro leaves

3 cups rice cooked in 6 cups water

Look for imported Italian Roma (cooked) tomatoes in a box for best results. We stock up, buying boxes and boxes of these whenever we're close to an Italian deli. The flavor and texture are superior and make this ultra-fast stew a winner.

PREPARATION TIME: 15 MINUTES

COOKING TIME: 30 MINUTES

MAKES 12 SERVINGS (RECIPE WORKS EQUALLY WELL CUT IN HALF TO SERVE 6)

May be made to the point of cooking the shellfish up to 2 days in advance. Reheat and add the shellfish 5 minutes before serving.

Film the bottom of a large stockpot with the oil, set over medium heat, then add the leeks and garlic. Sauté until the vegetables are translucent, stirring from time to time, about 10 minutes. Add the carrots, spices, and salt, and continue cooking for 4 or 5 minutes, stirring. Add the tomatoes, wine, and 1 cup of water. Bring to a boil, then lower the heat to medium and cook for 5 minutes. At this point the stew can be refrigerated for up to 2 days.

Before serving, reheat the stew and stir in the shellfish. Cook until the shrimp and scallops are opaque and until the clams, mussels, and oysters have opened, from 4 to 6 minutes. Discard any that don't open. Remove from the heat immediately and stir in the cilantro. Spoon over $^{1}/_{2}$ cup cooked rice in wide-rimmed soup bowls and serve at once.

BREAD AND BUTTER PUDDING

14 slices good white bread

5 tablespoons soft butter

2 cups milk

1 cup heavy cream

2 large eggs

3 egg yolks

$^{2}/_{3}$ cup sugar

1 cup raisins

$1^{1}/_{2}$ teaspoons vanilla extract

1 teaspoon cinnamon

This dessert is the ultimate in comfort food. We like to time it so that it comes out of the oven 10 minutes before it is served. For an added hedonistic comfort-food experience, serve it with heavy cream drizzled on top.

PREPARATION TIME: 10 MINUTES

COOKING TIME: 45 MINUTES

MAKES 12 SERVINGS

Preheat the oven to 350°. Thoroughly butter both sides of each slice of bread. Cut it into large squares and layer it in a well-buttered 13 × 9 × 2-inch pan. In a bowl, stir together the milk, cream, eggs, egg yolks, sugar, raisins, vanilla, and cinnamon. Pour the mixture over the bread and bake the pudding for 45 minutes, or until golden brown and puffed on the top. Serve warm or at room temperature.

Dr. Martin Luther King, Jr., Birthday Weekend Soul Food Dinner for Six

Our dear friend Barbara Askins inspired this menu. Barbara grew up in the South, where Sunday dinner is served at about two o'clock in the afternoon. Barbara says, "Sunday dinner in our house was about the smells . . . the smells that met you at the door when you got home from church." What better occasion to celebrate this wonderful tradition than on Martin Luther King, Jr., weekend. And it is true, the aroma from this dinner is great for your soul.

The Menu

BLACK-EYED PEA AND SWEET RED PEPPER SALAD WITH
FRESH THYME VINAIGRETTE

CALVIN'S CHERRY-GLAZED HAM

COLLARD GREENS

BLACK SKILLET CORN BREAD

SWEET POTATO PIE WITH PRALINE SAUCE

ICED TEA

Cooking Tips

One of the quickest ways to look like a pro is to pump up the flavors of your meal with fresh herbs instead of dried. Fresh thyme for the black-eyed pea vinaigrette makes the difference in this menu. We keep fresh herbs including bunches of thyme in the refrigerator in a cup of water, like a posy. Then, when a recipe calls for thyme, we simply strip the leaves off the stems by holding the stem at the top and stripping downward over a bowl to remove the leaves. When using uncooked fresh thyme, as in the vinaigrette, chop the herb fine to release the flavor. This rule holds especially true for salads. If you are going to cook with fresh thyme, the cooking will release the flavor, eliminating the need for chopping. Once you have discovered fresh thyme and other fresh herbs, you will never go back to dried. Next thing we know, you'll be starting your own kitchen herb window garden.

When using a raw red pepper, cut it into quarters and give it a cursory peeling with a potato peeler. We learned from Jacques Pepin that the pepper's peel can be tough and bitter. It takes only 1 more minute to peel it, and you don't have to get every bit of the peel off. The result is a much sweeter taste.

When baking a ham, line the roasting pan with aluminum foil. The foil lining will catch the glaze as it drips off the ham and carbonizes on the hot metal of the pan. After the pan is cool, peel off the lining and the pan will need only minimal cleanup without the carbonized mess.

All the Trimmings

The classic-looking ham features a diamond pattern accented by Maraschino cherries. The effect is easy to achieve by diagonally scoring the fat on the ham. When the ham comes out of the oven, place a halved Maraschino cherry secured with a toothpick in the middle of each diamond. The ham itself will be so beautiful you won't need a centerpiece. Let the ham rest then transfer to a platter set before the designated carver. Serve the rest of the meal family-style, passed in your best Sunday china.

Black-Eyed Pea and Sweet Red Pepper Salad with Fresh Thyme Vinaigrette

4 cups water (1 quart)

1 teaspoon salt

2 whole cloves

2 cloves garlic, chopped (1 teaspoon)

2 bay leaves

1 tablespoon fresh thyme (or 1 teaspoon dried)

1 (16-ounce) bag frozen black-eyed peas

Vinaigrette

¼ cup olive oil

3 tablespoons red wine vinegar

2 shallots, minced (3 tablespoons)

1 tablespoon fresh thyme, chopped
(or 1 teaspoon, dried)

2 red peppers, peeled, seeded, and diced

Salt and freshly ground black pepper, to taste

This recipe gives new life to black-eyed peas. It is best to use fresh thyme, but dried will do in a pinch.

PREPARATION TIME:	5 MINUTES
MARINATING TIME:	5 MINUTES
COOKING TIME:	20 MINUTES
MAKES 6 SERVINGS	

The black-eyed pea salad can be made up to 1 day in advance.

In a medium saucepan, bring the water, salt, cloves, garlic, bay leaves, and thyme to a boil. Add the black-eyed peas and cook, uncovered, for 20 minutes. Meanwhile, in a bowl, combine the olive oil, vinegar, shallots, thyme, and red peppers. When the peas are ready, drain, remove the bay leaves, and toss with the vinaigrette. Season with salt and pepper to taste. The salad can be chilled for 5 minutes or more, or it can be served at room temperature.

CALVIN'S CHERRY-GLAZED HAM

1 (7-pound) brine-cured fully cooked country ham (see below)

1 (8-ounce) jar apricot jam

1 8-ounce jar Maraschino cherry halves, drained

Flat-leaf parsley, for garnish

Calvin Rogers, Barbara's lifelong friend, has a successful catering business in New York. At holiday time, his regular clients request this mouthwatering, slow-cooked ham for their parties.

PREPARATION TIME: 5 MINUTES

COOKING TIME: ABOUT 2 HOURS. USE 20 MINUTES PER POUND AS A GUIDELINE, OR HEAT UNTIL THE INTERNAL TEMPERATURE IS 160° AS SHOWN ON A MEAT THERMOMETER.

MAKES 6 TO 8 SERVINGS (WITH LEFTOVERS FOR SANDWICHES)

Can be made a day in advance and warmed up in a 250° oven for 45 minutes.

Preheat the oven to 350°. With a sharp knife, score diagonal lines in both directions on the fat of the ham, making diamonds that are about 2 inches by 2 inches. Place the ham on a rack in a foil-lined roasting pan, fat side up, and bake for $1^1/_2$ hours. Spread the apricot jam on the ham and cook for an additional 30 minutes, for a total cooking time of about 2 hours or until a meat thermometer reads 140° when stuck in the center of the ham. Remove the ham and let it rest for 15 minutes. Cut the Maraschino cherries in half and place a cherry half in the middle of each diamond, secured with a toothpick through the middle. Arrange the ham on a platter surrounded by the parsley.

Calvin's choice for ham is sometimes known as country ham, which is slowly dry-cured with salt, then smoked and aged. Smithfield ham is a version of country ham. You can order a great Virginia country ham from S. Wallace Edwards and Sons Inc., 1-800-222-4267, or write P.O. Box 25, Surry, Virginia 23883.

If you purchase a ham labeled "cook before eating," it must be cooked to an internal temperature of the higher temperature, 160°. Place a meat thermometer deep into the meat without touching the bone, and cook about 20 to 30 minutes per pound, checking after an hour and a half, until the appropriate internal temperature is reached.

Most country hams are sold "bone-in" either by the whole, half, shank, or butt.

You'll get two to three servings per pound. You may also buy a boneless ham, fully cooked and usually in a rectangular or fake-ham shape. Figure four to five servings per pound. A semiboneless ham is easier to carve and has only the round leg bone to hold it together. You'll get three to four servings per pound, with leftovers for sandwiches. Deli ham is available cooked and sliced, and 2 ounces is sufficient for each sandwich serving.

Other popular hams include: Westphalian, a dry-cured German ham that's smoked with juniper twigs and berries; Tasso, a Cajun-style ham seasoned with pepper and spice; Capicolla, an Italian-style spicy ham made from the picnic (shoulder) and seasoned with cayenne and spices; Black Forest ham, a German-style dry-cured ham, heavily smoked with fir and pine branches; and prosciutto, an Italian-style cured ham that is air-dried and not smoked. Prosciutto is usually eaten without cooking and in thin slices.

Most hams you buy today are fully cooked and ready to eat. They can be served cold, or heated to an internal temperature of 140°. However, cooking the meat longer improves its texture and yields a tender, flavorful product without the gelatinous quality of meat cooked for a shorter period of time.

Store leftover ham, wrapped tightly and refrigerated, for up to a week. Don't freeze a ham unless you have to, and never for more than 60 days.

COLLARD GREENS

2 tablespoons salt

2 bunches collard greens, coarsely chopped
(about 2 pounds)

4 thick slices bacon, cut into 2-inch pieces

Collard greens give off a wonderful aroma as they cook. As long as you put in the bacon, you really can't ruin them. Don't pour out the liquid you cooked those greens in. We call that pot licker in the South and offer it only to our nearest and dearest, to be drunk right from the pot.

PREPARATION TIME: 5 MINUTES

COOKING TIME: 45 MINUTES

MAKES 6 SERVINGS

Bring a large pot of water to a boil with the salt. Add the collards and bacon and cook, uncovered, for 45 minutes. Lift the greens from the pot licker to a bowl and serve hot.

Black Skillet Corn Bread

2 (8-ounce) boxes corn bread mix   2 tablespoons butter (or bacon grease)

Ingredients called for on box

PREPARATION TIME: 5 MINUTES

COOKING TIME: 15 TO 20 MINUTES

MAKES 6 SERVINGS

If you prefer, simply buy corn bread muffins at a bakery.

Preheat the oven to 375°. Place butter in a 10-inch cast-iron skillet and preheat it either in the oven for 5 minutes or on top of the stove for 2 minutes. Spread butter around evenly to coat the bottom and sides of the skillet.

Meanwhile, prepare the mix according to the directions on the box. Pour the prepared mix into the hot buttered skillet, and bake for 15 to 20 minutes or until golden brown. Cut into wedges and serve hot from the skillet.

Sweet Potato Pie with Praline Sauce

1/2 cup heavy cream

1/4 cup sugar

1/4 teaspoon salt

2 (15-ounce) cans sweet potatoes, drained and mashed (with a fork right in the can)

1/4 cup (1/2 stick) unsalted butter, melted

3 tablespoons all-purpose flour

1 1/2 teaspoons cinnamon

1 1/2 teaspoons nutmeg

1 teaspoon vanilla extract

1 (9-inch) ready-to-bake piecrust

1/2 cup pecan halves

Praline Sauce:

1 tablespoon unsalted butter

1/4 cup sugar

1/2 teaspoon salt

1 1/4 cups heavy cream

1/2 cup chopped pecans

This sweet potato pie recipe made us realize (dare we admit) that we liked it better than pumpkin pie. The praline sauce is optional but outrageously good. We promise that there will be none left!

PREPARATION TIME: 10 MINUTES

COOKING TIME: 1 HOUR

MAKES 6 SERVINGS

The sweet potato pie and sauce can be made 1 day in advance.

To make the pie, preheat the oven to 350°. Whip the cream adding the sugar 1 teaspoon at a time. Add the salt, mashed sweet potatoes, melted butter, flour, cinnamon, nutmeg, and vanilla. Mix thoroughly in a large bowl, and pour the mixture into the uncooked pie shell. On the top of the filling, arrange the pecans halves in a pinwheel design. Bake for 1 hour.

Meanwhile, make the sauce. In a heavy saucepan, melt the butter and sugar until golden brown. Stir in the salt, cream, and pecans and continue to stir constantly for about 10 minutes, until the spoon leaves a trail through the sauce, revealing the bottom of the pan. Remove the sauce from the heat and let it cool a few minutes. To serve, drizzle some warm sauce over each serving of pie. If made ahead, store in a covered jar in the refrigerator. Remove the lid and reheat in microwave 1 minute, or on the stovetop in a boiling water bath until the sauce is hot and runny.

Super Super Bowl Italian Buffet

Entertaining football fans is easy. Provide one or more television sets with comfortable chairs and floor pillows, hand your guests a good microbrewed beer the minute they step in the front door, and offer brightly flavored hearty foods they can eat in front of the television. Make it easy on yourself by using good-quality paper plates and stadium beer cups.

To improve your odds for enjoying the game, and so that you don't miss the kickoff, choose this easy menu that requires mostly shopping and only a little cooking. And, if anybody asks you where the chips and dips are, penalize them 15 yards or send them straight to the showers. There are no cliché fast foods at this party—just classic Italian casual foods that are sure to please even the pickiest NFL scouts you know.

The Menu

COLD ANTIPASTI (SEE PAGE 304)

HOT PROSCIUTTO PANINI WITH FONTINA AND WATERCRESS

DEBRA PUCCI'S WHITE BEAN AND ESCAROLE SOUP

ASSORTED MICROBREWED BEERS

HAIL MARY SUPER BOWL SUNDAES

HOT COFFEE

Cooking Tip

When making soup with canned beans, taste and adjust the seasonings at the end of the cooking time, adding salt *only* if necessary. Most canned products have too much salt. The cannellini (white bean) soup recipe, which blends canned beans and juice with a large volume of cooked escarole and unsalted cooking water, is unlikely to need any additional salt, but then again, you never can tell. The beans you buy might not have enough salt to make a decent soup.

It's the golden rule for cooking: Cook and taste. Cook and taste. Season to suit yourself and think about the food while you're tasting. We like to get the soup made before the guests arrive, because it gets too confusing once people start milling around the kitchen, talking about home field advantages, the point spread, and so forth.

All the Trimmings

We try to set the mood at the front door, with a pair of pompoms for a decoration. Inside, we try to keep the action moving up and down our field by placing the food and drink in various parts of the house. In one room, set up the microbrewed beer bar by placing beers on ice—in an ice chest, a washtub, along with stadium cups, beer openers, and someplace to deposit the empties. In the dining area, arrange the buffet. Last year, we used a stadium blanket for a tablecloth and made a centerpiece out of an old football helmet we dug out of the front hall closet—and a sprinkling of confetti across the table in the colors of the teams that are playing. And, of course, serve the meal buffet-style.

HOT PROSCIUTTO PANINI WITH FONTINA AND WATERCRESS

2 (8 × 10-inch) focaccia breads (or large Boboli cheese-flavored pizza crusts)

12 ounces prosciutto, cut very thin

12 ounces Fontina cheese, shredded

4 cups watercress, washed and dried, roots discarded, plus additional for garnish

1 large red onion, peeled and cut into thin slices

1/4 cup balsamic vinegar

Salt and freshly ground black pepper, to taste

Buy the best-quality focaccia (Italian flat bread), prosciutto, and Fontina and these hearty sandwiches will satisfy the hungriest of football fans. Substitute arugula for watercress if you wish.

Make, wrap, and refrigerate these sandwiches just before the party starts, then pop them into the oven for a last-minute warm-up to serve at halftime.

Slice each bread in half, horizontally like a giant hamburger bun. Divide prosciutto slices between the bottom halves, then add the cheese, watercress, and onion slices. Drizzle vinegar over the sandwiches and season them with freshly ground black pepper and salt. Wrap the sandwiches tightly in aluminum foil and refrigerate them until serving time. Bake in a preheated 300° oven for 15 minutes. Remove the sandwiches to a cutting board and, with a sharp chef's knife, cut them into 2 × 4-inch sandwiches. Stack them on a serving plate, garnish with additional watercress, and set them out, with a stack of good paper plates, for guests to help themselves.

Debra Pucci's White Bean and Escarole Soup

8 cloves garlic, chopped (4 teaspoons)

1/3 cup extra virgin olive oil

1/2 teaspoon crushed hot red pepper flakes, or to taste

6 (1-pound) cans cannellini or Great Northern beans with their liquid (12 cups)

3 heads escarole, washed and chopped

Salt and freshly ground black pepper, to taste

Parmesan cheese, freshly grated

If your local market doesn't carry canned beans called cannellini, choose Great Northern or navy beans instead. Our friend Debbi Pucci serves this soup every week to her family, figuring on two 1-pound cans of beans and one head of escarole for a four-person dinner that's on the table in less than 20 minutes. This is one of those great, forgiving recipes that will blow up to feed the fans—a hearty rich winter soup that is ready to serve quickly, and will also stand on a sideboard in a crockpot or soup tureen and wait until you're ready.

Debbi's mother starts with dried beans, of course. Should you wish to start this way, cook up a pound of dried beans in salted water the day before, following package directions, then, just before the party, proceed with the recipe as given.

PREPARATION TIME: 1 0 MINUTES

COOKING TIME: 1 0 MINUTES

MAKES 1 2 SERVINGS

This soup can be made a few hours in advance. It just gets better with time. Keep warm in a crockpot or soup tureen in a 200° oven.

Place two large soup pots on the stove—one filled three-quarters full with barely salted water. Bring the water to a boil. Meanwhile, in the other pot, barely brown the garlic in the oil over medium heat, about 3 minutes, then toss in the red pepper flakes and stir. Now add all the beans and bean liquid, raise the heat, and bring to a boil.

Drop the escarole into the boiling water and cook until tender, about 10 minutes. Using a large slotted spoon, scoop the cooked escarole into the bean pot. Stir, then add enough escarole cooking water to the beans to maintain a thick, soupy consistency (usually about 3 to 4 cups). Taste and adjust the seasonings with salt and freshly ground black pepper. Transfer the soup to a preheated crockpot or soup tureen, cover, and place on the sideboard, or just serve from the stove.

Let guests scoop out individual bowls of soup, and have a bowl of grated Parmesan cheese handy.

Hail Mary Super Bowl Sundaes

Finally, in the kitchen, set up a Do-It-Yourself-Super-Sundaes-Bar with all the makings for ice-cream sundaes. Nearing the end of the game, nestle three different kinds of ice cream into a bowl of crushed ice. Near the ice cream, arrange bowls of bought sauces: chocolate, cherry, and butterscotch, as well as bowls of sprinkles, nuts, and candy toppings, whipped cream, sliced bananas, and Maraschino cherries. There are a lot of nontraditional things you can put out as well. We like real Vermont maple syrup, crunched-up oatmeal cookies, peanuts, coconut, and dried pineapple. Go for it. Add a stack of bowls and spoons, a couple of ice-cream scoopers, and let the guests make their own. Even if the game goes into sudden-death-overtime, serve with good coffee.

When Guests Just Sit

"I have had a great many letters complaining that the trouble with buffet meals, when there is no servant to pass anything, is that the guests sometimes refuse to help themselves and 'just sit.' The only thing to do then is to say to them, as you would to children at a party, 'Please go into the dining room and get something to eat.' And then, if they stand around the table and don't go back into the living room, say 'Won't you please go into the living room and sit down?'"

101 Common Mistakes in Etiquette and How to Avoid Them
Emily Post, 1939

Skiers Weekend Cassoulet Dinner

If there's anything as certain as sunrise and sunset, it's the roaring appetites of guests who've spent a day out on the slopes. Winter sports not only cheer people up, they put them in mind of an early dinner. Since we too like to spend our time outdoors, we usually make the cassoulet and the Chocolate Express at home the day before, then haul the whole thing to a rented condo on the mountain. When we come in from the cold, we set out the olives, peppers, and a loaf of country bread, along with a couple bottles of red wine, while we heat up the stew. We make and serve the quesadillas on the spot and by then the stew is ready. This hearty winter combination has become one of our standbys.

Knowing how ravenous we all get after a day in the snow, we usually cook twice as much food as we think we'll need. Strangely, it all seems to evaporate before we come down off the mountain. We usually transport the stew in the pot we cooked it in. You could, if you worry about spillage in the car, even freeze the stew at home right in its cooking pot. Once you're at the ski lodge don't worry if you don't have enough refrigerator space to hold that big pot. Just set it out by the back door in the snow. If the bears carry it off, we are not responsible.

Don't be surprised if the midnight ramblers, human or animal, don't clean out any remaining stew from the pot you set out in the snow, and we know from experience that the Chocolate Express never survives till breakfast.

The Menu

MIXED OLIVES AND PEPPERONCINI

LEEK QUESADILLAS WITH ARTICHOKES AND GOAT CHEESE

LAMB CASSOULET

RUSTIC COUNTRY BREAD AND SWEET BUTTER

CHOCOLATE EXPRESS BREAD PUDDING

VANILLA ICE CREAM

Wine Suggestions

Appetizers and Main Course—Both the appetizer and main course on this menu, goat cheese and lamb, have a predominantly gamy flavor, so you have a good opportunity to serve an earthy, deep red wine such as Italian wine from the Negro Amaro region, Primitivo (Italian Zinfandel), or from the Rhone region in France, grapes like Syrah and Mourvèdre. All of these wines have a wonderful herbal earthiness that will complement the earthy aromatic foods.

Dessert—A French, Banyuls region, late harvest Grenache, is the perfect wine for chocolate.

Cooking Tip

Cooking in a strange, rented kitchen is always an adventure. We find it's sort of like playing house. You never know what you'll find in the cupboards. Sometimes there's a spectacular pot you always wished you had. But more than likely, the cooking vessels will look like something rejected by Goodwill. Our advice is to take your own best 12-inch skillet. Not only will it come in handy for making the quesadillas, but you can use it the next morning for the flapjacks, and at noon for making bacon-tomato sandwiches. We always carry our own corkscrew too. A fate worse than you-know-what is to be snowbound with several good bottles of wine and no way to open them.

All the Trimmings

Here's a jolly good job for the little naturalists in your party. A just-gathered centerpiece of fir cones and pine boughs with candles nestled inside is all that's required. Even if you've been guaranteed a supply of firewood for the fireplace or stove, we advise you to take up one load of good dry firewood—just to be Boy Scout safe. And don't forget the kitchen matches. Once you get the fire roaring, you can toss on snow-packed wood and it will dry out and burn, but just try and get that first fire built with wet wood! Serve the leek quesadillas right off the stove to the hungry masses. Then set up a buffet and let everyone serve themselves!

Leek Quesadillas with Artichokes and Goat Cheese

2 tablespoons extra virgin olive oil, plus additional for the tortillas

6 garlic cloves, chopped (3 teaspoons)

1 bay leaf

1½ teaspoons dried thyme

1 large leek, washed thoroughly, then chopped, including most of the green

1 (12-ounce) package frozen artichoke hearts, thawed, drained, and coarsely chopped or 1 (6-ounce) can artichoke hearts, drained and coarsely chopped

Salt and freshly ground black pepper, to taste

3 tablespoons sherry vinegar

8 large (10-inch) flour tortillas

5 ounces fresh goat cheese

Cherry tomatoes, for garnish

Borrow a Mexican technique, cooking cheese and vegetables in a flour tortilla for a quick and delicious hors d'oeuvre to precede our rich lamb stew. If you wish, sauté the vegetable filling early in the day, then grill the quesadillas, at serving time, in less than 5 minutes.

PREPARATION TIME: 15 MINUTES

COOKING TIME: 5 MINUTES

MAKES 8 SERVINGS

Vegetables can be sautéed 1 day in advance. Transport in a tupperware container.

Heat the oil in a large skillet over medium-high heat, then cook the garlic until pale gold, less than 1 minute. Add the bay leaf and thyme and cook another minute. Now, stir in the leek, lower the heat to medium, and cook until the leek is soft but not brown, about 5 minutes. Add the artichoke hearts and cook 5 minutes. Discard the bay leaf. Season the vegetables to taste with salt and pepper, then toss with the vinegar and set aside.

Heat a 12-inch skillet over medium heat, then wipe it with olive oil and add a tortilla. Spread a heaping ¼ cup of vegetable mixture over the tortilla and crumble half of the goat cheese on top. Cover with a second tortilla, then press down with the back of a spatula. Brown on one side, about 3 minutes, then flip it over and brown the second side. Remove the finished quesadilla to a board and cut it into wedges, using a chef's knife or a pizza cutter. Repeat with the remaining ingredients, regulating the heat so the pan doesn't get too hot and adding more oil as needed.

LAMB CASSOULET

2 tablespoons extra virgin olive oil

1/4 cup all-purpose flour

2 pounds lamb stew meat, cut into chunks

1 large yellow onion, coarsely chopped

4 cloves garlic, chopped (2 teaspoons)

1 cup dry white wine

2 (14 1/2-ounce) cans chicken broth

1 (28-ounce) can tomatoes and their liquid

1 teaspoon dried thyme

2 bay leaves

Salt and freshly ground black pepper, to taste (start with 3/4 teaspoon of each)

1 stalk celery, coarsely chopped

1 small carrot, peeled and coarsely chopped

1/2 cup chopped flat-leaf parsley

2 (16-ounce) cans white beans (cannellini or Great Northern), drained

Make this hearty stew 1 or 2 days in advance, then reheat it for dinner after a vigorous day outside and you'll see how this traditional French country dish kept farmers safe from cold winter winds. The dish was invented by people who had lots of chores to do besides cooking, and although it cooks for a while, it doesn't require much of the cook beyond a good heavy stew pot and some patience. Like so many stews, the flavors marry and improve overnight. Ask your butcher to chop the lamb into chunks, use canned white (cannellini) beans, use your food processor to chop the vegetables, and this job is knocked into submission.

PREPARATION TIME: 20 MINUTES

STEWING TIME: 2 HOURS

MAKES 8 SERVINGS

Can be made a day or two in advance and refrigerated in the cooking pot. Reheat to boiling over medium heat on top of the stove.

Heat the oil in a large stew pot over medium-high heat. Put the flour in a bag, add the meat, and shake to coat it. Shake off the excess flour, then brown the meat on all sides in the hot pan. Add the onion and garlic and continue cooking 5 minutes longer, stirring until the onion turns translucent. Pour in the wine and deglaze the pan, stirring up any bits of browned matter from the bottom of the pan and reducing the liquid to about $^1/_4$ cup, about 5 minutes. Add the broth, tomatoes, herbs, salt and pepper, the celery, carrot, parsley, and beans, and simmer a final 90 minutes. Cover and set aside until serving time. Serve hot, in wide-rimmed soup bowls.

Chocolate Express Bread Pudding

1 cup heavy cream

1 stick ($^1/_4$ pound) unsalted butter

8 ounces best-quality bittersweet chocolate chips

$1^1/_2$ tablespoons instant espresso powder (or very strong brewed coffee)

5 large eggs

$^3/_4$ cup sugar

1 teaspoon vanilla extract

1 quart 1-inch bread cubes (day-old brioche, challah, or French bread)

Vanilla ice cream (optional)

Somewhere between a soufflé and a fudge, this quick and easy chocolate bread pudding takes a while to cook, but very little time to prepare. Don't bother cutting the crusts away from the bread and don't even consider making perfect cubes. The rich chocolate custard will transform them anyway into a heavenly punched-up chocolate espresso torte. And don't forget, it is better if the bread is one-day old.

PREPARATION TIME: 10 MINUTES

BAKING TIME: 60 MINUTES

MAKES ABOUT 10 SERVINGS

Yes, you can make it a day in advance and store covered, in its pan in the refrigerator. But don't blame us if it's all eaten up before the big event. Bring back to room temperature before serving.

Preheat the oven to 350°. Place a large roasting pan—at least 12 × 15 inches—on the bottom rack of the oven, and pour 1 inch of water into it. Butter a 10 × 13-inch glass baking dish or a $2^1/_2$-quart oval Le Creuset baking dish and set it aside.

Combine the cream, butter, chocolate, and espresso powder in a 1-quart glass measure and heat it in the microwave on high (100 percent power) for 3 minutes. Alternately, heat the mixture in a saucepan over low heat until the chocolate melts, about 3 minutes. Stir until smooth.

In a large bowl, beat the eggs and sugar with an electric mixer at high speed until thick, ropy, and well aerated (about 3 minutes). Beat a little of the hot chocolate mixture into the eggs. Then, beating constantly, very slowly pour the remaining chocolate mixture into the eggs. Stir in the vanilla extract.

Add the bread cubes and stir to mix. Transfer the mixture to the buttered baking dish, cover it with foil, then place it in the oven in the larger hot water bath. Bake until the pudding sets, about 60 minutes. Wiggle the pan. Once the pudding is cooked, it will no longer tremble in the center. Cool on a rack. Serve warm or at room temperature, in bowls with a dollop of vanilla ice cream, if you wish.

Winter Blues Pork Chop and Cheese Grits Lunch

Of course, the blues can hit any time of year, but they seem to be worst in the winter. And since misery loves company, why not make a party of it? For a blues party you just can't serve spa food. This menu was inspired by Meredith Pollack, a friend and frequent hostess in Houston, and it is designed for close friends who appreciate the real things in life! Whether you listen to the sounds of B. B. King, Al Green, Koko Taylor, Janis Joplin, Eric Clapton, or the Grateful Dead, a Sunday afternoon with a few beers, some friends, and your own homegrown Blues Fest just might help chase away those low-down dirty old blues.

The Menu

PRETZELS AND NUTS

PORK CHOPS WITH A CHILI DRY RUB

CHEESE GRITS WITH ROASTED GARLIC

BABY GREENS WITH THREE-CITRUS DRESSING (SEE PAGE 93)

DEEP-DISH CRUMBLE-TOP APPLE PIE (SEE PAGE 327)

ASSORTED MICROBREWED BEERS

Cooking Tip

For the juiciest pork chops, do not steam or overcook them. First use paper towels to thoroughly dry the chops. Then dredge them in the spice mixture. Don't worry, there will still be enough moisture for the rub to stick. Then, preheat a heavy cast-iron or Le Creuset skillet on high for 2 minutes. Spritz the pan with cooking spray and add the chops. Don't move them for 5 minutes, then turn and cook them without moving for 5 more minutes. The pork should be crisp on the outside and slightly pink on the inside. If you cover the chops or fail to dry them, they will steam and the meat will toughen.

All the Trimmings

The beauty of this dinner is in the sounds and, of course, the slow pace. Set the table before the guests arrive. Light lots of candles. Warm the plates. When the food is done and you are ready to eat, make up individual plates in the kitchen. Cut the grits into diamonds. Each plate should have a diamond of grits and a pork chop. Serve the salad on individual salad plates. Bring the extra salad to the table and people will want more! Serve the pie à la mode, casually, in the living room.

PORK CHOPS WITH A CHILI DRY RUB

3 tablespoons garlic powder

3 tablespoons paprika

1 tablespoon chili powder

2 teaspoons salt

1 teaspoon freshly ground black pepper, or to taste

Pinch of cayenne

4 (1-inch-thick) center cut pork chops

1 teaspoon peanut oil

This pork chop recipe is an old standby. Fast and flavorful, it really goes with anything. Make the rub weeks ahead, store in jars and use it for chicken, steaks, even oven-baked potatoes in a pinch. It makes great comfort food.

PREPARATION TIME: 5 MINUTES

COOKING TIME: 1 0 MINUTES

MAKES 4 SERVINGS

The chops are best if made and eaten immediately.

Combine the spices in a shallow bowl. Thoroughly dry the chops. Dredge each one in the spice mixture. Preheat a heavy cast-iron or Le Creuset skillet for 2 minutes. Spritz it with cooking spray or smear it with 1 teaspoon of peanut oil. Place the dredged chops carefully in the skillet, making sure they are not touching. Sauté for 5 minutes without moving them, then turn and cook for 5 more minutes, again without moving them. Check for doneness, since different stoves cook at different temperatures. The meat inside should be slightly pink and juicy. Don't worry. Pink is better than gray. Be careful not to overcook them.

CHEESE GRITS WITH ROASTED GARLIC

1 tablespoon peanut oil

1 tablespoon butter

1 onion, coarsely chopped

4 cloves garlic, peeled and chopped
(2 teaspoons)

1 (10^1/$_2$-ounce) can chicken broth

2^3/$_4$ cups water

1 cup quick grits

^{1}/$_2$ teaspoon salt

1 cup sharp Cheddar cheese grated

3 large eggs

1 tablespoon paprika

PREPARATION TIME:	10 MINUTES
COOKING TIME:	10 MINUTES
BAKING TIME:	45 MINUTES
MAKES 6 LARGE SERVINGS	

May be made the day before and reheated in the microwave 3 minutes or 300° oven for 10 minutes or so.

Preheat the oven to 350°. Spritz a 14-inch glass baking dish with cooking spray and set it aside.

In a medium saucepan set over medium heat, stir together the oil and butter. Add the onion and garlic and cook until the onion begins to turn translucent, about 3 minutes. Add the broth and water and stir in the grits. Add the salt, reduce the heat to low, cover, and cook for 4 to 5 minutes, stirring from time to time. Remove from the heat and mix in the cheese followed by the eggs. Pour the mixture into the prepared baking dish, dust the top with the paprika, and bake until the grits are puffed and brown on top, about 45 minutes. Cut into diamond shapes to serve.

Chocolate and Roses Valentine's Dinner
à Deux

Here's a celebration meal that's just for the two of you. Stretch this dinner out from seven to midnight if you wish, cooking the courses as you go along, and as the inspiration comes to you. Nothing takes long to cook and every single course of this meal will wait for you. While each course is a dazzler, the overall effect is fireworks.

The Menu

BROILED OYSTERS ON THE HALF SHELL

FOCACCIA

BABY GREENS WITH THREE-CITRUS DRESSING (SEE PAGE 93)

MAÎTRE D' HÔTEL BUTTER

BEEF MEDALLIONS WITH CRACKED PEPPERCORNS AND BOURBON SAUCE

POLENTA HEARTS

CHOCOLATE MOUSSE (SEE PAGE 256) WITH
GIANT DRISCOLL STRAWBERRIES

ESPRESSO

Wine Suggestions

Appetizer—a Prosecco from the Veneto region of Italy. This sparkling Italian wine is the official fizz from Venice, probably the most romantic place on earth. Not only will it be a great complement to the oysters, it is a more original choice than champagne.

Main Course—With beef on Valentine's, go for a northern Rhone Valley Syrah appellations Côte Rôtie, Hermitage, or any of the sub-appellations. The black peppery quality of the wine will be picked up by the peppercorn sauce and the tannins will cut the cream sauce. Plan on spending $20 to $40. Hey, it is Valentine's Day!

Dessert—From the South of France, the Banyuls region late harvest Grenache is the perfect wine for chocolate. Really original and really great. It is usually sold in a half bottle.

Cooking Tip

We wanted to serve the oysters raw on the half shell, but we couldn't get them open. In a moment of inspired desperation, we placed the unopened bivalves in a baking dish on a bed of kosher salt and ran them under the broiler. In 5 minutes, they were hot, the shells had popped open, and all we needed to begin our seduction dinner was a few drops of lemon juice on the steamy plump oysters, a glass of Veneto Prosecco, and hot focaccia.

All the Trimmings

Sprinkle rose petals on a white-linen-covered table for two and light candles, candles, candles all over the room. Use your best china, silver, and crystal. Play the music that made the two of you fall in love, and snuggle with your lover. Serve the oysters in the living room, then invite your guest into the kitchen to help sauté the steak and polenta. Compose beautiful individual plates. Serve the salad after the main course to clear your palate for dessert. That's all you need for a perfect Valentine's celebration, just between the two of you.

Maître d' Hôtel Butter

1/4 cup (1/2 stick) soft butter

2 tablespoons finely chopped flat-leaf parsley

1 teaspoon chopped garlic (2 cloves)

Freshly ground black pepper, to taste

Stir this spiked butter together at your convenience, roll, and refrigerate it. Then, when the steaks are done, put a $1/2$-inch thick pat on each medallion of beef and each polenta heart. It's even good melting over those hot, plump broiled oysters. The butter can also be used for hot bread, chops (for an instant sauce), or rice and pasta. The seasoning possibilities are also limitless. Always use fresh herbs that are well chopped to release their flavor!

PREPARATION TIME: 5 MINUTES

REFRIGERATION TIME: 30 MINUTES

MAKES 4 TABLESPOONS

May be prepared up to 2 days in advance.

Mix all the ingredients together with a fork, then roll the butter into a piece of waxed paper and refrigerate it until serving time.

Beef Medallions with Cracked Peppercorns and Bourbon Sauce

2 (4-ounce) fillets of beef (1 inch thick) $1/4$ cup beef broth

2 tablespoons cracked black peppercorns $1/4$ cup bourbon

$1/4$ cup dry vermouth

Crusty on the outside, pink in the middle, these little steaks are quick to fix and delicious to eat.

PREPARATION TIME: 5 MINUTES

STANDING TIME: 30 MINUTES

COOKING TIME: 10 MINUTES

MAKES 2 SERVINGS

Remove the steaks from the refrigerator and press the peppercorns into them about a half hour in advance so that they reach room temperature. That way, they will absorb flavors more easily and cook much more evenly and predictably.

Cut away and discard any fat from the meat. Pat the fillets dry with paper towels, and place them on a piece of waxed paper. Press peppercorns into both sides of the meat, using the heel of your hand or a mallet. Fold the paper over to cover the meat. Set the meat aside to come to room temperature.

Heat a 10-inch sauté pan over high heat, then place the meat in the pan. Without moving it, let the meat sear (this keeps the juices in), about 2 to 5 minutes, then flip the meat over, reduce the heat to medium, and cook the second side. After 2 minutes on the second side, place a small lid directly down over the meat and complete cooking, about 3 to 4 minutes. Cut into the meat. It should be crisp on the outside, pink in the middle.

Remove the steaks to a warmed plate and set them aside. Add the vermouth and broth to the pan, raise the heat to high, and boil until the mixture is reduced to 3 tablespoons, about 3 minutes. Add the bourbon and bring to a boil, then light it and burn the alcohol off, boiling the flaming mixture until it is reduced by half, about 5 minutes. Pour the pan juices over the fillets and serve at once, adding pats of butter.

Polenta Hearts

1 tube precooked polenta*

1 tablespoon extra virgin olive oil, butter, or Porcini oil

Salt and freshly ground black pepper, to taste

Maître d' Hôtel Butter

You've probably seen cooked polenta sold in supermarkets in sausage-like tubes. What could be handier for entertaining?

Preparation time: 5 minutes

Cooking time: 5 minutes

Makes 2 servings

* You can also make polenta for a big party by buttering a baking dish, then arranging the disks of polenta in the dish. Bake in a hot oven for 5 minutes or so, until crisp. A sprinkling of Parmesan cheese or a spoonful of your favorite marinara yields a trouble-free and dramatic side dish. Serve each disk with a pat of Maître d' Hôtel Butter.

Cut the polenta into 1-inch-thick slices. If you wish, just because it's Valentine's Day and just because you're in love, cut the polenta disks into hearts with a cookie cutter before sautéing. Heat the olive oil, butter, or Porcini oil over medium heat in a large, heavy skillet. Add the polenta and sauté until it's crisp on the outside, creamy smooth in the middle, about 5 minutes.

President's Day Weekend Brunch for Eight

It's hard to say whether American workers should cheer or jeer at the notion of combining Washington's and Lincoln's birthday celebrations into one holiday, but all we've got to say is to take advantage of the 3-day weekend. Now's a great time to throw a last-gasp-of-winter brunch for friends you might not otherwise have time to entertain.

Make a black skillet ham and vegetable dish, along with some stir-together corn muffins and a blood orange salad on a bed of watercress. Arrange the food at buffet stations, separating the main course from the I Cannot Tell a Lie Cherry Clafouti. The menu is ample. And you can feel content. You will have sent your friends out into the afternoon in a great mood.

The Menu

STARS AND BARS CHAMPAGNE BLUSH

BLOOD ORANGE AND CAPER SALAD

HOTCHA CORN BREAD MUFFINS

BLACK SKILLET ROASTED HAM WITH POTATOES, ONIONS, PEPPERS, AND TOMATOES

I CANNOT TELL A LIE CHERRY CLAFOUTI

COFFEE AND TEA

Wine Suggestions

Main Course—To make any champagne drink, use a Spanish or California vintage. If you want to be creative, try an Italian Prosecco from Veneto. It is really a bargain at $10 and makes a wonderful mixer.

Cooking Tip

Muffins are easiest to make if you use paper liners in the muffin pans. Remember to spritz the papers with cooking spray and the muffins will peel right out into your guests' hands. And besides that, the pan's not even dirty.

All the Trimmings

We like to set up brunches buffet-style. Serve the ham directly from its skillet. Make a station for champagne, coffee, and tea. Use red, white, and blue napkins. Wrap the silverware in a napkin and tie it up with a ribbon (see page 8), then place the packages in a cloth-lined basket for easy reach. On the dessert table, make an arrangement of red, white, and blue carnations. (We were going to incorporate a hatchet, but having invited both Democrats and Republicans to dine, we decided not to press our luck.)

You're Invited!

Fax your friends at least a week in advance with an invitation you've handwritten over a silhouette of Abe Lincoln, George Washington, a hatchet, stovepipe hat, wooden false teeth, or some combination thereof—whatever image works for you. Be sure to include not only the time the party is starting but also the time it will end (the big risk in a brunch is that some people will come and plan to spend the day). Include your own phone, fax, or e-mail number for people to RSVP.

Stars and Bars Champagne Blush

6 cups fresh or frozen pink lemonade

6 cups chilled cranberry juice cocktail

6 cups chilled dry champagne (Krug is a good choice or Spanish sparkling wine)

1 cup fresh blueberries

Optional ice ring

Champagne flutes filled with sparkling cranberry-champagne bubbly and speckled with fresh blueberries makes a salute to America that's suitably tart from lemonade, suitably sweet from cranberry juice, and suitably intoxicating to guarantee that no one tells a lie! If you're the kind who thinks ahead, make a fruited ice ring and serve the bubbly from a punch bowl.

PREPARATION TIME: 1 0 MINUTES

ICE RING (OPTIONAL) FREEZING TIME: 4 HOURS

MAKES 24 GLASSES OF BLUSH—3 (6-OUNCE) GLASSES PER GUEST

Now's your chance to use one of those Jell-O molds you inherited from your mother. We sometimes freeze a ring of fruit-studded lemonade to chill the punch bowl, but you could use a blob, a crown mold, or a square. Use your imagination and the contents of your pantry. Compose and freeze the ice ring as much as a week in advance. All you have to do is make up a small can of frozen pink lemonade, add some berries, and freeze. Then, just as the party starts, pop the ring into a punch bowl, make and serve the blush immediately. You can expand this recipe to the multitudes if you have sufficient supplies on hand. Just remember, the punch is equal parts lemonade, cranberry juice, and champagne. What could be simpler?

At serving time, combine all ingredients in a pitcher or punch bowl. Pour or ladle into champagne flutes, and serve.

Blood Orange and Caper Salad

8 small blood oranges

1 tablespoon capers, drained

¼ cup extra virgin olive oil

Juice and zest of ½ lemon (about 3 tablespoons juice)

½ teaspoon ground cumin

Salt and freshly ground black pepper, to taste

2 bunches watercress, washed, stemmed, and dried

½ teaspoon ground cinnamon

2 tablespoons confectioners' sugar

Sweet, savory, salty, and sunny in flavor and texture, this morning salad wakes up the sleepiest palate.

PREPARATION TIME: 10 MINUTES

CHILLING TIME: 30 MINUTES TO 24 HOURS

MAKES 8 SERVINGS

Find 10 minutes in your schedule to make and refrigerate this orange salad and dressing as much as a day in advance, holding separately in the refrigerator. If blood oranges aren't available where you shop, substitute seedless navel oranges.

Using a zester, remove the zest from one orange and place it in a large bowl. Peel the remaining oranges. Cut the oranges into thin rounds, discard the seeds, and add the flesh to the bowl. Sprinkle with the capers, cover, and refrigerate until serving time. Put the oil, lemon juice and zest, the cumin, salt, and pepper in a small jar. Shake to mix. Refrigerate until serving time.

To serve, pour the dressing over the watercress in a large bowl and toss to mix. Arrange the greens on a large flat platter, top with the oranges and capers, and drizzle with the juices from the bowl. Sprinkle the cinnamon and sugar over all and place on the sideboard.

Hotcha Corn Bread Muffins

1 cup fresh or frozen corn kernels

1/2 cup chopped onion

3/4 cup grated sharp Cheddar cheese

1/2 cup best-quality fresh hot salsa

1/2 cup milk

1 large egg

2 tablespoons bacon grease or vegetable oil

1 1/2 cups corn bread mix (White Lily* is the best but Jiffy will do)

Stir together corn bread mix, frozen chopped onions, corn kernels, and your favorite fresh salsa along with preshredded Cheddar, and you've got a winner of a quick bread to serve to guests.

PREPARATION TIME: 10 MINUTES

BAKING TIME: 20 TO 22 MINUTES

MAKES 18 MUFFINS

Best if eaten the same day they're made.

Preheat the oven to 425°. Line 18 muffin cups with paper liners, spritz each liner with cooking spray, and set aside.

In a medium mixing bowl, combine the corn, onion, cheese, salsa, milk, egg, and fat. Whisk with a fork, then stir in the corn bread mix. Stir to mix thoroughly, then divide among the muffin cups filling each 2/3 full. Bake 20 to 22 minutes or until browned.

Transfer the hot muffins to a cloth-lined basket and cover with a cloth. Place on the sideboard along with butter and various jams. Serve warm.

* To order White Lily, call 1-800-264-5459.

Black Skillet Roasted Ham with Potatoes, Onions, Peppers, and Tomatoes

1/4 cup extra virgin olive oil

3 pounds red new potatoes, cut in half (1 1/2 to 2 inches in diameter)

2 pounds yellow onions (about 4 medium), quartered

2 large bell peppers (1 red and 1 green) seeded, roughly peeled and quartered

8 cherry tomatoes

1 tablespoon fresh or dried rosemary needles

Salt and freshly ground black pepper, to taste

1 large fully cooked ham slice (about 1 1/2 pounds), cut into bite-size pieces

PREPARATION TIME: 1 5 MINUTES

ROASTING TIME: 40 MINUTES

MAKES 8 SERVINGS

May be made the day before, then reheated in the 300° oven 10 minutes or so at serving time.

Preheat the oven to 425° and wipe a 10- to 12-inch cast-iron (enameled or plain) oven-proof skillet with some of the olive oil.

Add the potatoes to the pan, then add onions, peppers, tomatoes, and rosemary. Drizzle the mixture with the remaining olive oil. Season generously with salt and pepper and toss to mix.

Roast, uncovered, about 40 minutes, nestling ham in among the vegetables during the last 10 minutes or so. Serve directly from the skillet, spooning any pan juices over the meat and vegetables.

To this station, you could also nestle containers of fruit-flavored yogurt and a side dish of good granola for the granola heads of your acquaintance.

I Cannot Tell a Lie Cherry Clafouti

1 tablespoon butter, for the pan

2 (17-ounce) cans sweet bing cherries, drained (not Maraschino)

³/₄ cup sugar

¹/₄ cup brandy or cognac

4 tablespoons unsalted butter, melted

1³/₄ cups milk

1 cup all-purpose flour

1 teaspoon salt

4 large eggs

Confectioners' sugar

A clafouti is wonderful French farmers' food. It is somewhere between a baked pancake and a custard, and it can be made with any fruit and liqueur combination. Here we call for canned cherries because fresh cherries are not available in the winter. This would, of course, be great in June with 2 pounds of fresh black cherries. Some clafoutis have a crust, though the classic clafouti does not. In honor of the busy host, we say leave it out. A clafouti can be served as a dessert or as a breakfast dish. For this brunch, it is really both.

PREPARATION TIME:	10 MINUTES
MACERATING TIME:	UP TO 30 MINUTES
BAKING TIME:	25 MINUTES
RESTING TIME:	10 MINUTES
MAKES 8 SERVINGS	

Can be made up 1 day in advance. Store covered in the refrigerator. Bring to room temperature to serve.

Preheat oven to 425°. Butter a straight-sided gratin dish or a 9 × 9 × 2-inch Pyrex dish. In the baking dish, toss the cherries with ¹/₄ cup of the sugar and the cognac. The longer the cherries macerate in the brandy, the better the clafouti will taste, up to 30 minutes. In a blender, mixer, or by hand, mix the melted butter with the milk, the remaining sugar, the flour, salt, and eggs. Pour this mixture over the cherries and bake for 25 minutes, or until a toothpick comes out clean. Allow the clafouti to rest for 10 minutes before serving. Serve it either warm or cold, sprinkled with confectioners' sugar just before serving.

Other Clafouti Suggestions:

Fresh cherries and kirsch

Cinnamon, apples, and raisins with Calvados (apples must first be sautéed in butter)

Pears, almonds, and Amaretto (pears and almonds first sautéed in butter)

Strawberries, rhubarb, and rum (rhubarb must first be sautéed in butter)

Blackberries, blueberries, and raspberries with Cassis

Strawberries, kiwis, and framboise

Clementine oranges and coconut with triple sec

Mangoes and cloves with triple sec

Arrange a separate table with coffee and tea service near the dessert to keep the guests moving. We use two coffee carafes—one marked regular and one for decaf, plus a separate hot pot for water, along with a selection of teas in a silver bowl for guests to choose from. Be sure to include sugar cubes or colored sugar on your shopping list, and don't forget the lemon and milk for the tea sippers. Place the teaspoons in a small glass, and set out your prettiest cups and saucers. Don't worry if they don't all match, or even if they're all different sizes. That just adds interest to the table.

Yearning for Summer
February Tropical Dinner

In most parts of the United States, February is a pretty dreary month. Where we live, there are almost no interesting vegetables at this time of year. Thank goodness for the Caribbean populations and the tropical fruits they've insisted we import. You can count on a mango or papaya anytime. So when the winter blues really start to get you down and you can't just hop down to the islands, try this menu to bring a little tropical sunshine into your life. Of course, you don't have to wait until winter. The great thing about tropical fruits is that they're always there.

We like this menu for two couples on a Friday night, because it comes together really fast. We have, however, made it for six or eight. The preparation and cooking times don't change—the grocery list just gets a little longer.

The Menu

AVOCADO SOUP

PLANTAIN CHIPS

PAN-GRILLED NEW YORK STRIP STEAK WITH PINEAPPLE-MANGO SALSA

SPICY BLACK BEANS

ROMAINE SALAD WITH THREE-CITRUS DRESSING

PAPAYA AND SPICE BLACK SKILLET CRISP

Wine Suggestions

Main Course—An Oregon Pinot Noir, low in alcohol (below 12.5 percent) and high in acidity and fruitiness, will complement both the strip steak and the Pineapple-Mango Salsa. Or, for a really festive wine, try a Yalumba Valley Brut Rosé from Australia. The fizzy and fruity character will match the tropical fruit flavors of the topping. You can serve it for dessert too!

Cooking Tip

The best way to cook a steak or chop when it's too cold to grill outdoors is to pan grill it on top of the stove. Most home broilers do not get hot enough to properly sear-in the juices of a steak or chop. Usually, the broiler just gets hot enough to steam a piece of meat, leaving it tough and dry. Remember that heat builds, so a preheated cast-iron or heavy copper-clad skillet is much hotter than your broiler. Always pat the meat dry with paper towels before placing it in the preheated skillet to prevent its steaming in the pan. And don't move the meat around. Let it sit in one hot place to sear and preserve the juices inside. Turn the meat with a spatula or tongs, not a fork. No need to stab the poor thing and watch it bleed to death before your very eyes.

All the Trimmings

This is a great opportunity to decorate the table with a tropical fruit basket. A Jamaican woman we know taught us to fill the bottom of the basket with wadded-up paper and rest the fruit on top, thus using less fruit. You can also tie an individual orchid to each napkin ring. Or make a simple arrangement of a few sprigs of orchids in a bud vase. The elegance is in the simplicity. Most importantly, turn up the volume on some calypso, mambo, or reggae music. We love Celia Cruz, the Cuban wonder! Close your eyes and think of turquoise water. Preset the table with the avocado soup before you sit down. Ask someone to clear the bowls while you make up the main course plates of steak topped with the mango salsa and a side of black beans. Pass the salad. Bring the dessert to the table in its skillet for a dazzling presentation.

Avocado Soup

2 large ripe avocados, sliced (reserve the best slices for garnish)

1/2 cup chopped scallions

1 cup half-and-half

1 (15-ounce) can chicken broth

1/2 teaspoon freshly grated nutmeg

1/4 cup freshly squeezed lemon juice

Freshly ground black pepper, to taste

Dollops of sour cream or sprinklings of cilantro, for garnish

PREPARATION TIME: 10 MINUTES

COOKING TIME: 5 MINUTES

MAKES 4 SERVINGS (MAY BE DOUBLED WITH NO CHANGE IN COOKING TIME)

May be made 1 day in advance and served cold or hot. Reheat 2 minutes on stovetop but do not allow it to boil.

In a food processor or blender, puree the avocados, scallions, and half-and-half. In a saucepan, bring the chicken broth to a boil with the nutmeg, lemon juice, and pepper. Turn the heat down and add avocado cream to heat through, but don't allow it to boil. Serve hot or cold, garnished with a dollop of sour cream or a sprig of cilantro.

Pan-Grilled New York Strip Steak

4 (6-ounce) New York strip steaks (may use fillets), thoroughly dried and peppered

Salt and freshly ground black pepper, to taste

A spritz of cooking spray or 1 to 2 teaspoons peanut oil

To get those good-looking grill marks in the kitchen, use a grill skillet with ridges. Preheat this skillet, just as you would any other.

PREPARATION TIME:	3 MINUTES
PREWARMING TIME:	15 MINUTES
COOKING TIME:	8 MINUTES
MAKES 4 SERVINGS	

Remove steaks from the refrigerator to warm to room temperature. Preheat a large cast-iron or copper-clad skillet for 2 to 3 minutes on high. Dry the steaks thoroughly with paper towels and season them well with black pepper. Spray the preheated skillet with cooking spray or put a little oil in the pan, and add the steaks. Do not crowd the skillet or the temperature will drop, the steaks will steam, and the meat won't sear properly. Cook for 2 to 3 minutes without moving, then turn and cook to the desired doneness.* Salt the steaks only after they are cooked or the meat will toughen.

* You can tell how well done a steak is by touch. A well-done steak should be as firm to the touch as the tip of your nose. For medium-rare, the steak should feel as firm as the lower palm of your hand when you make a fist; rare would be as relaxed as the lower palm of your hand when at rest. Rare steak cooks in about 2 minutes per side, medium-rare takes 3 to 4 minutes, and Gawd-forbid-well-done, 5 to 6 minutes per side.

Pineapple–Mango Salsa

1 (14-ounce) can pineapple chunks, drained

1 ripe mango, peeled, seeded, and cut into small chunks

4 scallions, white and green parts, finely chopped

3/4 cup loosely packed coarsely chopped cilantro leaves

1/2 teaspoon chopped garlic (1 clove)

1/4 cup rice wine vinegar

1 tablespoon extra virgin olive oil

1/4–1/2 tablespoon cayenne, or to taste

1/2 teaspoon salt

PREPARATION TIME: 10 MINUTES

MARINATING TIME: 15 MINUTES

MAKES 4 SERVINGS

Can be made 2 days in advance, covered and refrigerated until serving time.

Stir together all the ingredients in a salad bowl. Cover and marinate 15 minutes in the refrigerator, or until serving time.

Spicy Black Beans

2 (15-ounce) cans black beans, with liquid

1/2 teaspoon ground cloves

1 teaspoon ground cumin

Salt and freshly ground black pepper, to taste

PREPARATION TIME: 5 MINUTES

COOKING TIME: 5 MINUTES

MAKES 4 SERVINGS

The ingredients can be combined a day in advance, then brought to a boil in the microwave or on the stovetop before serving.

Cook this on the stovetop or in the microwave on high. Do what's easy for you. Stir together the beans and spices in a medium saucepan or microwave-proof bowl. Bring to a boil over high heat. Transfer to a serving bowl and serve hot.

ROMAINE SALAD WITH THREE-CITRUS DRESSING

8 to 10 large leaves romaine lettuce

Dressing:

Juice of ¹/₂ lemon
Juice of ¹/₂ lime

Juice of ¹/₂ orange
1 teaspoon rice wine vinegar
¹/₄ cup extra virgin olive oil
1 teaspoon sugar
Salt and freshly ground black pepper, to taste

Combining several citrus flavors makes a salad that sings. This is one of our standbys. We serve it with steak, chops, or pasta. Keep dressing in a jar, covered in the refrigerator up to 1 week. Works well with any tender greens as well as with edible flowers.

PREPARATION TIME: 10 MINUTES
MAKES 4 TO 6 SERVINGS

The dressing may be made 1 day in advance, but the salad itself is best if made and served immediately.

Wash and dry lettuce leaves and tear them into bite-size pieces. In a jar, mix the lemon, lime, and orange juices with the vinegar, oil, sugar, salt, and pepper, ƒ with a fork. Refrigerate until serving time. Toss the lettuce with the dressing and serve in a salad bowl immediately.

Papaya and Spice Black Skillet Crisp

1 (6- to 7-inch) very ripe papaya, peeled, seeded, and cut into ¼ inch strips

1 tablespoon lime juice

Zest of ½ lime

2 tablespoons dark rum

2 tablespoons butter

¾ cup brown sugar

Batter:

½ cup all-purpose flour

¾ cup sugar

¼ teaspoon baking powder

½ teaspoon salt

½ teaspoon ground cloves

1 large egg

1 teaspoon vanilla extract

2 tablespoons hot water

Vanilla ice cream or fresh cream (optional)

PREPARATION TIME: 5 MINUTES

COOKING TIME: 55 MINUTES

MAKES 6 SERVINGS

This cobbler may be made 4 hours in advance and cooked for 45 minutes, then warmed up for 15 minutes before serving.

Preheat the oven to 350°. Toss the papaya with the lime juice, zest, and rum, and set it aside. In a heavy cast-iron skillet, melt the butter and stir in the brown sugar. In a mixing bowl, stir together the flour, sugar, baking powder, salt, cloves, egg, and vanilla extract. Layer the papaya mixture over the brown sugar and butter mixture in the skillet, then pour in the batter. Bake for 55 minutes or until bubbly and brown, and serve warm directly from the skillet. Some people adore a dollop of vanilla ice cream or fresh cream drizzled on top.

Matching Food and Wine

Paul Bolles-Beaven is a managing partner of the Union Square Café. Part of his duties include overseeing the wine selections for the restaurant. He has tasted wines all over the country and paired wine with food for many renowned menus. He spoke with us in the afternoon from a table near the front window of Union Square Café about his advice for people who wish to enjoy wines with dinner.

How do you match wine with food? Just the basics.
Good wine tastes good with good food, and all of that tastes even better with good company. Having said all that, I believe the structural components in the wine are most important. If the wine's too big, it will overwhelm the food, and if the wine is too small, the food will overwhelm it.

So define too big? What does that mean?
With wine it's tannin, acid, and fruit—three things that can be imbalanced but relatively subdued or imbalanced but huge. If one were to take a big, mouth-numbing Cabernet and pair it with a delicately prepared piece of fish, it would be a waste of good fish.

How can you tell if you've done it right?
I really don't believe people should spend a lot of emotional energy making sure they're coming up with the perfect wine match. I have a yuck and yum philosophy. When I have a good wine and food combination, the wine makes me want to eat more, and the food makes me want to drink more. There's a synergy there.

Wine and food pairings fall into ways of looking at it. Either take things that are opposites to balance each other, or take things that are similar and they're going to create a wonderful harmony.

For example?
The simplest is cream in your coffee. The fat in the cream takes care of the tannin and bitterness in the coffee. Think of red meat as cream and the tannin in wine as the coffee. You can see how they balance each other. The fat in the meat softens the wine, and the tannin in the wine cleans up the fat.

How about hot and spicy? What would be the opposite?

That's tough, because hot and spicy doesn't really follow the rules. A lot of people say that sweeter, fruitier wines work well with spicy foods, but I don't necessarily find that to be the case. I like champagne with spicy food, and beer with spicy food, because the bubbles clean that burn off my palate and refresh the palate for the next bite. Fruity, sweet wine sometimes bonds the fire to the tongue and makes it more unpleasant for me.

What do you think people should serve with spicy food besides beer and champagne?

Rosés are wonderful. I like Vouvray or other Chenin Blanc–based wines with spicy foods. The sweet, tart thing that happens can be great with spicy food. I like a lot of Alsace wines—Rieslings—but then I always want to be careful with how much residual sugar is in that wine. Red wine is often forgotten with spicy food, and that's too bad, because there are a lot of wonderfully flushing, spicy reds that provide that sort of similarity combination. Some of the darker, more peppery wines and some of the warm-climate wines from the South of France that are not afraid of the more earthy flavor styles can be great with spicy foods.

Most restaurant wine lists seem loaded with Chardonnays. We've been stuck ordering some that really were disappointing. What's wrong with Chardonnays?

There are some wonderful Chardonnays from all over the world: California, France, you name it. They are great wines and they fit beautifully with foods. The problem is that wine, like so many things, has pendulum swings that have to do with public opinion and marketing and how comfortable people are. A lot of oak in wine sells wine, and allows people to charge a lot of money for it. So the wine maker says, "I'm gonna put a lot of oak in my wine"—and maybe it doesn't taste so great with food, maybe it tastes like you chewed on a two-by-four, but it sells. Oak is an intense flavor. It needs to be used like any seasoning, with discretion. If there's too much of it, like too much salt or pepper or garlic, it becomes monochromatic.

What about alcohol content? Are we better off with a low alcohol content for maximum food taste?

My personal gut reaction is to say that it's more important to balance wines to food. If the alcohol sticks out, it's gonna be a problem. The alcohol level should be below 13 percent if possible.

How do you know if it's sticking out?

It will seem hot on the tongue. Or you could start to blush, or your chest gets hot, or you sometimes can smell the alcohol. If red wine smells a little alcoholic, you can chill it a bit.

Because what's happening is that the alcohol is becoming volatile, so lowering the temperature is good.

Differentiate for us between champagne and other sparkling wines?
Real champagne comes from grapes grown in the Champagne area of France. But there are great sparkling wines from California. It's taken them about ten years, but some wonderful bubblies are being made in the West. Then there's Spain and Italy. Great sparklers from both countries. All good sparkling wines, because of the bubbles, and because they're so focused with intense fruit flavors, work very well with a lot of food. Plus, you can drink champagne all through the meal. The bubbles clean the palate and are not going to overpower much food. And frankly, since we're talking about feeling good, which is what champagne is all about, you'll feel good with every course.

Champagnes are nonvintage wines. You don't want to age them at your house for very long. Drink these wines quickly. People who have a bottle of White Star in their refrigerator five years—they might have a problem.

What about those very expensive champagnes that sometimes foam up in my mouth like I'm a rabid dog. What is that all about?
It's possible that something you ate is reacting to the CO_2 in the wine. It's also possible the wine isn't chilled enough. Maybe somebody dropped the bottle on the way to the table. You've got to be careful with sparkling wines.

What are your favorites?
Price is usually the biggest issue in champagne. My personal favorites are Billecart-Salmon, which is Union Square Café's house champagne; Krug; and Pol Roger. Amazing, but it is hard to find a fresh bottle of that in this town. Gosset is wonderful.

Back in the kitchen, what wine would you pair with salmon?
I always go red wine with salmon. But, the only rule you really have to follow is to do what you enjoy. There's a lot of fish that would be overpowered by some reds, but it's also true there's a lot of red wine that's perfect for fish: salmon, tuna, because they are oily and—depending on how it's prepared—even fried fish.

On the other hand, let's think about a cream sauce with a rich fish like salmon, such as a beurre blanc—that would call for a richer wine, like a wonderful white burgundy. The fat, nutty, rich quality of the white burgundy goes in harmony with the rich, buttery quality of the sauce.

So what exactly would you put with that salmon?

When I'm looking at a wine list and I know I'm ordering salmon, I look for Pinot Noir, or Barbera, or Conceto from Italy, and a rosé from anywhere.

We like some of those pink wines. For a long time we thought they were tacky, for the Boone's Farm crowd, but now we're trying some good ones.

See. There's a parallel here. Wines are like people. You can make generalizations about them and you're almost always going to be wrong sometimes. Wines are individuals. There are so many incredibly, wonderfully balanced delicious rosés on the market that you're missing something if you assume they're all sweet, syrupy, one-dimensional garbage.

What do you serve with Italian food?

Nobody in Italy made a conscious decision to make wine in a certain way, but they all knew what they liked. So, as the cuisine developed over the ages and the wine made progress and the viticulture developed, the wines they made went well with their food. So I say pair Italian food with Italian wines and you can't go wrong.

What are your favorite Italian wines?

Mmmm. I have so many. I love Tuscan Nodatavila, the super Tuscans as they're called. I love Barbaresco, and funky little wines that are inexpensive. A lot of wine geeks would say they're bad, but they're delicious, simple, earthy, and rustic. I love a lot of Italian wines, honestly. Besides Tuscany, there's Veneto and the absolutely wonderful wines of Quintarelli. Extraordinary.

What do you think about serving wine with dessert or chocolate?

You need to be really careful. We have a wonderful tradition here at Union Square Café of serving dessert wine by the glass. I encourage people to enjoy it separately from their dessert because oftentimes their sugar levels make it difficult for the wine and the dessert to be a good match. I think it's best to enjoy wine after the dessert or before—while you're waiting for it to come out of the oven. That's a great time to have a dessert wine.

The exceptions for me are Madeira and port, which I think are an undiscovered treasure in dining. Madeira, especially. It's a beautiful place to find extraordinary combinations. Madeira and banana desserts are remarkable. Sweeter Madeiras with chocolate are extraordinary.

I personally don't believe in this Cabernet with chocolate thing. It just doesn't do it for me. I believe you could have a glass of Madeira or port with chocolate and be a pretty happy camper.

What about a late harvest Grenache Noir from the Banyuls region of France? Isn't that the perfect wine to pair with chocolate?

Yeah. MMMM. Actually, Banyuls make chocolate seem pretty lackluster. A Banyuls is such a hedonistic experience. It's the kind of wine I want to pour over my head and rub all over my face. It's just so giving and so intense, so extraordinary, that you don't want to be too greedy in your aesthetic pleasures.

My mother is a fool for Sauternes so I have to ask you this—we hear they are an aphrodisiac.

Gosh. Maybe I should have a glass. It's something I would never have with dessert. But many people do and that's great. If I'm going to drink Sauternes it'll be with a moldy cheese.

Sauternes is one of the great gifts this world gives us, and it should be savored. Definitely not with chocolate cake. And, it's not to everybody's liking. Be careful who you serve it to. There's some cheeses that smell so bad, people think they're awful and there are people who love that. Save those cheeses for those people. It's the same with Sauternes.

When you're serving wines at dinner, is there a sequence, in terms of flavor, that you like to think about?

It's important not to be dogmatic about it. There are those odd exceptions, like starting with Sauternes. What better aperitif than a glass of chilled Sauternes? But generally, in my opinion, the wines should increase in body and go from white to red, and you should not follow a big wine with a white. The palate adjusts itself, and like going from a cold room to a warmer room, or vice versa—the difference makes the effect even stronger. The comparison can be quite jarring. So it's important to make some sort of progression.

I find people like to build to the oldest wine, let's say if you're drinking all reds, and I think that's a shame, because oftentimes the older wine is more subtle and your palate is tired by the time you get to it and you're gonna miss some of the nuances of the older wine. That happens a lot in wine tastings and at big dinners. It's like, by the time I get to it, I've already had all these icky purple young wines and I get to this graceful thing and I have nothing there to taste it with.

We hear they only release Beaujolais Nouveau on the third Thursday of every November. So let's talk about the hype around this wine. What is that stuff? What's the deal?

I personally think there's a lot of outstanding Beaujolais that's a better value and that I'd rather drink than Beaujolais Nouveau, but the seasonality of that wine and the harvest idea is kind of a neat thing—that the French Beaujolais harvest comes to this country in this sort of celebrated way.

So somebody shouldn't be drinking Beaujolais Nouveau that's a year and a half old, right?
I would say so. That wine is made to be consumed immediately. Actually, more and more wineries around the world understand that most wine is consumed the day it's bought and not laid down. So there's a trend, and it's an appropriate one, toward making wines that are approachable immediately. There is also a subset of wines that cannot age. They will fall apart.

Run through the wines that do not age.
Most white wines. There are exceptions. Some white burgundies and some California wines will go beyond their release dates, but most whites, certainly Beaujolais Nouveau and rosés.

People really shouldn't be aging wine in their homes, should they? Unless they know what they're doing, they're going to end up with vinegar.
Yeah. You might hurt the wine. It's affected by its environment, and most people don't have a home wine cellar that's temperature controlled. If you really want to invest in wine and buy something wonderful and lay it down when you have your first child because you want her to have two cases of vintage port from her birth year to celebrate her twenty-first birthday, there are places you can pay to store one or two cases for you. That's much better than opening that bottle to pour at her majority birthday party and finding out that it's been ruined by temperature changes at home.

Now, if you have an unheated basement, that's probably good. It would keep your wine for years, so long as there's not a furnace in the room.

With white wines, what types of grapes work best?
Well, I have a prejudice. I'm not a Chardonnay drinker. I've had wonderful Chardonnays with food, but for me, I like white wines with more pronounced, crisp tastes. They interact with foods better. They may not win blind tastings, but I generally choose Sauvignon Blanc, Chenin Blanc, Pinot Grigio from Italy, Rawaness, you name it. Basically any German wine.

I love German wines.
They're great with food.

There are two New York State Rieslings we've discovered. Dr. Konstantin Frank and Hermann J. Weimer. We think they're amazing.

They are amazing. We have, actually, a Weimer dessert wine on our list.

What is the best way to buy wine?

The best thing to do is find a wine merchant whom you trust and who listens to what you like, and doesn't try to sell you what he got the best deal on recently, but really understands who you are and what you like to drink. A merchant who is interested when you come back and say, hey, Joe, you sold me a bottle of this and I loved it, hated it, or thought it was just okay. Can you help me out today?

At the restaurant, I have this opportunity to taste through a lot of wines, but I know there are wine shops that know how to sell wine by helping the consumer. That's what you should look for.

Is it true that you should uncork red wines and let them breathe?

Generally, yes, but with certain wines, no. Any wine that's ready to drink will have enough breathing in the glass. It's one of those things that, if you did it every time, it would be pretentious, but if you do it based on the way the wine is, which means it's a little closed in and it needs some time to open up, it might not be a bad idea. It's completely worthless to do without decanting it, because wine is not going to get much breath through the neck of that bottle. If you want to breathe the wine, breathe the wine. Pour it and let it splash into a decanter. However, I must say, I don't like decanting older wines. You have to be careful.

What kind of wines would benefit from breathing?

Younger Cabernets that are maybe tense in structure. Any wine that's big enough to age well will benefit from breathing.

What about Burgundies?

No, I don't do that with Burgundies.

Spanish wines?

Riojas don't need it. They got plenty of time in the wood.

The point is, if you take a sip of the wine and it's not showing, and it's a young vibrant wine, pour it and splash it into a decanter and give it ten or fifteen minutes and maybe it will open up for you.

I know you think that a wine merchant is really important but, at the same time, people need to develop their own tastes. How can we quit depending on wine magazines and merchants and learn to trust ourselves?

Go to therapy. No. Go to a wine store and say, I like such-and-such Sauvignon Blanc. Do you have anything like that? I want to try something new.

So in other words, keep trying new wines?

Obviously. Trying wine and being honest and not feeling like you have to fulfill some obligation to some particular kind of wine that's currently in vogue is important.

How about buying wine in grocery stores?

Nobody would set out to make bad wine and nowadays, in this current wine market, most wine is good, not all of it great, but most of it's good. My parents live in Maine, and I go to the grocery store up there and see a lot of respectable, good values in wine.

Do people have to spend twenty dollars on wine to get a good one?

No. I don't buy wine for my home that's more than ten dollars a bottle unless it's a special occasion.

With all the different wines, what kind of glassware do you recommend?

Glassware is like stereo equipment. You can go crazy or you can be moderately sane. Whatever your budget allows. I personally like a straightforward goblet that bends in a little at the top, that's thin enough so I can enjoy it, but if I break three or four at a dinner I'm not gonna be very upset.

What about balloons; they are so beautiful.

They are beautiful. And they're loads of fun. The only thing about the balloon shape is that for some wines you won't be able to enjoy the bouquet and the wine will be less expressive in the nose.

What about the temperature of wines?

Temperature is a tough one, especially in the restaurant business because in general, in my experience, people in the United States like their white wines too cold, and their red wines too warm. Overchilling wine anesthetizes it. If, on the other hand, wine is too warm, it doesn't show its best qualities. I like reds that feel like a marble statue to the touch. Just a little bit cooler than room temperature, but not cold. I like white wine that's chilled but not cold. I mean, maybe in the fifties.

What is the temperature for reds?
Probably it's sixty-five.

What about rosés?
I like sparkling wines and rosés a little colder than whites, but not a lot.

So, if you were going to put white wine in your fridge, you might take it out how much before you serve it?
I generally throw white wines in the refrigerator well in advance, but take them out and open them and set them on the table a good half hour before dinner so they can sweat and warm up a little. The great way to get red wines the right temperature is to put them on top of a bucket of ice. Not in it, but on top. Or on an ice chest and not for more than twenty minutes or so before you're going to serve it.

Any final wine tips?
The most important thing about wine is that it's really beyond words. The bottom line is that wine is to be enjoyed. It doesn't matter how much you paid for it, or what glass you serve it in, as much as it matters that you enjoy it. Just taste, taste, taste, and trust yourself. Don't feel *obligated* to like anything.

  If I have the best wine in the world, it doesn't taste so good with people I don't enjoy spending time with. And I will say that any wine, no matter how cheap or awful, or what glass I serve it in—all wine tastes great when I'm drinking it with my wife.

Spring:

A New

Beginning

Eyes of Texas Feast: Rosemary and Habanero Pork Roast, and Corn Pudding

The Eyes of Texas Day, widely celebrated on March 2 in the Lone Star State with parties both indoors and out, marks Texas's Independence from Mexico. But the independence was—and is—in name only. Fortunately for Texans, and now the rest of the United States, the spirit of Mexico's President Santa Anna lives on in the great state. His influence is felt in many cultural norms, including the cuisine, which is arguably among the most delicious and flavorful in the fifty states. Of course, some people from Louisiana might take us to task for that statement, but we're both Texans, and we have our biases.

Tex-Mex, with its bright spicy flavors, is the original fusion cuisine, and it's good any time of year. The habanero roast in this menu is both sweet and spicy, its flavors offset by the corn pudding, the ultimate in comfort food.

Bock beer, sometimes known as green beer, is made and sold only in the spring. Sit out under the live oaks at Schultz's Beer Garden in Austin and, after a few beers, you'll feel independent too. For an easy finish to this celebratory meal, wherever you may be, cool off your mouth with best-quality vanilla ice cream drenched in Texas best pecan praline sauce, homemade or bought.

The Menu

LONE STAR AND SHINER BOCK BEERS

CHIPS AND SALSA

PICKLED OKRA AND JALAPEÑOS

ROSEMARY AND HABANERO PORK ROAST

MELISSA'S SWEET CORN PUDDING

JICAMA AND ORANGE SALAD WITH CILANTRO

PRALINE SAUCE (SEE PAGE 101) OVER VANILLA ICE CREAM

Yellow roses are a must for the center of the table. We use a gingham tablecloth with ban-
dannas for napkins. Make a napkin ring out of a piece of burlap twine, a fresh jalapeño
pepper, and a sprig of rosemary. Texans do still consider hides, horns, and feathers to be
high art. They're fond of deer antlers, rattlesnake rattles, longhorns, horseshoes, and other
western paraphernalia. Make do with what you've got! This meal is best served family-style.
Set the tables and preset the salad. Serve the pork roast on a platter, surrounded with the
carrots and potatoes, and pass the corn pudding.

Cooking Tip

Raw habaneros can burn your skin and eyes. Use a fork to handle them and wash your
hands, the cutting board, the fork, and the knife thoroughly with soap after touching the
peppers! Whatever you do, don't rub your eyes.

ROSEMARY AND HABANERO PORK ROAST

3 cloves garlic, sliced

1 (3- to 4-pound) boneless center-cut rolled
pork loin

Freshly ground black pepper, to taste

2 teaspoons peanut oil

2 pounds new potatoes

1 pound carrots, peeled

1/4 cup fresh rosemary leaves, left whole

Glaze:

1/2 cup apricot jam

3 cloves garlic

1 fresh habanero pepper, seeded

1 tablespoon red wine

1 teaspoon salt

Freshly ground black pepper, to taste

*Melissa Schenker, Katherine's former New York party cohort and now a great entertainer in Austin, Texas, knows
the value of an easy dish that wows the audience. This pork roast fits the bill.*

PREPARATION TIME: 15 MINUTES

COOKING TIME: 2 HOURS FOR MEDIUM

STANDING TIME: 10 MINUTES

MAKES 6 TO 8 SERVINGS

May be made 1 day in advance and warmed up in the microwave 1 minute or in a warm oven about 10 minutes.

Preheat the oven to 350°. Insert slivers of garlic into the folds of the pork roast and pepper generously. In a large roasting pan set over medium-high heat, sear all sides of the pork roast in the peanut oil. Remove from the heat and nestle the potatoes, carrots, and rosemary around the roast. Roast, uncovered, in the preheated oven for 1^1/$_2$ hours.

Meanwhile, in a food processor, pulse the apricot jam, garlic, habanero pepper, wine, salt, and black pepper. Pour the glaze over the roast and return it to the oven for another 30 minutes. If you wish, test the roast with a meat thermometer. It should read 160° for medium and 170° for well done. Let the roast stand 10 minutes before serving. Slice the loin and fan out the slices on a platter. Surround with the potatoes and carrots.

MELISSA'S SWEET CORN PUDDING

^{1}/$_2$ cup all-purpose flour

^{1}/$_4$ cup yellow cornmeal

^{1}/$_4$ cup sugar

2 tablespoons baking powder

^{1}/$_2$ teaspoon salt

^{1}/$_4$ to ^{1}/$_2$ teaspoon cayenne (to taste)

5 large eggs

^{1}/$_2$ cup heavy cream

^{1}/$_4$ cup (^{1}/$_2$ stick) butter, melted, plus 2 tablespoons for greasing pan

1 (8^1/$_2$-ounce) can cream-style corn

1 cup fresh or frozen corn kernels

1 small red bell pepper, roughly peeled, seeded and chopped

1 small green bell pepper, roughly peeled, seeded and chopped

Melissa developed this recipe to go with the habanero pork roast. It is such a knockout dish that we renamed it after her!

Preparation time: 10 minutes

Cooking time: 45 minutes

Makes 6 to 8 servings

May be made a day in advance and warmed up in the microwave a minute or so, or in a warm oven 10 minutes.

Preheat the oven to 350°. In a large mixing bowl, stir together the flour, cornmeal, sugar, baking powder, salt, and cayenne. Then add the eggs, cream, melted butter, cream-style corn, corn kernels, and green and red bell peppers. Mix thoroughly and pour into a buttered 9 × 13-inch baking dish. Bake for 45 minutes or until golden brown on top.

Jicama and Orange Salad with Cilantro

1 large jicama, peeled and cut into matchstick julienne (2 cups)

2 medium oranges, peeled, pith and seeds removed, and cut into chunks

³/₄ cup cilantro leaves, whole, loosely packed

Dressing:

¹/₈ cup fresh lime juice

¹/₈ cup rice wine vinegar

¹/₄ cup extra virgin olive oil

Salt and freshly ground black pepper, to taste

Preparation time: 15 minutes

Makes 6 to 8 servings

Toss all salad ingredients together in a large salad bowl. Whisk dressing in a small bowl or jar and sprinkle over salad. Serve at once or cover and refrigerate up to 30 minutes.

March Madness Basketball Play-Off Corned Beef Buffet Dinner

"March Madness" starts around the fifteenth day of the month, when college basketball play-off games can be heard blasting from televisions across the country. Katherine usually tries to have a party on one of those weekend days in front of the TV. Send out a "play-off pool sheet" with the invitations to spice things up.

This menu is no hoop dream; it's good enough for a prince (Hakeem Olajuwon, of course), and it all goes together in advance, so the host can watch the game too. The flavors of the apricot and fresh rosemary blend together and really complement the mellow corned beef. And the aroma throughout your house will drive the sports fans wild. Definitely a slam dunk!

The Menu

ROSEMARY AND APRICOT-GLAZED CORNED BEEF WITH NEW POTATOES

VIDALIA ONIONS AND CABBAGE, PICKLED IN RICE WINE VINEGAR

BLACK PUMPERNICKEL BREAD

CHEESE BOARD (SEE PAGE 287)

CRUDITÉS, CHIPS, AND DIP

GRANDNONNIE'S SPICE BUNDT CAKE (SEE PAGE 353)

DARK BEER

Cooking Tip

Proteins in meat begin to firm up at 120° and begin to toughen at 170°. However, if cooked over low heat for a long period of time, the protein in meat begins to break down and tenderize again. That is the principle behind the cooking method for this corned beef. By simmering the meat for an hour and a half first, you really tenderize it. Finishing the corned beef in the oven gives it a nice glaze and guarantees flavor.

All the Trimmings

Serve this meal buffet-style. Serve the corned beef on a platter, sliced and surrounded by the baked new potatoes. The Vidalia onions and cabbage pickle will look great over a bed of red-tipped lettuce on a separate platter. The cheese board (see page 287) and black bread should be next to one another. The crudités, chips and dips can be in the TV room. Make sure there is a knife for each type of cheese, and precut the bread.

Decorate the buffet table with pennants, and use napkins in your alma mater's (or other) school colors.

You're Invited!

This is a great opportunity to make a collage from newspaper or sports magazine headlines. Be sure to copy the tournament roster to include with the invitation. Ask your guests to use this to RSVP, filling in their picks. Remind them they must get it back to you before the tournament begins. You determine the ante and come up with a prize for the winner. Let the losers wash the dishes after the game.

Rosemary and Apricot-Glazed Corned Beef with New Potatoes

1 (6-pound) corned beef

16 whole cloves

8 juniper berries

16 black peppercorns

12 cloves garlic, peeled and cut in half

24 small whole new potatoes (about 2 pounds; medium size can be used if cut in half)

2 tablespoons extra virgin olive oil

Salt and freshly ground black pepper, to taste

1/4 cup fresh whole rosemary leaves, very loosely packed

Glaze:

3/4 cup apricot jam

1/4 cup brown sugar

1/4 cup, loosely packed, chopped fresh rosemary leaves

PREPARATION TIME:	10 MINUTES
BOILING TIME:	1 1/2 HOURS
ROASTING TIME:	30 MINUTES

Makes 8 servings, with leftovers for sandwiches

The corned beef can be boiled 1 day in advance. Store it covered and refrigerated, then finish in the oven at serving time.

Place the corned beef, cloves, juniper berries, peppercorns, and garlic in a large stew pot. Add cold water to cover, bring to a boil, and boil gently for 1 1/2 hours. To make the glaze, in the microwave on medium (50 percent), heat the jam for 30 seconds to melt it or stovetop over low heat for a minute. Stir in the brown sugar and the rosemary. Set aside. Toss the new potatoes with the olive oil, salt, pepper, and the rosemary leaves. Set aside. After 1 1/2 hours, remove the corned beef from the water and drain it thoroughly. Preheat the oven to 350°. Place the corned beef in a roasting pan, and brush it with the glaze mixture. Place the new potatoes around the corned beef. Bake for 30 minutes to cook potatoes and caramelize the glaze. Slice the corned beef and serve hot or at room temperature, with the potatoes.

Vidalia Onions and Cabbage, Pickled in Rice Wine Vinegar

1 cup rice wine vinegar

¼ cup extra virgin olive oil

¼ cup sugar

1½ teaspoons salt

Freshly ground black pepper, to taste

2 Vidalia, Walla Walla Sweet, or Texas 1015 onions, peeled and thinly sliced

1 head green cabbage, finely sliced

1 carrot, peeled and grated

PREPARATION TIME:	15 MINUTES
BOILING TIME:	10 MINUTES
MARINATING TIME:	15 MINUTES
REFRIGERATION TIME:	1 HOUR TO 2 DAYS
MAKES 8 SERVINGS	

May be made up to 2 days in advance.

Combine the vinegar, olive oil, sugar, salt, and pepper in a serving bowl. Toss with the onions, cabbage, and carrot. Cover and refrigerate until ready to serve. This tastes best if allowed to marinate at least 15 minutes, and it will hold for up to 2 days.

Cooking Tip

We call for a lot of shortcuts in this book, but one that we cannot abide is prechopped cabbage in a bag. We have tried it several times and have found it stale and dry. The cells on the prechopped cabbage have long since closed up, admitting no vinegar and exuding no juice. There are also questions of nutrient loss not yet answered to make the inconvenience worth it.

St. Patrick's Day Salmon Dinner

March 17 is the date when the Irish remember their patron saint—Patrick. And while the Irish may stress the religious significance of the day, Irish Americans make it a day for fun and good feelings about the Emerald Isle.

When Linda went to Ireland to see how Bushmills Irish Whiskey was made, she learned that the Irish love nothing more than a party, and that good food and good drink are as central to their lives as shopping malls are to ours. Bushmills's Eily Kilgannon introduced the visiting group to genuine Irish celebration food. Salmon and other seafood prevailed. But the *new* old discovery was champ, an onion-laced mashed potato dish that's easy to make and provides a new taste sensation for many Americans.

Linda went rattling around the green Irish countryside with Alisa Donato and Nancy DeKalb, easing the way with shots of Black Bush, and sampling new and comforting Irish dishes in wayside pubs strung out across the Irish lanes like pearls on a string. They agreed that about the only souvenir they wished they could bring home was an Irish cow. The dairy products from that green paradise cannot be duplicated. But other than that, Americans can make a perfectly lovely Irish celebration meal. After that trip, nothing would do but a St. Patrick's Day dinner—and plans for another visit to the Emerald Isle at the earliest possible moment.

Because St. Paddy's Day is the first springtime holiday, it often outraces the weather, and if you want a really green event, you have to plan ahead. Last year, it snowed heavily in Oregon on St. Patrick's Day, but our party went ahead as scheduled, with forced blossoms of quince and forsythia in tall glass vases on the mantle and on various tables everywhere—from the living room to the downstairs bath—to remind us that the good green world would soon come our way again.

Linda and Joe kissed everybody, whether they were wearing green or not. We played Irish jigs on the stereo. We started the festivities at the front door with flutes of Black Velvet Cocktails—a delicious blend of equal parts Guinness Stout and champagne, or straight shots of Black Bush, the best Irish whiskey there is. By the time the party ended, every guest was claiming some Irish blood.

The Menu

BLACK VELVET COCKTAILS AND BLACK BUSH

STILTON CROCK AND IRISH SODA BREAD

PAN-GRILLED SALMON WITH MINT

CHAMP

SPINACH PEAR PUREE

BUSHMILLS SUNDAES

All the Trimmings

Green is the theme for St. Patrick's Day. Use forced blooms in the living room and little pots of shamrocks on the dining table. Be sure there's Irish music, the scent of candles, and the aroma of great food in the air from the moment the guests walk in.

A couple of spools of green satin ribbon in varying widths and a box of cream-colored candles is all that's required to make your table gorgeous. We like a white tablecloth with green ribbon runners and green confetti sprinkled about. Use white linen napkins tied with green ribbon bows. Light the room with candles placed strategically on the sideboard, the table, even the top of the china cabinet—and tie every one with a simple green bow.

It is easiest to make up plates of salmon, potatoes, and spinach in the kitchen just before dinner. Pass the bread and butter separately.

STILTON CROCK

1 pound English Stilton cheese   Irish soda bread
¼ cup best-quality port wine

A wedge of Stilton and a decanter of port wine are served in the drawing rooms of Irish country houses for high tea, along with Irish water biscuits (crackers). But you can combine the port and cheese in a crock—or buy it ready-made at fine cheese shops—and be ready with instant hors d'oeuvre at the drop of a shamrock. If you're hosting a large party, buy a whole 10-pound wheel of blue-veined Stilton, slice off the top, scoop out some of the cheese, leaving a cheese "bowl," then mash the scooped-out cheese with the port and refill the wheel. Cover and age the "crock" for up to a week. This makes an impressive buffet centerpiece and will serve up to 100 wedding or holiday guests.

PREPARATION TIME: 1 0 MINUTES

MARINATING TIME: 1 HOUR TO A WEEK

MAKES 2 CUPS (UP TO 1 5 COCKTAIL SERVINGS)

Mix and crock the Stilton and port up to a week ahead.

In a medium bowl, crumble the cheese into the port wine and mash to combine with the back of a wooden spoon. Pack into a 2-cup crock, cover, and refrigerate to age for up to a week.

Bring the cheese to room temperature before serving it with the Irish soda bread.

Pan-Grilled Salmon with Mint

1 cup rice wine vinegar

1/4 cup honey

1 tablespoon vegetable oil

1/2 teaspoon sesame oil

6 (4-ounce) salmon fillets (each about 1 inch thick)

Salt and freshly ground black pepper, to taste

Fresh mint leaves, for garnish

Choose best-quality inch-thick Chinook or Irish salmon fillets, marinate them in a Ziploc bag until you're ready to cook, then quickly pan grill them in a big skillet for a real luxury dinner from Ireland.

PREPARATION TIME:	10 MINUTES
MARINATING TIME:	10 TO 40 MINUTES
COOKING TIME:	10 MINUTES
MAKES 6 SERVINGS	

Combine the vinegar, honey, and oils in a gallon-size Ziploc bag or a glass dish. Add the salmon, cover, and refrigerate for 10 to 40 minutes. (Longer marination and fish may break down.) Preheat a large nonstick skillet over medium-high heat, then film it with additional vegetable oil. Lift the fish out of the marinade and pat it dry. Sauté for 5 minutes, adding salt and pepper to taste; then use a spatula to turn the fillets. Pour the reserved marinade over the fish, salt and pepper the second side, and cook 5 minutes more, or until the fish flakes easily with a fork. Place the fillets on warmed dinner plates. Spoon the pan juices over the fish, garnish with the mint leaves, and serve.

CHAMP

3 pounds russet or Yukon gold potatoes, peeled and cut into large chunks

1½ cups milk

1 bunch green onions and tops, finely chopped

Salt and freshly ground black pepper, to taste

Butter, for the soufflé dishes

Without potatoes, it wouldn't be Ireland. These easy, traditional mashed potatoes, served in mini-soufflé dishes, can be made up in advance and reheated in the oven just before dinner. An old-fashioned potato masher and a wooden spoon will give you the slightly lumpy results you're after. The final timing is not critical. Place the little dishes on a baking sheet for ease of handling, then put them in the oven 5 minutes before you start grilling the salmon. The main idea is to give form to these single servings of ancient comfort food.

PREPARATION TIME:	15 MINUTES
COOKING TIME:	20 MINUTES TO BOIL POTATOES
BAKING TIME:	15 MINUTES
MAKES 6 SERVINGS	

Can be prepared in the morning and reheated.

Boil the potatoes in water to cover for about 15 minutes, or until tender. Drain them in a colander, then return them to the pan, place it back over the turned-off burner, and allow the potatoes to dry a couple minutes.

While the potatoes boil, simmer the milk and onions in a second pan. Mash the drained and dried potatoes with a potato masher, then use a wooden spoon to whip them together with the milk mixture. Season to taste with salt and pepper.

Butter six 8-ounce ramekins or mini-soufflé dishes, then divide the mixture among them. At this point you can cover the dishes with plastic wrap and refrigerate them until dinnertime.

To serve, uncover the ramekins, place them on a baking sheet, and bake in a 350° oven for about 15 minutes, or until heated through and lightly browned on top. Serve hot.

SPINACH PEAR PUREE

3 bunches fresh spinach (about 2 pounds) or
3 (10-ounce) fresh washed or frozen packages

2 tablespoons salt

3 ripe Comice or Bartlett pears (2 cored, peeled, and chopped, plus 1 left whole, for garnish)

3 tablespoons butter

Freshly grated nutmeg

3 tablespoons half-and-half

Make this easy puree in advance, then reheat it in the microwave or oven just before dinner. The subtle perfume of the pear offsets the bitter undercurrent of the greens in a surprising finish for familiar creamed spinach. Although we have constant arguments about this, Katherine swears by the virtues of frozen spinach and Linda would never begin with anything but fresh. Cooking fresh spinach is easy if you use a big pot—the spinach should have plenty of water and never be covered. Right after boiling, quickly refresh the spinach under cold water. This sets the color. Squeeze out water and chop. Using frozen, on the other hand, cuts out the whole first step of the process. Either way, you'll get that luscious St. Patrick's Day green.

PREPARATION TIME: 10 MINUTES

COOKING TIME: 10 MINUTES

MAKES 6 SERVINGS

Can be prepared a day ahead of time, refrigerated, and reheated on top of the stove or in a microwave before serving.

Chop the root ends off the fresh spinach bunches, then wash the leaves thoroughly under cold running water to remove the sand. Meanwhile, bring a large soup pot of water to a rolling boil with 2 tablespoons of salt. Add the spinach and bring it back to a full boil. Instantly, scoop the spinach into a colander and rinse it under cold tap water. Squeeze out the excess water with both hands. (If you're using frozen spinach, simply start here and thaw and drain the spinach before making the puree.)

Place the 2 chopped pears and the drained spinach in the food processor and reduce to a fine puree, about 30 seconds. Meanwhile, heat the butter in a 12-inch skillet until it foams, then add the spinach mixture. Season to taste with salt and nutmeg, and stir with a wooden spoon until the mixture bubbles. Add the half-and-half and stir to heat through. Transfer to a warmed vegetable dish. You may serve now, or cover and refrigerate the spinach until dinnertime.

To serve, reheat the spinach in the oven (about 15 minutes at 350°) or in the microwave (on high—100 percent power—for about 3 minutes). Garnish with half of the remaining pear, peeled, sliced almost to the stem end, then pressed into a fan shape.

Bushmills® Sundaes

1 tablespoon cornstarch

1 tablespoon honey

1 (8-ounce) can crushed pineapple and juice

$^1/_2$ cup Bushmills Irish Whiskey

1 pint good-quality vanilla ice cream

6 mint sprigs, for garnish

These tasty sundaes finish off this meal with an easy-to-prepare flourish.

MAKES 6 SERVINGS

Make the sundae topping the day before the party.

In a 2-cup glass measure, combine the cornstarch, honey, and enough water to measure $^3/_4$ cup. Add the crushed pineapple. Whisk, then microwave on high (100 percent power) for 2 to 3 minutes, whisking every 30 seconds or so, until the mixture is bubbly and thick. Now whisk in $^1/_4$ cup Bushmills and microwave on high (100 percent power) for 30 seconds. Alternatively, stove top, over medium heat, cook and stir until mixture is thick, about 5 minutes, then whisk in Bushmills. Whisk again, adding the remaining Bushmills, cover, and refrigerate. Just before serving, reheat in the microwave on high (100 percent power) about 2 minutes, or stovetop to boil, about 5 minutes, then spoon about $^1/_4$ cup of the hot, molten golden sauce over a scoop of vanilla ice cream in a balloon wineglass or ice cream coupé. Repeat with five other wineglasses. Top with a sprig of mint and serve.

After the Hunt Easter
Lamb Chop Dinner for Eight

Dyeing, hiding, and hunting for Easter eggs is a splendid way to celebrate this rite of spring. It's amazing to see how much normally staid grown-ups get into the act of decorating and dyeing the eggs. We don't let them hunt though—that we reserve for the kids.

We like to have our main meal at noon on this holiday, and if the kids don't eat all the Easter eggs before they get brought into the house, we incorporate them into both the decor and the hors d'oeuvre. For little kids, who may be too hungry to wait, we sometimes make Goldenrod Eggs on Toast (see page 124). Using a white gravy mix out of a package, we can have a plate of kid-friendly food on the table in 10 minutes.

But for the grown-ups, the flavors of spring—lamb, tender mesclun with edible pansies, asparagus, and the season's first berries—make this a menu that will enchant. The preparation is simplicity itself. Stir together the molded dessert a day or two before, while you're hard-cooking the eggs, then, when you come inside after the hunt, all you have to do is roast the chops and the asparagus, toss the salad, and serve.

The Menu

AD-LIB DEVILED EASTER EGGS (SEE PAGE 124)

MESCLUN SALAD WITH EDIBLE PANSIES AND THREE-CITRUS DRESSING
(SEE PAGE 93)

GARLIC-CRUSTED LAMB CHOPS

ROASTED ASPARAGUS WITH LEMON CURLS

HOT FRENCH BREAD AND SWEET BUTTER

PANNA COTTA WITH SPRING'S FIRST STRAWBERRIES

Main Course—a French Madiran from the Languedoc region. The dry yet tannic quality of this wine stands up to the gamy aspects of lamb chops.

Dessert—From the Piedmont region of Italy try Moscato d'Asti la Spinetta. This wonderful wine bears no relation to the disgustingly sweet Asti Spumante that America knows all too well. Be careful that the Moscato is not more than 8 months old.

Cooking Tip

To easily peel hard-cooked eggs, lightly crack them in a few places. Drop them into a pan of cold water and let stand for at least 30 minutes or until you are ready to peel them. They can sit in cold water overnight. The water will get between the shell and the egg and the shells will just drop off.

Easter Eggs Made, Hunted, and Recycled

Dyeing Easter eggs needn't mean a trip to the store for a bunch of special dyes. All you need is a few drops of food coloring mixed in a custard cup with a teaspoon of white vinegar and enough water to completely cover the egg. Remember—to prevent that green line from forming between the white and yellow portion of the egg, the operative word is hard-cooked, not hard-boiled. This means you should place a dozen or so eggs in a pan covered with cold water, *then* bring the water to a simmer and cook the eggs for 15 minutes. Let the eggs cool in the water, then replace them in the egg carton and refrigerate until decorating time.

For food safety, keep cooked eggs in their carton in the refrigerator until time for hiding, and don't use eggs for eating that have been out of the refrigerator for more than 2 hours.

The easiest way to use hunted eggs is in a table centerpiece. But there are those of us who can't stand to let them go to waste. Learn to make deviled eggs and goldenrod eggs, and you've added two preparations to your repertoire for use all year long.

Ad-Lib Deviled Easter Eggs

You can make an easy ad-lib deviled egg mixture by simply peeling the hard-cooked eggs, then cutting them in half and removing the yolks to a small bowl. Mix the yolks with an equal amount of mayo, a jot of Dijon mustard, and a little salt, pepper, and cayenne. Add drops of rice vinegar and stir with a fork. Taste and adjust the seasonings, then stuff the yolks into the egg whites, cover, and refrigerate until serving time. Want to get fancy? Add a little curry powder, or capers, or pickle relish, minced red pepper, minced red onion. You can even use a pastry bag to pipe the mixture back into the eggs. You decide. A jot of caviar on the top makes it a feast.

Easy Goldenrod Eggs

Instead of deviled eggs, you can make goldenrod eggs. First, make a white sauce, then add the chopped, cooked egg whites. Make toast and serve each person a piece of toast covered with egg white sauce, then sprinkled with crumbled cooked egg yolks. Kids love this for a quick Easter brunch. This year, Linda made a sauce using White Lily's Pepper Gravy Mix, following the directions on the back of the package, then chopped the whites into that. Look in the supermarket for gravy mixes and give it a shot.

All the Trimmings

Serve the salad on individual plates, arrange the chops and asparagus on warmed dinner plates, and put the bread in an Easter basket. Pass the deviled eggs on a large platter.

Decorating the table for Easter is a cinch. Use an Easter basket filled with eggs—real or faux—for the centerpiece, then finish the theme with various pastel colored ribbons running the length of the table. You can also add fresh flowers picked while hunting the eggs, or picked-out while hunting the groceries. Buy a chocolate egg or another fancy faux egg for the big hunt prize. As for us, if we get the food coloring in the custard cups and get it onto the eggs and the eggs into the backyard for a ritual hunt without spilling the dye all over the floor, we count ourselves successful.

You're Invited!

Handwrite and photocopy the invitations onto pastel paper, then place them in envelopes, along with some Easter grass. Remind your guests to bring their own Easter baskets for hunting. You could—to speed things up—ask each guest to bring a dozen hard-cooked eggs, too. Figure on at least twelve eggs for each kid. Some will get lost. Some will get broken. All will be enjoyed.

GARLIC-CRUSTED LAMB CHOPS

Extra virgin olive oil

2 large whole garlic heads, tops sliced off

$\frac{1}{2}$ teaspoon salt

2 tablespoons whole black peppercorns

8 thick center-cut loin lamb chops (4 ounces each)

Sprigs of rosemary, for garnish

2 tablespoons traditional whole seed mustard, for garnish

A mound of crisp, glistening, roasted garlic and crushed black pepper tops a tender, flavorful lamb chop. This is an easy way to prepare chops because you don't have to watch the cooking every second. Great for harried dinner-party cooks. Technique is everything here. Be sure to completely preheat the skillet so that the moment the chops hit the hot surface they begin to sear and caramelize. Don't move the chops around; let them brown completely before you turn them. It only takes a couple of minutes per side to completely glaze the meat and seal in the good juices. Coat the chops with roasted garlic and peppercorns you've just smashed, and the flavor is completely developed. Make them a couple hours ahead to this point, cover and set aside, then pop them in the oven to finish when you're ready to serve.

Once the chops are roasted, no sauces need apply. A jot of seeded mustard is sufficient. The flavors will explode in your mouth. You can allow the roasted chops to stand 20 minutes or so before serving with no loss of flavor or finish.

May be prepared and pan grilled up to 1 1/2 hours in advance of final baking.

Preheat the oven to 400°. Wipe a shallow 8½ × 11-inch gratin or baking dish with olive oil and set it aside.

Dab the garlic with olive oil and salt. Place the garlic heads in a microwave-safe dish, cover with plastic wrap, and cook in the microwave on high (100 percent power) for 2 to 3 minutes, or until tender. Alternatively, roast uncovered in a 400°F oven about 45 minutes. Remove the garlic and let it stand, covered, for 5 minutes. Wrap a paper towel around the bottom of the garlic head so it won't burn your hand, hold it over a small bowl, and squeeze the soft, cooked garlic out of its papery husks. It will squish out like toothpaste.

While the garlic is cooking and cooling, preheat a large skillet over high heat. Trim the excess fat from the lamb chops and dab them with olive oil. Sear the chops in the hot skillet, taking care to allow them to brown and caramelize thoroughly before you move them, then turn and brown the second side, about 3 to 4 minutes total. Salt lightly.

Remove the chops to the prepared baking dish. Use a mallet or the side of a chef's knife to crush peppercorns in a Ziploc bag, then press crushed pepper firmly into both sides of the lamb chops.

Coat the chops on both sides with the cooked garlic, rubbing it into the seared surface of the meat. Don't worry if some of the topping falls off the chop when you turn it over, just scoop the pepper-garlic mixture under the chop and press the chop into the mixture. The flavor essences will permeate the meat quite effectively. The chops may be made a couple of hours ahead and held covered until final cooking 10 to 15 minutes before serving time.

Bake, uncovered, in the preheated 400° oven for 10 to 15 minutes to complete the cooking (10 minutes for rare, 15 minutes for medium). To serve, run a spatula under the chops and scoop them onto warmed dinner plates. Garnish each plate with a sprig of rosemary and a jot of mustard.

ROASTED ASPARAGUS WITH LEMON CURLS

2 pounds fresh asparagus spears

1 tablespoon extra virgin olive oil

Zest curls and juice of 1 lemon

Freshly ground black pepper, to taste

Roasting asparagus concentrates its flavor better than any kind of water cookery, plus it's as easy as the proverbial pie. Choose thick or thin asparagus, according to your preference. Asparagus jumps out of the ground the thickness it will be, so don't think that pencil-thin asparagus is "younger" or more tender. Test the tenderness of asparagus in the market by running your thumbnail into the flesh. If it's too woody and hard to penetrate, that means the asparagus is old and you shouldn't choose it. For a very special occasion, order asparagus from Mr. Spear in California. Every stalk is perfect, as thick as your thumb, and ready to cook. Call 1-800-677-7327 to order.

PREPARATION TIME: 10 MINUTES

ROASTING TIME: 10 MINUTES

MAKES 8 SERVINGS

Roast the asparagus at your convenience up to two hours ahead and serve at room temperature if you wish.

Preheat the oven to 400°. Wash the asparagus. Hold each spear between your fingers and break it where it naturally snaps, or peel the woody stems with a potato peeler.

Coat a gratin or glass baking dish with the olive oil. Place the asparagus in the dish and roll it around to coat with oil. Roast in the preheated oven for exactly 10 minutes, then cool on a rack.

Add the lemon zest and juice to the asparagus. Cut the lemon in two, and, using your hands as a strainer, squeeze the juice of the lemon through your fingers into the asparagus, discarding the seeds and pulp you catch with your hands. If you, like Katherine, are a chicken, use a lemon juicer.

To serve, place about 3 large or 5 small asparagus spears on each dinner plate, along with a lamb chop, and sprinkle with freshly ground pepper to taste.

PANNA COTTA

2 cups (1 pint) heavy cream

²/₃ cup sugar

2 teaspoons (2 envelopes) unflavored gelatin

2 cups (1 pint) half-and-half

1 teaspoon vanilla extract

1 teaspoon almond extract

Fresh strawberries and mint leaves, for garnish

Pure white and silky, this perfect little molded dessert is fast replacing tiramisu as the trendy new finish to high-end New York restaurant meals. And why not? It's made with nothing more than cream, sugar, gelatin, and flavoring. It goes together as fast as your grandma's Jell-O and fruit cocktail special, and it makes a fine finale to a lush meal, with just a few fresh berries and mint to accompany it. You can make it a day or two in advance; then all you do at serving time is to unmold it onto chilled plates, garnish, and serve.

PREPARATION TIME: 10 MINUTES

REFRIGERATION TIME: AT LEAST 2 HOURS

MAKES 8 SERVINGS

May be made 2 days in advance.

Coat eight small ramekin dishes or custard cups with cooking spray and set them aside. Combine the cream and sugar in a medium saucepan and heat over medium heat to just under the boil, stirring from time to time to dissolve the sugar. Meanwhile, sprinkle the gelatin over the half-and-half, stir, and let it stand to dissolve. Once you can see little bubbles around the edge of the cooking cream, stir in the gelatin mixture and cook and stir— but do not boil—until the gelatin is completely dissolved, about 3 minutes.

Strain the cream mixture into a 4-cup liquid measure, then stir in the vanilla and almond flavorings. Pour into the prepared dishes, cover, and refrigerate for at least 2 hours or until set.

Alternatively, you can pour the cream mixture into a 13 × 9 × 2-inch Pyrex cake pan. When the panna cotta has chilled and solidified, cut it into rectangles and serve it with Jackson Pollock swirls of chocolate syrup on top.

To serve, run a knife around the edge of each ramekin, then dip the bottom of the ramekin into hot water, shaking to completely loosen the cream. Invert each mold onto a chilled dessert dish and serve garnished with the fresh strawberries and mint leaves.

Spring Has Sprung:
Rosemary-Lemon Chicken Picnic

Linda gave a party for one of our outdoorsy pals by inviting friends to a kite-flying picnic high on the top of the ski mountain outside of town, once the Alpine flowers had burst into bloom.

Flowers aside, the true beauty of this party is that all the good cooking begins in the market. With this menu, there's no cooking at all. We shopped, mixed, chilled, and transported these brightly flavored dishes to the picnic site in a box.

The menu is really forgiving. Find the right 10 minutes in your schedule and you can make and chill each of the dishes, then simply assemble them at picnic time.

This gives you all the time in the world for kite flying and other portable sports you and your friends enjoy.

Serve this picnic to four or double the amounts for eight friends, depending on the length of your guest list.

The Menu

CHILLED CUCUMBER SOUP

FENNEL SALAD WITH ORANGE, CUMIN, AND CHILIES

ROSEMARY-LEMON CHICKEN

TABOULI PITA SANDWICHES

ANGEL FOOD CAKE WITH THREE-BERRY FOOL (SEE PAGE 215)

Wine Suggestions

Main Course—Offer a lemony sauvignon blanc either from the Loire in France or from New Zealand and/or Austria. The Austrian sauvignon blancs, when you can find them, tend to be very lemony and fruity, while the French tends to be a bit drier. The New Zealand wines have a distinct tropical fruit quality that is great with the citrus flavor of this meal.

All the Trimmings

Lay out the food buffet-style and enjoy. Serve the soup in plastic tumblers for easy cleanup. Uncork the wine, and don't forget to display the Three-Berry Fool. Wine always tastes better in wineglasses than in plastic tumblers. Carry them to the picnic site wrapped in colorful cloth napkins to be used during the meal. Decorate the picnic table with spring flowers and leaves. If you're in the wild, gather the flowers on the spot. If you're in the city park and don't wish to finish off your picnic with a stint in the local pokey, bring flowers from the supermarket, then just cast them out over the table to make a veritable bed of spring blossoms and greenery.

You're Invited!

If kite flying is your theme, send various parts of the kite in the mail, along with a xeroxed invitation and directions to the picnic site. Send the kite itself to the best flier on your list. Send a ball of twine to another guest. Rip up colorful cloth for the kite's tail and send each invitation folded over its own scrap of colorful cloth. Tell your intended guests that the kite can't fly without them. Be sure to include the date, time, a map of the location, and a phone number to RSVP. What would we do without answering machines to take down messages?

CHILLED CUCUMBER SOUP

4 cups peeled, seeded, and coarsely chopped cucumbers (about 4 medium)

1 clove garlic, peeled

16 ounces (2 cups) plain yogurt

1/4 teaspoon salt

1/8 teaspoon cayenne

1/2 teaspoon sugar

Celery swizzle sticks

PREPARATION TIME: 10 MINUTES

REFRIGERATION TIME: 30 MINUTES

MAKES 4 SERVINGS (MAY BE DOUBLED WITH NO CHANGE IN PREPARATION OR CHILLING TIME)

May be made a day ahead, covered, and chilled.

Process the cucumbers and garlic together in a food processor or blender until pureed, then stir in the yogurt, salt, pepper, and sugar. Transfer the soup to a clean jar or thermos bottle, cover, and refrigerate until serving time. Serve in stemmed balloon wineglasses with decorative celery swizzle sticks.

FENNEL SALAD WITH ORANGE, CUMIN, AND CHILIES

1 medium fennel bulb, thinly sliced to make about 2 cups, feathery tops reserved

1 tablespoon fennel seeds, crushed

1/2 teaspoon ground cumin

1/4 teaspoon crushed hot red pepper flakes

Zest curls and juice of 1/2 orange

Zest curls and juice of 1/2 lemon

2 teaspoons extra virgin olive oil

Salt and freshly ground black pepper, to taste

PREPARATION TIME: 10 MINUTES

REFRIGERATION TIME: 30 MINUTES

MAKES 4 SERVINGS (MAY BE DOUBLED WITH NO CHANGE IN PREPARATION OR CHILLING TIME)

May be made a day ahead, covered, and chilled until serving time.

Toss the fennel with the seeds, cumin, and red pepper in a medium bowl. Combine the remaining ingredients in a jar and shake to mix. Pour the dressing over the fennel, cover and let the salad rest at room temperature 30 minutes or so. At serving time, chop about $^1/_2$ cup of the feathery fennel tops, toss with the salad, and serve.

ROSEMARY-LEMON CHICKEN

2 tablespoons chopped sun-dried tomatoes in olive oil

1 (4- to 5-pound) roasted chicken

Juice and zest of 1 lemon

3 sprigs of fresh rosemary

Splash of dry vermouth

Here's something to carry to the picnic or to a potluck supper. It looks as if you slaved over a hot stove all day to make it, but actually, all you did was season a deli-cooked bird and let time do the rest.

PREPARATION TIME: 10 MINUTES

REFRIGERATION TIME: 30 MINUTES

MAKES 4 SERVINGS (MAY BE DOUBLED SIMPLY BY USING TWICE THE INGREDIENTS)

Best if composed and eaten the same day.

Sprinkle the tomatoes in a gratin dish. Quarter the cooked chicken and arrange it on top of the tomatoes. Add the lemon juice and zest. Arrange the rosemary artfully and splash a little dry vermouth over all. Cover with plastic wrap and refrigerate for at least 30 minutes or until serving time. Spoon the herbs and tomatoes over the chicken pieces and serve.

Tabouli Pita Sandwiches

3/4 cup bulgur (#1 fine grain)

1 cup chicken broth

1/2 cup minced fresh flat-leaf parsley leaves

1 absolutely ripe tomato, seeded and diced

2 green onions with tops, finely sliced

1/2 cup finely chopped, seeded, peeled cucumber

1/8 cup fresh mint leaves (or 1 tablespoon dried)

Zest and juice of 1/2 lemon

2 tablespoons extra virgin olive oil

Salt and freshly ground black pepper, to taste

4 pita breads

An Arabic salad made with bulgur—the steamed cracked wheat that needs nothing more than soaking—this dish requires little more than chopping, mixing, and soaking. To really save time, buy a boxed tabouli mix, follow the directions, and add the fresh parsley, green onions, tomatoes, mint, and lemon zest and juice. In fact, the fresh vegetables in the tabouli are the greater part of this salad.

PREPARATION TIME: 10 MINUTES

SOAKING TIME FOR BULGUR: 30 MINUTES

MAKES 4 SERVINGS

Filling may be made up to 4 days in advance, covered, and refrigerated. Do not fill sandwiches until ready to transport so pita doesn't get soggy.

In a large bowl, thoroughly combine the bulgur with the broth, then pat the mixture down with your fingers. Cover and set it aside in the refrigerator for 30 minutes while you prepare the remaining ingredients.

Toss the bulgur with all the remaining ingredients except the pitas, tasting and adjusting the seasoning with salt and pepper. Cover and refrigerate until serving time. Cut the pita breads in half, and stuff each half with about 1/2 cup filling. Pack the sandwiches, cut side up, in a basket lined with a colorful cloth, and place them on the buffet table.

Alternatively, prepare a tabouli mix, following the directions on the box. Toss in the fresh vegetable ingredients and adjust the seasonings to taste.

Spring's Bounty Weekend
Bouillabaisse Lunch for Eight

Once the Shakespeare season starts in Ashland, Linda begins to have company drive down from San Francisco for weekend visits. Most of them love the possibility of eating outside in a gorgeous park, as we can do so easily, provided the famous Oregon rain doesn't interrupt the festivities and it's not too cold. But this menu works equally well served at home, at the park, inside or out. You can use all of it or build your own menu around the bouillabaisse, adding store-bought products to suit your time and temperament.

Because the flavors of spring are so intense here in the cool Northwest, where farms and gardens produce flowers and fruits slowly and perfectly, a stroll through the farmer's market for the very best of local strawberries, rhubarb, asparagus, and artichokes puts us well on the way to humming "The flowers that bloom in the spring, tra la." Decorating is easy. Swoop down on bunches of spring flowers and use copious amounts of pastel ribbon. You can even make yourself a maypole from a dowel stuck in a flowerpot; your guests will return from their spring visit with smiles on their faces.

The Menu

ARTICHOKE AND FENNEL BITES WITH SAFFRON GARLIC SAUCE
(SEE PAGE 260)

EILEEN'S BOUILLABAISSE

HOT CRUSTY FRENCH BREAD AND BUTTER

ROASTED ASPARAGUS WITH LEMON CURLS (SEE PAGE 127)

COLD THIN-SLICED HAM WITH STEWED RHUBARB SAUCE

PECAN SUGAR PAPER-THINS WITH STRAWBERRIES AND
VANILLA ICE CREAM

Wine Suggestions

Appetizer, Main Course, and Dessert—The classic wine the French serve with bouillabaisse is a rosé from Provence. These lovely pink wines have no relation to the cloyingly sweet rosés popular in the States during the seventies when disco was king. A good rosé from Provence (and now some California rosés—though be careful it is not a retro rosé) are dry, fruity, and perfect for this fish dish. It is no accident that Provençal rosés marry perfectly with bouillabaisse—part of the cuisine of the region—the flavor of the wine developed along with the local cuisine. It is a natural complement!

Cooking Tip

Parchment paper prevents foods from sticking, is greaseproof, and can be used as a pan liner for baking sheets, casseroles, and pots. When baking cookies, feel free to use the same piece of parchment over and over. Then just wad up the paper and throw it away. No baking sheet to wash!

All the Trimmings

Use little clay pots of spring flowers to create a centerpiece that can be broken up for party favors when your guests leave. For a little drama you may want to use a white tablecloth and several varieties of white flowers. This is the time of year we like to use paper doilies under the bread and our favorite pastel-colored napkins, and, if the weather is decent, serve the meal outside. Serve the Artichoke and Fennel Bites in the living room as an appetizer if the weather forces you inside.

The bouillabaisse should be preset at the table when the guests sit down. Pass the bread in a basket. Hold the ham and asparagus in the kitchen until ready to serve. The asparagus will be served at room temperature.

Next time you visit a museum, pick up a stack of art postcards. They make wonderful keepsake invitations. Handwrite the time, date, and RSVP phone number, and your guests will have a lovely reminder of your party they can turn over to enjoy.

ARTICHOKE AND FENNEL BITES
WITH SAFFRON GARLIC SAUCE

1 extra-large artichoke
Juice of ¹/₂ lemon
1 large fennel bulb, trimmed, feathery tops
reserved

Saffron Garlic Sauce (see page 260)

An easy stir-together dish that starts with the best-quality mayonnaise, tangy enough to stand up to the intense spring flavors of a steamed artichoke and fresh, raw fennel.

PREPARATION TIME: 10 MINUTES

COOKING TIME: 40 MINUTES ON THE STOVE OR 12 TO 16 MINUTES IN THE MICRO-
WAVE ON HIGH (100 PERCENT POWER).

MAKES 8 SERVINGS

You may steam the artichoke the day before and chill it until serving time.

To cook the artichoke, bring a little water to a boil with the lemon juice in a medium saucepan fitted with a steamer basket. Alternatively, choose a deep microwave-safe bowl for microcooking. Meanwhile, trim the artichoke stem so that the artichoke will stand up straight. Cut off spiny tips by chopping off the top end of the artichoke, then add it to the pan. To steam on the stove top, cover and cook in the steamer basket over medium heat until the stem is tender and a leaf will pull free with no resistance, about 40 minutes. Alternatively, to cook in the microwave, cover the bowl with plastic wrap and microwave on high (100 percent power) for 12 to 16 minutes.

Let the artichoke stand until cooled, then place it in a bowl, cover, and refrigerate it until serving time.

To serve, make a bed of feathery fennel tops then cut the fennel bulb into bite-size pieces and arrange them around the artichoke. Place a small bowl of Saffron Garlic Sauce alongside and don't forget an empty bowl to catch the artichoke leaves.

EILEEN'S BOUILLABAISSE

1 large sweet potato or yam

2 tablespoons extra virgin olive oil

2 medium onions, chopped

1 teaspoon chopped garlic (2 cloves)

3 cups chicken broth

2 cups dry white wine

1 (14$^1/_2$-ounce) can chopped tomatoes and juice

Zest of $^1/_2$ orange

1 teaspoon dried thyme, crushed

1 teaspoon fennel seeds

$^1/_4$ teaspoon saffron

1 pound codfish or other firm white-fleshed fish such as halibut, grouper, snapper, or haddock, cut into bite-size chunks

$^1/_2$ pound rock shrimp or peeled, deveined, medium shrimp with tails

24 mussels and/or clams in their shells

Salt and freshly ground black pepper, to taste

1 loaf French bread, cut into thick slices and toasted

Because the terrible truth is that spring is chilly and damp in more places than we'd care to name, we serve this comforting, clear, flavorful French-style soup to begin our easy spring weekend lunch. We got the recipe from our favorite nurse friend, Eileen, who not only thinks about what's healthy and good but also has a daughter living in France who sends her recipes fairly regularly. Eileen shared this recipe with Carol, Linda's favorite fishmonger, who shared it with us. Don't you love how recipes move around?

Don't be daunted by the long ingredient list. This goes together in a flash, and it's hearty enough to be offered as the main course, if you wish.

PREPARATION TIME: 15 MINUTES

COOKING TIME: 15 MINUTES

MAKES 8 SERVINGS

May be made 1 day ahead and refrigerated until serving time. Reheat on the stove top or in a microwave to just under boiling.

Cook the sweet potato in the microwave on high (100 percent power) for 5 to 6 minutes, or until tender. Alternatively roast in a 400°F oven about 45 minutes. Peel and cut into bite-size pieces.

Meanwhile, in a large stew pot, heat the oil over medium heat, then sauté the onions until translucent, about 5 minutes. Add the garlic and cook 2 more minutes. Pour in the chicken broth, wine, tomatoes, orange zest, thyme, fennel, and saffron. Bring to a boil, then add the fish, shrimp, and mussels. Return to a boil, then reduce heat and simmer, covered, 3 to 5 minutes. Add the sweet potato. Adjust seasonings with salt and pepper.

To serve, place a piece of toasted French bread in a rimmed soup bowl and ladle the soup over it.

COLD THIN-SLICED HAM WITH STEWED RHUBARB SAUCE

4 to 5 ribs rhubarb, chopped

¹/₄ cup sugar

³/₄ pound Black Forest or other high-quality baked ham from the deli

This is a simple side dish that can be served on the same plate as the asparagus. The tastes complement each other. The sauce is also lovely over vanilla ice cream.

PREPARATION AND STANDING TIME: 35 MINUTES

COOKING TIME: 15 MINUTES

MAKES 8 SERVINGS

The rhubarb sauce should be made a day in advance for full flavor release, but can be made days ahead for convenience.

Put the rhubarb in a medium saucepan, sprinkle it with the sugar, and set the pan aside for 30 minutes or so to allow the sugar to draw the juices from the rhubarb. Then cook over low heat until the rhubarb is tender, about 15 minutes. Transfer it to a clean jar, cover, and refrigerate.

Put a dollop of this sauce on thinly sliced ham and serve it with the asparagus if you wish.

PECAN SUGAR PAPER-THINS

¹/₂ cup (1 stick) butter

¹/₂ cup (1 stick) margarine

³/₄ cup tightly packed light or dark brown sugar

1 large egg yolk

1 tablespoon vanilla extract

³/₄ cup all-purpose flour

¹/₄ teaspoon salt

1 cup chopped pecans

Bake the cookies on parchment as the cookie stores do, and you'll have no trouble at all peeling them off. Plus, you'll have one less pan to wash. Combining butter and margarine guarantees a proper texture. Serve these with a dish of vanilla ice cream nestled over fresh strawberries, with a sprig of mint for decoration.

PREPARATION TIME: 20 MINUTES

BAKING TIME: 9 TO 11 MINUTES PER BATCH

MAKES 3 DOZEN

May be made 1 week ahead and stored in a tin. The tin will protect the cookies from the damaging effects of humidity and the fingers of family interlopers.

Preheat the oven to 350°. Arrange racks in the two middle positions in your oven. Line two large baking sheets with parchment paper (see Cooking Tip). Lay out a cooling rack. Line a large tin with a paper napkin.

Cream the butter and margarine in the food processor until smooth, then add the brown sugar and process for 5 seconds. Add the egg yolk and vanilla and process 5 seconds, scraping down the sides of the bowl with a rubber spatula. Remove the lid and add the flour, salt, and pecans. Pulse to barely mix these ingredients.

Use two teaspoons to push off dough by the spoonful onto the baking sheets, leaving about 3 inches between cookies. Bake 9 to 11 minutes, or until brown around the edges. Cool on the parchment paper on the rack until hard, then peel off the paper and store in the tin.

Oscar Night Hors d'Oeuvre for Twenty

The Oscars have become the new American traditional party. Citizens of the cocktail nation stand up and celebrate. And we celebrate them with two of America's great contributions to world cuisine—cocktails and hors d'oeuvre! Bon vivants and demimonde habitués alike will love this party even if the Oscars aren't playing on a television screen nearby. If the Oscars *are* on, you have to organize a pool to see who can most closely guess what movies the Academy will select. We also like to have our own categories for awards. "Most Insipid Movie Likely to Win for Political Reasons," or "We laughed-at-it-not-with-it." "Most predictable Hollywood ending," "Best T&A," "Best statue clutching by an Actress in a Ridiculous Dress," etc. There are always a few that deserve this such recognition.

The disadvantage to hors d'oeuvre is that they involve more putting-together than most main-course dishes. The advantage is that most can be made well in advance and arranged half an hour before anyone arrives. With a little bit of advance planning, you can really act like a guest at your own finger-food party.

You should figure that each person will want three pieces of each type of hors d'oeuvre (for shrimp figure a little more). When we are serving hors d'oeuvre as the meal, we try to make sure that we do not serve too many fat-laden selections. We do not want to hand out Rolaids for party favors on the way out. Also, if you see to it that your guests get a little protein, they will feel full faster. This is important when you are counting on the hors d'oeuvre to serve as a meal. If you are just having cocktails from 5:30 P.M. to 7:30 P.M. as a prelude to dinner, reduce the amount of food you serve. This menu is meant to be a meal.

The Menu

ASSORTED COCKTAILS

ARTICHOKE CRAB BITES

SCANDINAVIAN SHRIMP AND BLACK OLIVES

CHERRY TOMATOES STUFFED WITH TROUT PÂTÉ WITH BLACK OLIVE TOPS

CELERY FILLED WITH BLUE CHEESE AND ORANGE

ENDIVE TIPS WITH CREAM CHEESE, BLUE CHEESE, AND A RED GRAPE

MINI CORN MUFFINS WITH HAM AND HONEY MUSTARD

GRAPES* AND COOKIES

Wine Suggestions

Hors d'Oeuvre—For this meal try a good Riesling either from Germany or one of our Finger Lakes favorites, Dr. Konstantin Frank or Hermann J. Wiemer from upstate New York. The fruity, slightly sweet flavor will go with all of the hors d'oeuvre. And since everyone will be standing around drinking, it will be easier on the carpet than any red wine!

All the Trimmings

When planning a finger-food party, there are a few simple things to think about. You want to have a variety of colors, textures, and flavors on the trays. When we are entertaining more than six, we make a large, abundant presentation on a buffet table that encourages people to dig in.

Mingling is important to a cocktail party. No sitting! Set the TV or TVs up high so people can stand to watch. Move chairs and couches to the sides of the room. Stand-up cocktail parties die if people start to sit! Consult a bartender's book for how best to set up a bar like a pro. Be sure to have lemons, limes, cherries, olives, and little pearl onions ready to go into the glasses. You don't want to be cutting up lemons while people are waiting.

Of course, those little square cocktail napkins are a must at a cocktail party, along with toothpicks with cellophane hats, olives stuffed with pimentos, and Maraschino cherries. As far as equipment is concerned, we like swizzle sticks and ice buckets. And don't forget plates full of votive candles for atmosphere. Vive le cocktail party!

* Grapes should always be served either cut into small "individual-size bunches" or with a pair of scissors next to the bowl. It is in the poorest taste to ask people to tear off grapes by hand from the stems!

For a guest list of	They'll consume	If drinks are 1½ oz you'll need
6 people	12 – 18 drinks	2 fifths
8	16 – 24	2
10	20 – 30	2
12	24 – 36	3
20	40 – 60	4
30	60 – 90	6

How to Stock the Bar

Because spirits keep for years, we like to have a well-stocked bar. Here's our list of bottled goods:

Bourbon, scotch, rye, gin, rum, vodka, dry and sweet vermouths, brandy, and liqueurs. Add cold beer for those who prefer it. The basic liquid mixers include orange and tomato juice, ginger ale, club soda, tonic water, Collins mix, and cola. Buy some fancy waters for your nondrinking guests. Now add more ice than you could ever imagine people would use (about a pound per person), to the above and you're ready to roll.

Set the bar up away from the food station and either make it self-serve, or snag a friend or a bartender to keep things pouring along. Be sure to include an ice bucket, bottle openers, a corkscrew, and napkins.

One good general rule is to say that the larger the party, the more limited the selection. This prevents bottlenecks at the bar and trouble for the bartender (who just might be a snagged guest). It's better to serve two or three well-made drinks than to attempt to pretend you're a professional bartender. If you're having more than about a dozen guests, get

6 people	12 – 18 drinks	3 fifths of wine
8	16 – 24	4
10	20 – 30	5
12	24 – 36	6
20	40 – 60	10
30	60 – 90	15

help. But remember, nothing makes guests feel worse than irritatingly weak or unmercifully strong drinks. Use a jigger measure and pour appropriate amounts.

Here's a generous drink estimator:

Artichoke Crab Bites

1 cup grated Gouda or other semi-soft cheese

2 (6-ounce) jars marinated artichoke hearts, drained

6 ounces fresh or canned crabmeat, drained and picked over

3 green onions with tops

1/4 cup Italian-seasoned dry bread crumbs

1/4 teaspoon hot pepper sauce

6 large eggs

PREPARATION TIME: 10 MINUTES
BAKING TIME: 30 MINUTES
COOLING TIME: 15 MINUTES
MAKES 60 HORS D'OEUVRE

May be made in the morning, covered and refrigerated. Bring back to room temperature before serving.

Preheat the oven to 325° degrees. Spritz a 7 × 11-inch baking dish with cooking spray and set it aside.

Pour the grated cheese in the prepared baking dish. In a food processor fitted with the steel blade, coarsely chop together the artichoke hearts, crabmeat, and green onions. Add the bread crumbs and pulse to mix. Pour this mixture over the cheese. Add the hot pepper sauce and eggs to the processor and process to beat the eggs. Pour over the other ingredients in the baking dish and stir to mix thoroughly.

Bake until the mixture is golden brown on top and the center feels firm to the touch, about 30 minutes. Cool on a rack for about 15 minutes, then cut into squares or diamonds (about 1 × 1 1/4 inches). Cover until serving time. Serve warm or at room temperature. Reheat 10 minutes in a 325°F oven if desired.

SCANDINAVIAN SHRIMP AND BLACK OLIVES

$1^1/_2$ pounds peeled and cooked shrimp*

$^3/_4$ cup extra virgin olive oil

1 cup freshly squeezed lemon juice

Zest of $^1/_2$ lemon

$^1/_4$ cup coarsely chopped fresh dill

$^1/_2$ red onion, chopped

1 (16-ounce) can medium black pitted olives, drained

PREPARATION TIME: 5 MINUTES

MARINATING TIME: 1 HOUR

ASSEMBLY TIME: 20 MINUTES

MAKES ABOUT 60 HORS D'OEUVRE

May be made 1 day in advance and refrigerated.

In a large bowl, combine the shrimp, olive oil, lemon juice, lemon zest, dill, and red onion. Cover, refrigerate, and marinate for at least 1 hour. Remove the shrimp from the marinade and skewer on toothpicks with an olive in the curve of the shrimp. Be sure to use cellophane-topped or other decorative toothpicks! Cover and refrigerate until serving time.

* We sometimes buy precooked and peeled shrimp to save time and effort.

Cherry Tomatoes Stuffed with Trout Pâté with Black Olive Tops

2 pints cherry tomatoes

1 pint smoked trout pâté*

1 (15-ounce) can small black pitted olives, drained

Preparation time: 15 minutes

Assembly time: 15 minutes

Makes about 60 hors d'oeuvre

May be made up to 3 hours in advance, covered, and refrigerated.

Using a very sharp knife, cut a slice off the bottom of each tomato so it will stand upright. Using a melon baller, hollow out the tomatoes. Fill them with the smoked trout pâté, and cap each one with half a black olive.

Celery Filled with Blue Cheese and Orange

8 ounces cream cheese, softened

4 ounces blue cheese, softened

1 cup raisins

1 orange, seeds and pith removed, cut into small chunks

15 stalks celery

1 cup pecan halves

Preparation time: 10 minutes

Assembly time: 20 minutes

Makes 60 hors d'oeuvre

* Available at gourmet shops.

May be made up 3 or 4 hours in advance, covered, and refrigerated.

Mix the cream cheese and blue cheese thoroughly. Mix in the raisins and orange chunks. Fill celery stalks with the mixture. Cut each stalk into 4 pieces and top each piece with a pecan half.

ENDIVE TIPS WITH CREAM CHEESE, BLUE CHEESE, AND A RED GRAPE

3 to 4 heads green Belgian endive, leaves separated from the stalk

8 ounces cream cheese, softened

4 ounces blue cheese, softened

1 pound red seedless grapes

This recipe uses the same blue cheese/cream cheese mix as the one above, minus the raisins and orange. So you could just double the cheese recipe above and make it all in one batch. It may also be made 3 to 4 hours before serving.

PREPARATION TIME: 10 MINUTES
ASSEMBLY TIME: 20 MINUTES
MAKES 60 HORS D'OEUVRE

Thoroughly mix cream cheese and blue cheese. Spoon a teaspoonful onto the bottom of each leaf of endive. Top with a red grape. Cover and refrigerate until serving time.

Mini Corn Muffins with Ham and Honey Mustard

1 cup clover honey

1 cup Dijon mustard

5 dozen mini corn muffins from the bakery

2 pounds ham, thinly sliced

PREPARATION TIME: 5 MINUTES

ASSEMBLY TIME: 20 MINUTES

MAKES 60 HORS D'OEUVRE

May be made 1 hour in advance. Best if covered loosely with a damp dish towel, then with plastic, and refrigerated until serving time.

Thoroughly combine the honey and mustard. Slice the muffins in half horizontally, fill them with honey mustard and ham slices, and put back the tops.

May Day Cornish Hen
Formal Dinner for Four

We believe in any excuse for a dinner party, and May Day is as good a reason as any. This menu can be prepared after a long day at the office, a Sunday hike, or even after a Saturday full of chores. It can easily be doubled to serve eight. Borrow a popular French trick: Rub curry on the poultry, bake, and serve it with fruit for a subtly complex taste. Spinach and Garlic Custards are the perfect complement to the easy and elegant hens.

The Menu

MESCLUN SALAD WITH THREE-CITRUS DRESSING (SEE PAGE 93)

FRUITED CORNISH HENS

COUSCOUS

SPINACH AND GARLIC CUSTARDS

STRAWBERRIES WITH CHOCOLATE SAUCE

Wine Suggestions

Main Course—A German Mosel, Riesling, Kabinett, or Spätlese. This delicious wine with a low alcohol content, slightly acidic and sweet, will be the best complement to the spicy curried birds surrounded by fruit.

Dessert—From Santa Cruz California, Bonny Doon Framboise. The rich strawberry flavor of this sweet dessert wine is a nice complement to the strawberries with chocolate sauce on the dessert menu.

Many kitchen accidents are caused by dull knives, so make sure your chef's knife is very sharp. To sharpen a knife properly, use a stone or steel rod and run the blade along it at a 45-degree angle six times on each side. A chef typically sharpens a knife several times a day. It is much easier to split the Cornish hens and rub them with the curry powder when they are very cold or not completely thawed. Besides, presentation is improved by a well-cut bird, not one that looks as if it had a run-in with an ax murderer.

All the Trimmings

Decorate a white tablecloth with little bouquets of spring flowers and ribbons. Serve each half bird slightly overlapping the couscous, surrounded with the fruit mixture. Place the custards next to the birds and couscous. Pour the chocolate syrup into a handsome bowl, place the bowl in the middle of a serving plate, and surround it with the whole strawberries. You don't even have to remove the stems—they add color and provide a useful handle for dipping.

Fruited Cornish Hens

2 (18- to 22-ounce) Cornish hens

2 tablespoons Indian curry powder, for rubbing

1/2 cup mango chutney

1/4 cup freshly squeezed lemon or lime juice

2 medium tart cooking apples (Granny Smith or Jonathan or Red Delicious), coarsely chopped

2 kiwi fruit, peeled and coarsely chopped

3/4 cup dried cranberries or cherries (optional)

Cornish hens are so rich, we find that just half a bird makes a generous serving. Throw in an extra bird should you expect big eaters at your table.

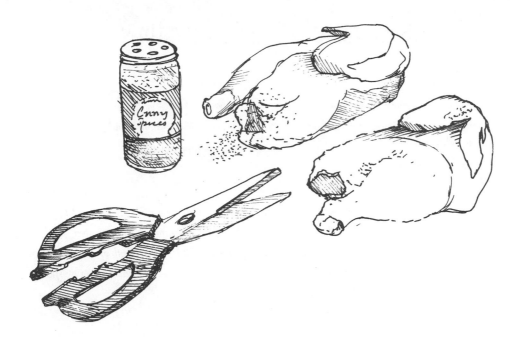

PREPARATION TIME: 5 MINUTES

BAKING TIME: ABOUT 1 HOUR

MAKES 4 SERVINGS

Best if made and served promptly, although we do admit—the leftovers are luscious the next day, zapped in the microwave on high (100 percent power) for a minute or two.

Preheat the oven to 450°. Lightly grease or spritz a shallow roasting pan. Remove and discard the giblets from the hens. Rinse and thoroughly dry the game hens. With a very sharp chef's knife or poultry shears, split the hens lengthwise. Each half should have a leg and a wing. Rub the hens with the curry powder inside and out. Place the hens, skin side up, in the prepared pan. Bake, uncovered, for 25 minutes. Meanwhile, mix the chutney with the lemon juice. After 25 minutes, reduce the heat to 350° and baste the birds with the chutney mixture. Continue baking, uncovered, 25 more minutes. Now, scatter the chopped apples and kiwis around the birds and cook 10 more minutes. Arrange the birds and fruit slightly overlapping the couscous, next to the spinach custards, on warmed dinner plates.

Spinach and Garlic Custards

2 tablespoons extra virgin olive oil

2 cloves garlic, chopped (1 teaspoon)

1 (10-ounce) box frozen spinach, thawed, excess water squeezed out

1/4 cup heavy cream

2 large eggs

1 teaspoon cornstarch

1/4 teaspoon salt

1/2 teaspoon freshly ground black pepper

1/2 teaspoon ground nutmeg

The flavor and texture of these custards, cooked in a water bath in the oven, are a perfect complement to the Cornish hens or any roasted meat. Traditionally, the water for the bath is boiled on top of the stove, then added to the pan in the oven. We have eliminated this extra step by placing the Pyrex dish with the bath of water in the oven 25 minutes before we add the custards. Be sure to fill the Pyrex dish only one-third full to avoid overflow.

Preparation time:	10 minutes
Water preheating time:	25 minutes
Cooking time:	40 minutes
Makes 4 servings	

Make these up to a day in advance, refrigerate in the ramekins, then reheat in a microwave on high (100 percent power) for 1 to 2 minutes, or 10 minutes in conventional oven set at 350°, and turn out onto dinner plates at serving time.

Place a square Pyrex baking dish one-third full of water in the oven and preheat to 350° for 25 minutes. Butter four individual ramekins or custard cups. Combine the oil and chopped garlic and microwave on high—100 percent power—for 2 minutes. Transfer to the bowl of a food processor, add the spinach, cream, eggs, cornstarch, salt, pepper, and nutmeg, and process until nearly pureed, 1 to 2 minutes. Divide the mixture equally among the four ramekins and cover with foil. Place the ramekins in the water bath and bake until the centers are firm, about 40 minutes. Just before serving, loosen the edges with a butter knife and invert the custards onto the dinner plates.

Alternatively, this savory custard can be made with about 1 1/2 cups mixed mint, peas, and spinach; or cauliflower and carrots; or broccoli and Parmesan cheese.

Strawberries with Chocolate Sauce

1 (8-ounce) can chocolate syrup
2 pints strawberries, washed and dried, stems
not removed

May is a great time of year to buy spring's first, beautiful strawberries. Remember, the smaller the berries, the better the taste. This recipe is so easy, it is embarrassing. Of course, you can use any type of fruit that can be eaten with your fingers. We prefer Hershey's syrup.

PREPARATION TIME: 5 MINUTES

MAKES 4 SERVINGS

Wash and dry the strawberries as much as 3 hours in advance and arrange them around a bowl of chocolate for dipping. Cover everything with plastic wrap and refrigerate.

Pour the chocolate syrup into a beautiful bowl. Place the bowl in the middle of a platter and surround it with the strawberries. Place the platter in the middle of the table and let everyone dip their own fruit. This is a very warm and communal way to have dessert. You may want to garnish the serving plate with a bunch of fresh mint or a Jackson Pollock-like splatter design that you can make by dusting the plate with confectioners' sugar and drizzling chocolate syrup in a swirly pattern, as described below.

You can keep a tea strainer in the confectioners' sugar sack, and when you want to create special effects, just scoop out some sugar, hold over the dessert plate, knock it against the heel of your hand, and out comes a drifting of sugar onto the plate. To achieve the chocolate drizzle, drip syrup from the tip of a teaspoon, or squirt it from a plastic ketchup or mustard dispenser—as the restaurants do. You'll get a free-form design.

Spring Fever: Black Skillet Chicken Supper for Four

Even a bad case of spring fever can be cured with this brightly flavored dinner. Leeks, fiddleheads, rhubarb, and friends are all good antidotes for the fever we all know comes when the calendar says "spring" and the weatherman says "snow." It is a great season for casual dinner parties. Catch your friends before they start to spend weekends in the country. For this simple menu we like to have just a few close friends and a few good bottles of wine. Serve the chicken right out of the black skillet. The presentation is both dramatic and rustic, and will make your guests feel right at home. As always, light the candles, open the wine, and enjoy a glass before your guests arrive. A relaxed host is the most important element at any party.

The Menu

FIDDLEHEAD SOUP

BLACK SKILLET ROAST CHICKEN WITH LEMON, TOMATOES, NEW POTATOES, AND KALAMATA OLIVES

BRAISED LEEKS WITH HERBES DE PROVENCE

RHUBARB AND STRAWBERRY COBBLER

Wine Suggestions

Main Course—A dry Spanish Albariño, if you can find it, with its lemony note, will pick up the lemon of this dish and complement the meal. You might also try a dry fino sherry. Though most people don't think to serve sherry with food, the results can be wonderful. You might try the Tio Pepe on the less expensive side or the Emilio Lustaw on the more pricey side. Both are good. We love those Spanish wines!

Dessert—Rhubarb and strawberries always present a great dessert wine opportunity. Try a late harvest Sémillon from Australia.

Leeks are a terrific ingredient because of their mild onion taste and fibrous texture. But they do require some care in washing because sand gets down into the lower leaves. To prepare leeks, remove all outside and withered leaves. Trim the roots as if you were trimming a beard, being careful to leave the base that holds the leaves in place. Cut off the top part of the leaves, leaving about 8 inches of the white and green end of the leek. Wash the leeks well under running water, spreading the stalks to get all the sand out.

All the Trimmings

You can decorate the table if you want, but for a casual dinner, food, candles, and good wine are all that adorn our table. The food on this menu is so beautiful on its own that you don't have to do anything extra.

Fiddlehead Soup

1 large onion, chopped

4 tablespoons butter

1 pound fiddleheads, washed and drained

2 (13-ounce) cans chicken broth

1 cup dry white wine

1 cup heavy cream

$1/2$ teaspoon nutmeg

Juice of 1 lemon

Salt and freshly ground black pepper, to taste

Fiddleheads are the tips of a young fern. Their taste is similar to that of asparagus with an earthy overtone. Available only for a short period in the spring, they are not to be missed. Don't try to gather your own unless you are a botanist. Some varieties of fiddleheads are poisonous. Most gourmet stores have them available in the spring.

Preparation time: 10 minutes

Cooking time: 40 minutes

Makes 4 servings

Can be made 1 day in advance. Cover and refrigerate until serving time. Reheat in the microwave 2 minutes or stove top over medium heat 5 minutes or so. Don't reboil.

In a large soup pot, sauté the onion in the butter, until the onion is translucent, about 3 minutes. Add the fiddleheads and sauté for 3 more minutes. Remove and reserve one fiddlehead to garnish each bowl of soup. Add the chicken broth and wine to the remaining fiddleheads and simmer for 30 minutes. Let the soup cool a few minutes, then blend in blender or food processor until the fiddleheads are finely chopped. Return the soup to the pot, add the cream, nutmeg, lemon juice, salt, and pepper, bring to a boil, then set aside, covered, until time to serve. Refrigerate overnight and reheat in the microwave or stove top to just under the boil. To serve, ladle the soup into wide rimmed soup bowls and float a reserved fiddlehead on top.

BLACK SKILLET ROAST CHICKEN WITH LEMON, TOMATOES, NEW POTATOES, AND KALAMATA OLIVES

4 tablespoons extra virgin olive oil, divided

1 large lemon, thinly sliced

6 large cloves garlic, chopped (3 teaspoons)

$1/4$ teaspoon salt

Freshly ground black pepper, to taste

Juice and zest of $1/2$ lemon

8 boneless, skinless chicken thighs

1 pound red new potatoes, scrubbed and quartered

10 cherry tomatoes

15 Kalamata olives

1 teaspoon chopped fresh rosemary leaves, plus a sprig of fresh rosemary

The colorful food set against the black skillet eliminates the need for any centerpiece.

PREPARATION TIME: 10 MINUTES

BAKING TIME: 1 HOUR

MAKES 4 SERVINGS (CAN EASILY BE DOUBLED—JUST USE A SECOND SKILLET)

Preheat the oven to 450°. Wipe a 10-inch cast-iron ovenproof skillet with olive oil, then overlap the lemon slices on the bottom.

In a medium bowl, stir together 2 teaspoons of the chopped garlic with $^1/_4$ teaspoon salt, pepper, lemon juice and zest, and I tablespoon of the olive oil. Toss the chicken pieces in this mixture, then arrange them in one layer over the lemon slices. Top with any garlic mixture left in the bowl.

In the same bowl, stir together the remaining teaspoon of garlic and remaining olive oil. Add the potatoes, tomatoes, olives, and fresh rosemary leaves. Season generously with salt and pepper and toss to mix. Arrange the vegetables around the chicken and lay the rosemary sprig over the top.

Roast, uncovered, for 60 minutes, or until a meat thermometer inserted into the chicken reads 175°. Serve immediately, from the skillet, spooning any pan juices over the meat and vegetables.

Braised Leeks with Herbes de Provence

6 leeks, cut in half, roots trimmed short but left on, thoroughly washed (see Cooking Tip, page 155)

1 (13-ounce) can chicken broth

2 cups water

4 tablespoons butter

1 tablespoon herbes de Provence

Salt and freshly ground pepper, to taste

This leek recipe is another of our secret weapons. Leeks are associated with spring but are available all year round. They are really wonderful with many dishes, such as lamb chops or roast beef.

PREPARATION TIME: 5 MINUTES

COOKING TIME: 20 MINUTES

MAKES 4 SERVINGS

May be made 1 day in advance if removed from broth and warmed in the microwave a moment or stovetop a couple minutes.

In a 10-inch skillet with a lid, place the leeks cut side down and pour in the broth, water, butter, herbes de Provence, salt, and pepper. Simmer on low for about 20 minutes or until a fork easily pierces the leeks. Set aside, covered, until ready to serve. Serve on a warmed platter.

RHUBARB AND STRAWBERRY COBBLER

½ cup (1 stick) butter, melted

1 cup diced rhubarb

1 cup sliced strawberries

1 cup sugar

1½ cups biscuit mix

½ cup (1 pint) heavy cream, plus additional for serving

1 egg

Rhubarb and strawberries just say spring. This cobbler has a light texture and is delicious and easy. Pass the cream, please.

PREPARATION TIME: 15 MINUTES

BAKING TIME: 25 MINUTES

MAKES 4 TO 6 SERVINGS

Preheat the oven to 400°. Melt the butter in a saucepan over low heat or in the microwave on high (100 percent power) for 1 minute. Drizzle half the butter (4 tablespoons) into an 8 × 8 × 2-inch Pyrex dish and stir in the rhubarb, strawberries, and ¼ cup of the sugar. In a separate bowl, combine the biscuit mix, the remaining melted butter, remaining ¾ cup of sugar, the heavy cream, and the egg. Pour the batter over the fruit and bake for 25 minutes, until hot and bubbly. Serve with additional cream drizzled on top.

Polenta Lasagna Graduation Feast for Eight

The day baby brother Jay graduated from NYU, we all gathered, after freezing to death in Washington Square on that late May afternoon, for a lunch with some of his friends. Katherine and Linda made the lunch before hopping on the subway from Brooklyn to Manhattan so that once they returned—chilled, exhilarated, and hungry—all they had to do was reheat the lasagna and stir together the salad and the chiffonade. One thing is certain—kids may graduate from college, but they still fall on home-cooked food like a pack of hungry wolves. This menu is ideal for hungry teenagers or kids of any age. It's easy to put together, it's comforting, and it's not too costly to prepare.

The Menu

ASSORTED OLIVES AND FRESH RAW FENNEL SLICES

POLENTA LASAGNA WITH ITALIAN SAUSAGE AND ARTICHOKE HEARTS

CHIFFONADE OF LETTUCE AND PEAS

ROMAINE SALAD WITH THREE-CITRUS DRESSING (SEE PAGE 93)

HOT CRUSTY BREAD

CHOCOLATE SWEETHEART CAKES WITH SOFT CENTERS

Wine Suggestions

Main Course—Our cardinal rule is Italian wines with Italian food. Barbaresco has the highest acidity and will go nicely with this dish. On the other hand, Sangiovese is fruitier and great for a celebration. People love these wines.

Dessert—A California late harvest Zinfandel is a good match for chocolate, though we are really crazy about Banyuls region wines from the South of France made from late harvest Grenache Noir.

All the Trimmings

Mortar boards and school colors make decorating for this event easy. We like to strew some festive confetti on the buffet table. Serve the olives and fennel bites in the living room. Set up the buffet with the hot food on one end and the salad on the other.

POLENTA LASAGNA WITH ITALIAN SAUSAGE AND ARTICHOKE HEARTS

Polenta:

1½ cups coarse yellow cornmeal

4 cups water

2 teaspoons salt

4 tablespoons butter, cut into chunks

¼ cup freshly grated Parmesan cheese

Sauce:

1½ pounds hot Italian sausage

2 medium onions, peeled and chopped

2 cloves garlic, chopped (1 teaspoon)

2 tablespoons extra virgin olive oil

1 (6-ounce) jar artichoke hearts, drained and finely chopped

1 (26-ounce) jar marinara sauce (we like Barilla's)

2 teaspoons fresh oregano (1 teaspoon dried)

½ pound fresh mozzarella cheese, grated (2 cups)

PREPARATION TIME:	10 MINUTES
SAUTÉ TIME:	10 MINUTES
COOKING TIME:	12 MINUTES (IN A MICROWAVE) OR 18 TO 20 MINUTES ON THE STOVE
SAUTEEING AND BAKING TIME:	25 MINUTES
MAKES 8 SERVINGS	

Can be made a day ahead up to the point of baking, covered, refrigerated.

Preheat the oven to 350°. Spritz a 12 × 8 × 2-inch glass baking dish with vegetable oil cooking spray. Add the cornmeal, water, and salt, then let sit for 3 minutes. Cook, covered, in the microwave on high (100 percent power) for 6 minutes. Alternatively, cook on the stovetop, in a saucepan over medium heat, stirring, until thick, about 10 to 12 minutes. Stir in the butter and Parmesan cheese and cook in the microwave or on the stove 6 more minutes.

Meanwhile, in a large skillet over medium-high heat, sauté the sausage, onions, and garlic in the oil for 5 minutes, or until the meat is browned and the onions are translucent. Add the artichoke hearts, marinara sauce, and oregano, raise the heat, and bring to a boil. Pour the sauce over the cooked polenta, sprinkle with the mozzarella cheese, and bake in the oven until bubbly and brown, 20 minutes. This reheats very nicely in 10 minutes or so in 350°F oven.

CHIFFONADE OF LETTUCE AND PEAS

3 tablespoons unsalted butter

1 head iceberg lettuce

1 teaspoon sugar

4 cups frozen green peas, thawed

Salt and freshly ground black pepper, to taste

2 tablespoons heavy cream

The French, famous for their "waste not/want not" philosophy, roll up less-than-perfect lettuce leaves into fat cigars, then cut them into fine strips for use in raw and cooked dishes. That's what's meant by a chiffonade. It's easier than making a good Havana cigar, and is one more use for iceberg lettuce besides picking up broken glass. The result is a bright green, luscious side dish you'll want to make again and again.

PREPARATION TIME: 10 MINUTES

COOKING TIME: 5 MINUTES

MAKES 8 SERVINGS

Best if made at serving time.

Heat the butter in a large skillet until it foams. Meanwhile, stack lettuce leaves, roll them into fat cigars, and cut into thin strips. (You should have about 16 cups of strips from one large head of lettuce.) Add the lettuce to the skillet and cook about 3 minutes, or just until it wilts, stirring frequently.

Stir in the sugar, peas, salt, and pepper, and continue to cook about 2 minutes more, or until peas are heated through. Stir in the cream and serve at once.

Chocolate Sweetheart Cakes with Soft Centers

$^3/_4$ cup ($1^1/_2$ sticks) butter

6 ounces semisweet chocolate chips

$4^1/_2$ tablespoons all-purpose flour

2 tablespoons Dutch-process unsweetened cocoa

5 large eggs, separated

$^1/_3$ cup sugar

$1^1/_2$ tablespoons Kahlúa (or cold espresso)

$^1/_2$ teaspoon vanilla extract

$^1/_2$ cup raspberry sauce

1 cup fresh raspberries

Confectioners' sugar and cocoa to dust plates

Vanilla ice cream

Individual cakes with warm, soft hearts of deep, dark chocolate, these are perfect for a sentimental send-off dinner for graduates. Make them in big Texas-size cupcake cups for grade school graduation parties, or in buttered ramekins for the college crowd. The surprise of a warm, runny center encased in a tender chocolate cake makes these easy desserts a hit with children of all ages. And don't forget these love cakes when you want to top off a romantic dinner with a great dessert.

PREPARATION TIME:	15 MINUTES
BAKING TIME:	10 TO 12 MINUTES
COOLING TIME:	5 MINUTES

MAKES 8 TEXAS-SIZE CUPCAKES (OR 16 REGULAR-SIZE)

Make these cakes the day before, cool them in the muffin tins, then cover and chill. At serving time, reheat in a 300° oven, uncovered, about 10 minutes, then turn out onto dessert dishes.

Preheat the oven to 375°. Line 8 large Texas-size cupcake cups with paper liners (or 16 regular-size cupcake cups) or arrange 8³/₄-cup ramekins in a large baking dish. Spritz ramekins or paper cupcake liners with cooking spray and set them aside.

Combine the butter and chocolate chips in a microwaveable bowl. Melt in the microwave on high (100 percent power) for 2 minutes, then whisk thoroughly. If not completely melted, continue to microwave at 15-second intervals, and whisk until you have a smooth, melted mixture. (Alternatively, stir the butter and chocolate together in a small saucepan set over low heat. Cook and stir until melted and smooth, about 3 minutes.)

Stir the flour and cocoa together in a small bowl.

In a large bowl, beat the egg whites on high speed until foamy. Add the sugar by the spoonful, and beat until the whites hold stiff, shiny peaks.

Stir the liqueur, vanilla, egg yolks, and cocoa-flour mixture into the melted butter and chocolate until smooth, then stir in about a quarter of the beaten egg whites. Fold the remaining whites into the chocolate mixture, leaving no white streaks. Divide the batter evenly among the prepared baking pans or ramekins.

Bake just until the edges feel firm but the centers are still soft when pressed gently with your forefinger, about 10 or 12 minutes. Cool for 5 minutes.

While the cakes are baking, artfully swirl the raspberry sauce onto 8 dessert plates, using a plastic ketchup bottle or the tip of a spoon, and scoop a mound of raspberries onto each plate.

Invert each cake onto a dessert plate, then dust with confectioners' sugar and cocoa. Add a small scoop of vanilla ice cream.

The Grill's Opening Night:
Rosemary Pork Chops

Late spring, just when the nights begin to be warm enough to sit outside, is a great time to initiate the grill for the season. The smell of fresh rosemary on the grill will make your guests' mouths water in anticipation. The pork chop recipe takes 5 minutes to put together, a day or two to marinate, and no time to eat. The ingredients in the pork chop marinade are unusual, but well worth the initial investment.

The neat thing about this menu is that three of the items need marinating. So the cucumbers, bruschetta topping, and chops can all be made up at once, and refrigerated to marinate a day or two in advance.

The Menu

FRESH TOMATO BRUSCHETTA

ROSEMARY PORK CHOPS

ORZO WITH SPINACH

CUCUMBERS AND ONIONS IN TARRAGON VINEGAR

BRAISED RUM PINEAPPLE VANILLA ICE CREAM

Wine Suggestions

Main Course—This dish is really aromatic with the clove and juniper berry flavors, which are, of course, Germanic or Alsatian. So try a German Auslese riesling or an Alsatian wine. Be careful to check the alcohol content of Alsatian wines, and remember that over 13 percent really overwhelms food. Or, you can try those two New York State favorites of ours, Hermann J. Wiemer or Dr. Konstantin Frank. The dry and semi-dry Rieslings are really great. You might even try them for breakfast!

Cooking Tip

To get those great grill marks on the chops—like those you see in restaurants—begin with a perfectly clean grill, then preheat it until you can't hold your hand over it for more than a count of one-thousand-and-one. Slap the chops onto the hottest part of the grill and cook them for 3 to 4 minutes. Then turn them clockwise a quarter turn and continue to grill them another minute or so before flipping them. Move them to a cooler part of the grill and finish cooking the second side.

For medium-rare, press down on the top of the chop with your thumb. It should no longer feel soft, like raw meat, but should begin to firm up. For well-done, continue to cook until the chop feels firm to the touch.

All the Trimmings

Candles and lanterns do more than make a patio dinner romantic. They also keep mosquitoes at bay. Place candles and lanterns on every available surface. Make your patio a magical place. The dinner will taste even better.

You have to buy fresh rosemary for this meal anyway, so why not tie a sprig of it to each napkin with a piece of burlap string for the napkin ring. Also, a few sprigs of rosemary on the grill will fill the air with an incredible aroma and help flavor the chops. We suggest serving the chops on a large platter on top of the orzo and spinach.

Fresh Tomato Bruschetta

Topping:

3 large tomatoes, seeded and coarsely chopped

1 medium red onion, minced

1/3 cup extra virgin olive oil

2 tablespoons red wine vinegar

1 teaspoon salt

Freshly ground black pepper, to taste

1/4 teaspoon Tabasco sauce

1/2 cup chopped fresh basil

1 large baguette, sliced

1/4 cup extra virgin olive oil

Start with great bread and this appetizer will do exactly what hors d'oeuvre are supposed to do—it will make your guests fall on their dinner with wild abandon.

Cooking Tip

To seed tomatoes, cut them in half and use your fingers or the tip of a spoon to remove the seeds and watery flesh.

PREPARATION TIME:	10 MINUTES
MARINATING TIME:	AT LEAST 30 MINUTES TO 2 DAYS
COOKING TIME:	5 MINUTES TO TOAST THE BREAD
MAKES 8 SERVINGS	

The topping can be made up to 2 days in advance and refrigerated.

Combine all of the topping ingredients in a large bowl, cover, and marinate in the refrigerator 30 minutes or for up to 2 days, until ready to serve. Brush the bread lightly with olive oil and toast in the oven or a toaster oven. Top with the tomato mixture just before serving.

Rosemary Pork Chops

Marinade Mixture:

2¼ cups water	½ teaspoon white peppercorns
¾ cup fresh rosemary leaves	12 coriander seeds
2 tablespoons sugar	12 juniper berries
1 tablespoon salt	4 allspice berries
1 teaspoon dried thyme	2 bay leaves

8 thick-cut loin pork chops	4 sprigs of rosemary, for grill
Salt and freshly ground black pepper, to taste	

Choose thick-cut loin pork chops and remember to set out the steak knives. Don't be daunted by the long list of spices. This will soon become your standard chop marinade! Substitute thick veal chops if you wish.

PREPARATION TIME:	5 MINUTES
MARINATING TIME:	1 TO 2 DAYS
COOKING TIME:	5 TO 10 MINUTES
MAKES 8 SERVINGS	

For these chops to be really tasty, marinate them as long as possible—up to 2 days before. Make sure you have all the ingredients before you start.

Mix all marinade ingredients in a Pyrex dish or Ziploc bag. Add the pork chops and turn several times. Cover the dish or zip the bag tight and refrigerate 1 to 2 days, turning occasionally. When ready to cook, remove the chops from the marinade and pat them dry. Salt and pepper generously. Preheat the grill for at least 5 minutes. Place the sprigs of rosemary on the grill, then add the chops and grill them for 3 to 4 minutes on each side, turning ¼ turn, or until cooked as desired.

Orzo with Spinach

4 cups chicken broth

2 cups uncooked orzo (12 ounces)

1 tablespoon butter

1 1/2 teaspoons chopped garlic (3 cloves)

1 (1 1/2-pound) box frozen chopped spinach, thawed

3 tablespoons freshly grated Parmesan cheese

3 tablespoons toasted pine nuts*

Orzo is that lovely pasta that looks like thick grains of rice. Take care not to overcook it and orzo will soon become one of your favorites.

PREPARATION TIME: 5 MINUTES

COOKING TIME: 1 0 MINUTES

MAKES 8 SERVINGS

We usually make this up in advance and reheat it in the microwave a minute or so just before serving. You can also reheat on the stove top to just under the boil.

Bring the broth to a rolling boil. Add the orzo and cook for 7 minutes, or just until *al dente.* Meanwhile, in the serving bowl, microwave the butter and garlic for 1 minute, add the frozen spinach, and microwave on high (100 percent power) for 5 more minutes. Alternatively, do this in a pan on top of the stove over high heat, stirring frequently until heated through. Toss the cooked orzo with the spinach, add the Parmesan, and top with the toasted pine nuts.

* To toast the pine nuts, place them in a small hot skillet and, watching them constantly, shake the nuts over medium heat until they begin to brown. Immediately transfer them to a glass dish so they do not burn. They will continue to cook after they are removed from the heat.

Cucumbers and Onions in Tarragon Vinegar

2 large seedless cucumbers, peeled and thinly sliced

1 large red onion, thinly sliced

¼ cup tarragon vinegar

⅛ cup extra virgin olive oil

1 teaspoon salt

Freshly ground black pepper, to taste

We like to think this is one dish that delivers more than the effort you put into it.

PREPARATION TIME: 5 MINUTES

MARINATING TIME: AT LEAST 30 MINUTES

MAKES 8 SERVINGS

May be made a day or two in advance.

Combine all the ingredients in a medium bowl. Cover and chill at least 30 minutes or until ready to serve.

Braised Rum Pineapple Vanilla Ice Cream

4 tablespoons butter

1 (14 ounce) can pineapple chunks, drained

$1/2$ teaspoon ground cloves

$1/2$ cup rum

1 pint best-quality vanilla ice cream or frozen yogurt

One good question to ask of any dessert is whether it's better than a bowl of plain vanilla Häagen-Dazs ice cream or frozen yogurt? Although we do adore that plain vanilla ice cream—sometimes straight out of the container—for company, we gild the lily with a hot rum pineapple sauce that slides down the rounded sides of the ice cream like a volcanic eruption.

Preparation time: 5 minutes

Cooking time: 6 minutes

Makes 8 servings

Make this sauce after dinner, just before you serve it.

Melt the butter in a large skillet set over medium heat. Add the pineapple and sprinkle with the ground cloves. Boil for about 3 minutes, then turn the pineapple and continue cooking 2 more minutes. Add the rum and heat for 1 more minute to just under the boil. Using a match, light the rum to flambé. Serve over best-quality vanilla ice cream or frozen yogurt.

The Ubiquitous Shower for Twenty

Here's a menu of light little bites that makes a smashing buffet for bridal, baby, or other showers. We've included plenty of fruit for those who have no time to cook and no desire to eat heavy foods. Add or subtract dishes according to the length of your party list and the amount of time you have to prepare.

If your guest list is long, begin with passed hors d'oeuvre. This is particularly nice to do if you can fling open the doors to the outside and move the party from the house to the garden. Set up the buffet inside or out, on snowy white linen festooned with ribbons in baby or the bride's chosen colors. Arrange platters of finger sandwiches among bowls of speared fresh fruits, cashews, roasted asparagus, olives, and cornichons. Intersperse glorious flowers from your garden or the florist: peonies, pink roses, or daffodils, for example. A scattering of single blooms in silver and glass containers fits the festive mood.

Set up the dessert and drink stations in another part of the house or backyard. Besides peach lemonade in tall glasses, remember that some guests desire nothing more than a glass of icy mineral water with a lemon slice floating on top.

A third table with a flower centerpiece and fluttering ribbons can hold the gifts. When to open? We like to have the gift opening between the main course and dessert. That leaves plenty of time for you to make coffee, and allows those guests who might have to get back to work the opportunity to have a leisurely lunch, visit with the honoree, and see the gifts opened.

The Menu

WHITE PEACH LEMONADE

ENDIVE TIPS WITH CREAM CHEESE, BLUE CHEESE, AND A RED GRAPE
(SEE PAGE 147)

CRANBERRY SCONES WITH SMOKED TURKEY AND SWEET HOT MUSTARD

FOCACCIA BASIL ROAST BEEF MINI SANDWICHES

CASHEWS, OLIVES, CORNICHONS

ROASTED ASPARAGUS WITH LEMON CURLS (SEE PAGE 127)

STRAWBERRIES WITH BROWN SUGAR AND CRÈME FRAÎCHE
(SEE PAGE 187)

PEACH MELBA AND VANILLA ICE CREAM

COFFEE AND TEA

Wine Suggestions

All Courses—All these foods will go nicely with an Australian Yalumba Valley brut rosé and everyone will be amazed at this pink bubbly. The slightly tropical feel to this wine will make everyone feel great. Excellent for a party.

Cooking Tip

Once again, great cooking begins with great shopping, and never has this been more true than with this Ubiquitous Shower menu. Choose only ripe, perfumed fruit, then prepare the buffet with great deli meats, breads, pickles, and olives. It's that easy.

Making the Party Go Smoothly

Count out your silver. Borrow from the neighbors. Here's the party that calls for real china, gleaming silver, and champagne flutes. Of all times to hire the neighborhood kid to pass food and bus tables, this is it. Usually you can get a fourteen- to sixteen-year-old to happily act as a waiter for reasonable wages. Be sure to give explicit directions about what you want. Of course, you'd like your waiter to pass trays of fruits and finger foods. Give instructions about picking up used plates, where to put them, whether or not you want your waiter to wash plates and silverware or pour drinks. If you decide in advance just what will help you, you'll be sure to get the help you need.

All the Trimmings

Buy bolts of inexpensive ribbon from a craft shop and tie bows to everything: the trees in the backyard, the front gate, the stems of footed serving trays. Festoon the table with more ribbons to flutter over the white linen cloth. Pass the endive tips on a tray and serve the rest of the meal buffet-style.

You're Invited!

For bridal parties it is best to send out written invitations two to three weeks ahead. Consult with the bride about inviting her out-of-town aunties. And remind her to ask the groom about his old aunties too. Wouldn't want to snub anybody at a time like this! White vellum paper and nice handwriting are a bonus. A telephone RSVP will let you to know how much shopping and cooking awaits you.

WHITE PEACH LEMONADE

1 (16-ounce) package frozen peaches (or 6 very ripe peaches, peeled, see page 178)	4 quarts ice water
	2 cups white rum (optional)
1 (12-ounce) can frozen lemonade concentrate	Fresh mint sprigs, for garnish
2 cups sugar	Shaved ice
Freshly squeezed juice of 3 lemons	

Serve the lemonade in tall narrow glasses full of shaved ice, with mint sprigs for garnish, and you'll find guests returning again and again for more of this refreshing drink.

PREPARATION TIME: 10 MINUTES

REFRIGERATION TIME: 20 MINUTES TO OVERNIGHT

MAKES 40 GLASSES

Can be made several hours ahead of party time.

Puree the peaches with the frozen lemonade and I cup of the sugar in a food processor fitted with the steel blade. Pour the mixture into a large pitcher, then add the lemon juice and the remaining sugar and refrigerate until serving time. When ready to serve, mix with the ice water, taste, and adjust the sugar. Add the rum if desired. Fill tall narrow glasses with shaved ice and pour the peach lemonade over the ice. Garnish with sprigs of fresh mint.

CRANBERRY SCONES WITH SMOKED TURKEY AND SWEET HOT MUSTARD

3 cups baking mix, such as White Lily, Bisquick, Jiffy, Pioneer*

1/4 cup sugar, plus additional for sprinkling

2 large eggs

2/3 cup milk

1/2 cup dried cranberries

Scones can be made from a mix. Pat the dough out into a big Frisbee-like circle on a baking sheet, score it for cutting into sixteen to twenty wedges, and bake. This is easier than biscuits, which must be rolled and cut into circles. Make these early in the day, then fill them with smoked turkey and a smattering of great mustard just before serving. We've experimented with Bisquick, Krusteaz, Jiffy, and White Lily, getting equally good results. You can even use a low-fat baking mix if you're trying to cut back on the fat grams.

PREPARATION TIME: 15 MINUTES

BAKING TIME: 12 TO 15 MINUTES

ASSEMBLY TIME: 10 MINUTES

MAKES 16 TO 20 SERVINGS

* If you use White Lily instant flour instead of baking mix, add 1/3 cup canola oil.

Scones, biscuits, and muffins are always best if made the day you plan to serve them. They don't freeze well and by the second or third day are more suited for use as hockey pucks. But beginning with a mix, they're not too much trouble to make the day of the party.

Preheat the oven to 425°. Spray a large baking sheet with cooking spray and set aside. Pour the baking mix and $^1/_4$ cup sugar into a very large mixing bowl and stir with a fork to aerate. Stir in the eggs (and oil, if needed, see asterisk, page 174) and milk with a fork, and mix only until the dry ingredients are moistened. Blend in the cranberries. Wet your hands, gather the dough into a ball, and press so that it holds together.

Transfer the dough ball to a baking sheet and press it into a 14-inch circle, about $^1/_2$ inch thick. Using a sharp knife, cut the dough into sixteen to twenty pie-shaped wedges. Separate the wedges with a spatula so the wedges don't reconnect as the dough rises in the oven. Sprinkle the top with additional sugar and bake about 12 minutes or until golden brown. Cool on the baking sheet on a rack. At serving time, split the scones and insert the sandwich ingredients.

Honey mustard
1¹/₂ pounds deli smoked turkey breast, thinly sliced
1 bunch watercress, washed, stemmed, and patted dry

Smear a little honey mustard on the scone, then top with turkey and watercress. Arrange the sandwiches on a platter, cover with plastic wrap, and refrigerate until serving time.

Focaccia Basil Roast Beef Mini Sandwiches

2 bunches fresh basil (about 2 cups per bunch), plus additional for garnishing the platters

1 cup best-quality mayonnaise

1 loaf bakery-style focaccia (8 × 1¹/₂ inches)

1 (12-ounce) jar sun-dried tomatoes in olive oil (about 1¹/₄ cups), drained and chopped

1¹/₂ pounds rare deli roast beef, sliced paper-thin

A round silver platter with a circle of rosy-hued bite-size sandwiches set around a posy of basil leaves tastes as good as it looks. Here's a shortcut to a punched-up Mediterranean mayonnaise. You can make different flavors by choosing different herbs and spices. The classic, aioli, is nothing more than lots of garlic stirred into a mayonnaise. This luscious green-flecked version makes a beautiful bed for sun-dried tomatoes and deli roast beef.

PREPARATION TIME: 10 MINUTES
REFRIGERATION TIME: 1 HOUR OR OVERNIGHT
MAKES 20 SANDWICHES

Make the herbed mayonnaise as much as 3 days before serving, if you wish. Compose and cut the sandwiches, assembly-line fashion, 24 hours ahead of time, then cover with plastic wrap and stack in the refrigerator. To serve, just uncover and slide the composition onto your best tray, decorated with fresh basil leaves.

Bring a medium pan of water to a boil. Place 1 bunch (2 cups, loosely packed) basil leaves in a colander and lower it into the boiling water. Blanch for 30 seconds, then remove to the sink and run cold water over the leaves until they feel cold to the touch. Drain and squeeze dry. Place the leaves in a food processor and process until smooth. Add the mayonnaise and pulse to mix. Transfer to a clean jar, cover, and refrigerate while you prepare the bread.

With a long, serrated knife, split the focaccia in half horizontally. Line up the two bread halves on the countertop with their sides touching. Use a spatula to generously coat the bread with basil mayonnaise. Arrange the sun-dried tomatoes over the flavored mayo, then add the whole basil leaves and top with the roast beef. Cover and wrap the focaccia securely with plastic wrap, and refrigerate it for 1 hour or overnight.

To serve, remove the focaccia to a cutting board and cut into finger sandwiches. Cut each bread lengthwise into five strips, then each strip into $1^1/2$-inch lengths. Arrange the sandwiches in circles on platters, with a bunch of whole basil leaves in the center—like a flower.

Peach Melba

15 large ripe cling-free peaches or
3 (16-ounce) packages frozen peaches, thawed
Juice of a lemon
$^1/_2$ cup sugar
1 pint fresh raspberries

2 quarts best-quality vanilla ice cream
20 fresh edible pansies or Johnny-jump-ups
2 cups Quick Melba Sauce (recipe follows)

Here's a make-it-on-the-spot dessert for the sideboard. Offer a bowl of sliced peaches—fresh or frozen—decorated with edible pansies, a bowl of vanilla ice cream, scoop, your own homemade melba sauce, and fresh raspberries. Either compose one dessert dish with ice cream, peaches, Melba sauce, and a perfect pansy and raspberry garnish as an example, or ask your neighbor-kid waiter to act as dessert host/bartender and get him to compose desserts. A stack of dessert dishes, spoons, and extra cocktail napkins are a good idea at this station.

PREPARATION TIME: 15 MINUTES
MAKES 20 SERVINGS

If you're starting with fresh peaches, prepare and refrigerate them as much as 1 day before serving, then simply arrange the elements of the dessert at party time. If you're using frozen peaches, just compose this dessert when you're ready to eat.

To peel fresh peaches, bring a large pot of water to a boil, then drop in the peaches, a few at a time, and blanch for about 30 to 45 seconds. Remove the peaches to a dish towel to drain, then pinch up the skins (they'll look like they're blistered), and pull them off. Holding each peach over a bowl, slice and drop the peaches into the bowl, adding lemon juice and sugar as you go. Once you've sliced all of them, toss to mix thoroughly, cover, and refrigerate until serving time.

To serve, transfer the peaches to your best-looking glass bowl and place them on the sideboard, along with a bowl of raspberries, one of vanilla ice cream, and a pitcher of Melba sauce. Each serving is made up of a splash of sauce topped with ice cream, peaches, and a perfect raspberry. An edible pansy on top is perfection.

QUICK MELBA SAUCE

1/4 cup red currant jelly	2 tablespoons cornstarch
1 pint fresh or frozen raspberries	2 tablespoons cold water

PREPARATION TIME: 10 MINUTES

COOKING TIME: 3 MINUTES

REFRIGERATION TIME: AT LEAST 30 MINUTES

MAKES 2 CUPS

Make this fabulous sauce up to a week before party time, cover, and refrigerate.

Place the jelly in a 4-cup glass measure and microwave on high (100 percent power) for 1 minute or until boiling. Add the raspberries and microwave on high (100 percent power) for 2 minutes, or until boiling. Meanwhile, dissolve the cornstarch in the water. Stir it into the raspberry mixture and microwave on high (100 percent power) for 1 minute more, until slightly thickened. Pour into a clean jar, cover, and refrigerate.

Alternatively, you can make this in a saucepan on the stove top: Bring the jelly to a boil over medium heat, then stir in the raspberries and bring them to a boil, stirring constantly. Stir in the cornstarch mixture and boil until the liquid turns clear, about 3 minutes.

Easy Southeast Asian Dinner

Entertain in style on a weeknight with this quick-to-assemble, brightly flavored Southeast Asian dinner. Yes, it takes some planning, some advance purchases, but not very much time to get on the table, thus allowing you to stay at the office and complete those critical end-of-day tasks. The menu owes its unique flavor to Vietnamese cuisine, and can be completed in 1 hour. Reflect the Vietnamese-French culinary tradition and serve good crusty European bread with the meal.

The Menu

WASABI PEAS*

HANOI BEEF CUBES

MARINATED VIDALIA ONIONS (SEE PAGE 218)

CRUSTY EUROPEAN BREAD AND BUTTER

COLD ASIAN NOODLE SALAD

VANILLA ICE CREAM OR FROZEN YOGURT WITH MANGOES

* These are a Japanese snack food and can be purchased at Asian markets.

Wine Suggestions

Main Course—Asian food is usually best paired with a good German Riesling, Auslese, or Spätlese. You really can't go wrong.

Cooking Tip

Stir-frying is Asian cooking's most memorable, and difficult-to-master technique. You don't have to have a wok to cook in—any large heavy skillet will do—but you do have to have the nerve to turn the heat all the way up and to watch the food and take it out when it looks and smells right.

This cooking method goes fast, so it's important to have all your ingredients measured, chopped, marinated, and ready before you begin. Done properly, stir-fried foods are not greasy or overcooked. Remember to keep the food moving at all times, tossing and turning, and soon you'll have a well-cooked product that's tender and juicy, with all the flavors intact and a texture that's heaven.

Heat the skillet or wok dry—with no added oil—over high heat until it's so hot that a drop of water will jump off it screaming. Add the oil and distribute it evenly over the surface of the pan. It should be almost smoking before you add the food. If you're flavoring the oil—with garlic, ginger, or chili—add the flavoring first, toss a few seconds, then remove it. Then add the food as described in the recipe. Allow meat to rest a few moments before stirring to properly seal the surfaces (the same way the French say to leave meat alone in the pan when you're sautéing, to sear it), then finish by stirring and continuing to cook as directed in the recipe.

All the Trimmings

Displaying this dinner is easy and the result looks great because of all the intense colors. Light candles, put on a bright pretty tablecloth, and enjoy this light tangy meal. The beef cubes should be placed on Boston or Bibb lettuce leaves, then garnished with mint or basil and shredded carrots. Arrange tomato wedges around the lettuce leaves, and you will have covered most of the color wheel. Add a serving of Cold Asian Noodle Salad and you're done. Serve good crusty bread and butter. Continue the tropical theme with vanilla frozen yogurt or ice cream topped with mangoes.

HANOI BEEF CUBES

$1^{1}/_{2}$ pounds boneless beef steak (sirloin, London broil, or fillet)

3 cloves garlic, chopped ($1^{1}/_{2}$ teaspoons)

3 teaspoons Vietnamese fish sauce (*nuoc mam*)

$1^{1}/_{2}$ teaspoons sugar

$1/_{2}$ teaspoon salt

4 tablespoons peanut oil

$1/_{2}$ teaspoon crushed hot red pepper flakes

4 whole large Boston or Bibb lettuce leaves

1 cup mixed shredded carrots, basil and mint leaves

1 large tomato cut in wedges

This recipe can be used successfully for hors d'oeuvre, serving the beef cubes on skewers or toothpicks.

PREPARATION TIME:	5 MINUTES
MARINATING TIME:	AT LEAST 30 MINUTES
COOKING TIME:	10 MINUTES

MAKES 4 SERVINGS FOR DINNER OR 8 FOR HORS D'OEUVRE

Buy or cut the steak into bite-size cubes and marinate up to 24 hours before the meal.

Using a sharp chef's knife, cut the steak into 1-inch cubes, removing excess fat. In a large bowl, combine the beef, garlic, fish sauce, sugar, salt, and 2 tablespoons of the peanut oil. Marinate at least 30 minutes, or for up to 24 hours.

Preheat a large skillet or wok over high heat. Add the remaining 2 tablespoons of peanut oil and turn the pan to coat it evenly. When the oil is very hot, lift the beef cubes from the marinade, add to the pan, and stir-fry, turning frequently until brown on all sides yet still pink in the middle, about 10 minutes. Arrange a lettuce leaf on each of four plates and pile the beef cubes onto the leaf. Garnish with mint sprigs and shredded carrot. Arrange tomato slices and the Marinated Vidalia Onions around the lettuce leaf and serve with the Cold Asian Noodle Salad.

Cold Asian Noodle Salad

3 quarts water

3 tablespoons salt

12 ounces fresh Chinese flat noodles (can substitute ½ pound dried linguine)

Dressing:

3 tablespoons vegetable oil

2 tablespoons rice vinegar

2 tablespoons freshly squeezed lime juice

½ teaspoon Vietnamese fish sauce (nuoc mam)

1 teaspoon sesame oil

1 teaspoon freshly grated gingerroot

½ teaspoon salt

Pinch of crushed hot red pepper flakes

1 large cucumber, peeled, seeded, and julienned

½ carrot, peeled and julienned

1 cup shredded iceberg lettuce

2 cups bean sprouts

½ cup fresh basil leaves, cut into chiffonade

PREPARATION TIME: 10 MINUTES

MARINATING TIME: AT LEAST 5 MINUTES

MAKES 4 GENEROUS SERVINGS

Can be made up to 1 day in advance.

In a large pot of 3 quarts well-salted boiling water (3 tablespoons of salt), cook the noodles just *al dente* (2 minutes for fresh, 7 to 8 minutes for dried). Remove and reserve 1 cup of the pasta cooking water. Drain pasta, return the noodles to the empty pot, and stir in tablespoons of the pasta cooking liquid until the noodles stop absorbing liquid.

To make the dressing, in a large bowl, mix together the oil, rice vinegar, lime juice, fish sauce, sesame oil, grated gingerroot, salt, and red pepper flakes. Add the warm noodles and toss well. Taste and adjust the seasonings. You may need to add more lime juice.

Layer the cucumber, carrot, lettuce, bean sprouts, and basil on top of the dressed noodles. Cover and refrigerate until ready to serve. For maximum crispness for the vegetables, toss just before serving.

Fish sauces vary from deep mahogany to light amber in color. When we first ate this salad in a Philadelphia Vietnamese restaurant known as My Huong, we were advised to buy Squid brand, which is the color of strong tea and has an intense salty, fishy taste. It's made in Bangkok from nothing more than anchovy extract, water, and salt. You'll be able to identify the brand without being able to read any of the four Asian alphabets represented on the label. It has a big picture of—guess what—a swimming squid in among all the words. We bought a 24-ounce bottle in a Chinatown grocery store for less than a dollar and a half. Look for the green plastic cap, the red, blue, and green letters on the white label. The glass bottle is even embossed with the image of a squid for the visually impaired. A kind of Thai Braille. Close inspection reveals the manufacturer has won a double gold medal something for this sauce. Not that we could understand more than the symbol. But what we can understand is the clean, intense flavor of the sauce. We like it and use it interchangeably with Vietnamese fish sauce.

Mother's Day Breakfast in Bed:
Easy as One-Two-Three

This has got to be easy. The day the kids make Mom's breakfast to honor her day, the menu needs some automatic safeguards. Like a waffle iron that blinks when the waffles are ready to serve, or using the microwave to heat up the spicy cider so that it turns off automatically, or using the oven or microwave to cook bacon so that you don't have to worry about grease splashing on little fingers. This is a menu that even preschoolers—with some able and surefooted help from Dad—can make for Mom. It's ready to serve in less than half an hour, it contains flavors that will please both parents and kids, and it's the sort of gift that mothers will never forget.

The Menu

BROWNIE PECAN WAFFLES WITH RASPBERRY JAM

OVEN-ROASTED PEPPER BACON

STRAWBERRIES WITH BROWN SUGAR AND CRÈME FRAÎCHE

HOT SPICY APPLE CIDER

COFFEE AND/OR TEA

All the Trimmings

Perhaps the most important element of this meal is a camera—either the throwaway kind or your own—loaded and ready to document the event, from the kids making the waffle batter, to the tray made up for Mom, all the way through to the carnage left in the kitchen. Make a small album. This can become one of the moments you'll treasure long after the kids are grown.

As to the preparations by Dad, when buying the groceries for this breakfast, don't forget fresh flowers for Mom, maybe even a single red rose in a bud vase. Serve Mom her breakfast on a tray in bed. Line the tray with a colorful napkin, then, using your best dishes, serve the waffle on the main plate with a dollop of raspberry jam in the middle. Present a dessert bowl of strawberries, with small bowls of crème fraîche and brown sugar, and a big mug for the hot cider. Take the pictures and make a gift to Mom of those. Nothing could please her more. In fact, as we all know, she'll probably be the one who ends up taking a good many pictures herself—just to get the looks on the faces of her budding chefs as they make their debut.

Brownie Pecan Waffles

2 cups baking mix	1 large egg
1/4 cup unsweetened cocoa powder	3 tablespoons vegetable oil
1/4 cup sugar	1/2 cup chopped pecans
1 2/3 cups milk	Raspberry jam

Start out with your favorite baking mix—White Lily, Pioneer Lowfat, Krusteaz, Bisquick, or Jiffy. Then stir in cocoa and pecans and you'll have a spectacular easy waffle mix to please the chocolate lovers in your household.

PREPARATION TIME: 10 MINUTES
BAKING TIME: 15 MINUTES
MAKES 4 SERVINGS (6 7-INCH WAFFLES)

Best if made and eaten at once.

Plug in the waffle iron to preheat. Spritz the hot iron with cooking spray. Stir all ingredients except the jam in a large bowl until blended. Use a soup ladle to pour the batter onto the hot waffle iron. Bake until the steaming stops and the waffle iron signals that they're done. Keep the finished waffles warm in a low oven while preparing the rest. Serve on a warmed dinner plate with a dollop of raspberry jam in the middle.

Oven-Roasted Pepper Bacon

1 pound thick-sliced bacon   **1 teaspoon cracked black peppercorns**

Use this method anytime you want to cook bacon in a trouble-free way. It's great for kids, because they're not likely to splash themselves with hot bacon fat. However, we do recommend that you ask Dad to help turn the bacon and to lift the cooking pan from the oven.

PREPARATION TIME: 5 MINUTES

BAKING TIME: 22 MINUTES

COOLING TIME: 1 0 MINUTES

MAKES 4 TO 6 SERVINGS

Best if cooked and eaten immediately.

Place the oven rack in the middle of the oven and preheat it to 400°. Line a $15 \times 11^{1}/_{2} \times$ 2-inch baking sheet with foil. Place a baking rack on the foil. Arrange the bacon slices in a single layer on the rack, then sprinkle with the cracked peppercorns.

Bake for 12 minutes, then turn the bacon with tongs and finish cooking, about 10 minutes more, or until the bacon is brown and crisp. Remove from the oven and cool on the rack for about 10 minutes before serving.

Alternatively, cook bacon in the microwave 1 minute per slice.

Strawberries with Brown Sugar and Crème Fraîche

1 pint strawberries

4 tablespoons brown sugar

4 to 6 ounces crème fraîche

No tricks to this one. In 5 minutes, Mom will be eating the specialty of Wimbledon.

PREPARATION TIME: 5 MINUTES

MAKES 4 SERVINGS OF ABOUT 3 TO 6 STRAWBERRIES EACH.

These berries can be prepared the night before.

Wash and hull the berries and allow them to dry. Arrange the berries on a plate or in a small bowl, and serve the crème fraîche and the brown sugar in separate bowls alongside. Dip the berries in the crème fraîche and then the brown sugar.

Hot Spicy Apple Cider

6 cups fresh or frozen or canned apple cider

1/2 cup dried apple slices

4 cinnamon sticks

1 teaspoon chopped crystallized ginger (optional)

Simmer this in the microwave while you're making breakfast, and soon the whole house will smell spicy and sweet.

PREPARATION TIME: 3 MINUTES

SIMMERING TIME: 10 MINUTES

MAKES 6 CUPS

Make this ahead if you wish. It's also delicious cold, so save any leftovers in the refrigerator and serve them with lunch. Reheat to just under the boil in the microwave.

Combine all ingredients in a 2-quart microwavable glass measure and heat on high (100 percent power) for 10 minutes. Alternatively, simmer on the stove top in a saucepan. Serve hot, in large mugs.

Catering Wisdom from Suzanne McCray

Suzanne Tinker McCray has been a caterer for fifteen years. For the past eight years she owned and operated Celebrations by Suzanne Catering in Lexington, Kentucky, and is now the catering director for Lexmark International Computers Restaurant Dining Services. She trained in Los Angeles, worked at the Beverly Hills Country Club, apprenticed at Hyatt Hotels, and worked for a movie catering company called Along Came Mary, doing movie premieres, movie set lunches, and parties in stars' homes. Ms. McCray still does contract catering with Lundy's Special Events, which most recently catered the 1996 Atlanta Olympics. Nepotism rules, and we are fortunate that Suzy is also Katherine's cousin.

Suzy, you've been throwing parties for years and years. What advice could you give to the beginning entertainer? How would you allay the fears of a person just starting out?

Let me give you an example. I've got a friend who is still single. She wants to have her fiancé's folks over as well as some other people, including some of her close friends. She calls me up and I'm trying to talk her through it. I'm willing to help her pull it off. So the first thing I'd say is call up a couple of your good friends and make sure they're available on the date you've chosen because you want to make sure you don't have a room full of strangers.

So you think it's okay to ask for extra help?

Sure. If you have a good friend who you know is better at this sort of thing than you are, ask her (or him) to lend a hand. From what I've been reading in *Bon Appétit* the past year or so, it's perfectly okay to involve your guests in the cooking. I don't actually do that myself, but it's an acceptable way to entertain.

What's your idea of the ideal size for a party?

It depends on the type of party. If you're having an informal party with cocktails, invite just as many as your house can comfortably hold. If it's a more formal dinner, invite only as many as you can comfortably seat at the table. For potluck, where the food probably won't require cutting with a knife and fork, you can invite as many as you can comfortably seat in the living room.

A couple of years ago I was hired to cater a wedding by a woman who was a major control freak. She gave me checklists for everything. But she forgot one thing. The menu she created featured prime rib. Now, she hadn't planned on where all those people were going to sit. People were wandering around, plates in hand, wondering where to plant themselves. Some even went outside and were sitting on the steps. They were trying to balance plates on their knees. It was a major faux pas, in my opinion. I was not happy with the way that turned out. Just remember, if you need a knife to cut it, you've got to have a place to set it down.

When should you send out written invitations?
Depends on how upscale you want to be. If it's for something formal, send out written invitations two weeks ahead. For a wedding or big holiday event, even longer, like a month.

How much advance planning do you need to do?
That depends on the person. If you're a type A and need to have control of everything—or if you get flustered easily, say the soufflé falls and you freak—then I'd say give yourself a couple of weeks. Work out a schedule for yourself. Monday, I'll do the shopping. Tuesday, I'll make this certain dish ahead and freeze it. If you're more comfortable in the kitchen, you can call friends on a Thursday and say "Come on over Friday night."

What are your tricks for staying organized?
Lots of notes. I make detailed notes for when things are to be done. When I first started out, I'd even lay out the platters empty the night before, and put little Post-it notes in them saying what went in what dish. I'll tell you what. No other part of my life is organized. But when I'm at work, I am totally organized. My staff knows. I keep a manila envelope on every event, with checklists. The staff will come in and say, "Where's the envelope?" I list quantities. How many chafers. How many glasses, linens . . . the works. I make notes about what goes in the oven when, and when it comes out. I know what I want, and making notes keeps me calm and organized.

How long should a party last?
If you're having a cocktail party, the rule of thumb is to plan for a couple of hours, then know that no one will leave when you think. You'll still have stragglers. For a dinner party, allow forty-five minutes to one hour for hors d'oeuvre and drinks—you don't want them to overeat or overdrink before dinner—and about an hour at the table for the dinner, then they'll probably stay and mingle for another hour. So usually, three hours is good.

So how do you get your guests to go home when the party's over?
I talked it over with my mom and she says you can't. But sometimes I pull a good friend aside and say, "You've got to get these people out of my house." Will you be the first to go

so they'll go? And if it's a case of somebody who has drunk too much, call a cab or get somebody to drive that person home.

Would you ever ask your guests to help with the dishes?
Mother says it's never correct. But you know, if it's casual, friends will offer. Otherwise, I usually just get the dishes into the kitchen, scrape them off, and let them wait until the next day. And other times it's okay. For instance, we usually ask people over to watch basketball and I'm not into it, so I don't mind coming into the kitchen to wash up. But for a business or more formal dinner, no. I think it's rude to disappear into the kitchen and start cleaning up; it makes your guests uncomfortable, like they should leave.

It sounds like you consult with your mother a lot about entertaining.
You know, my mom says she can't entertain, but I learned everything from her. She taught me there's no such thing as an empty refrigerator. That there's always room for one more at the table. And when she and Dad had to do all that business entertaining and I was just a little kid, I used to be in awe of my mom.

Let's talk party specifics. What's your favorite kind of party?
I love brunches. As a caterer, I love brunch food. Starters can be made ahead. You can go to the best bakery in town and buy muffins and fruit breads. It doesn't take a lot of effort. You can keep the drinks simple: Bloody Marys, mimosas, coffee. I think brunches are fun. You can keep them informal and do a lot of stuff ahead of time like buy prepared foods and fresh fruit.

I like to set up a coffee bar with lots of coffees. Somewhere, you put a cinnamon stick into the basket with the coffee grounds. It gives a wonderful smell throughout the whole room. Get flavored creamers, liqueurs, whipped cream, chocolate chips, and chocolate sticks with fruit fillings. I like to keep the beverages away from the food to avoid bottlenecks.

Can you talk about your dream party? What would you serve and who would you invite?
I've already had it. My wedding reception. It was a brunch. I had it planned years before I met my husband. In fact, I'd picked out my wedding cake—from an old edition of *Chocolatier* magazine. I had my dress picked out. Everything.

I was twenty-nine years old when I met Danny. I'd decided that maybe I'd never get married after all, and that was okay. But when we decided to get married I said, "Here's what we're going to do."

Danny's a caterer and special events planner, too. So, we did it all ourselves. I had a sous chef from the hotel who did a crêpe station; we had another seafood station with cold boiled shrimp and smoked salmon and bagels; and a carving station with roast beef. We catered it ourselves. We did it all. The night before, Danny and I worked until midnight, getting the tables set up, then the next day, my staff took over. We had two hundred people and it was wonderful. But for a big event, I say hire a professional. Unless you are one.

Now, can we talk about making a party look great. How do you do it?
People eat with their eyes first. Food service is 90 percent presentation. If you want to look like you picked up deli trays at the grocery store, then just serve everything flat. For me, I use a lot of height and elevation. If I have to turn a milk crate upside down and cover it with a cloth, I'll do it to get some of the food up off the table. I use a lot of cake stands. That would be a good thing to collect, if you ask me. You can never have too many.

And colors. You have to plan a menu to make sure everything isn't green, let's say. At hotels they put a cherry tomato on the plate when all else fails. I personally can't stand bare space on a buffet table. If I have to, I get heads of flowering kale and intersperse them with the food. I'll use a bowl of beautiful fruit. At holiday time, I've gone so far as to spray paint artichokes a beautiful gold. I'll put votive candles into artichokes and apples I've hollowed out. I've even taken asparagus and put a pillar candle in the middle of several spears then tied the whole thing up with raffia. It's inexpensive and it's dramatic.

I like a lot of color on the table—different-colored linens. Go to the fabric store and pick up colorful fabric. I use lots of baskets. You know many people do veggies and dips, but it makes all the difference in the way you present it. Instead of laying everything flat, line the platter with purple kale, tilt it, then let the food just spill out onto the tablecloth.

Danny says I just pour food on the table. But I like things to look bountiful. If I'm doing a cheese board, for example, I'll arrange cheeses on several levels, using cake stands, then finish it off with cubes of cheese that spill off a tray onto the tablecloth, and grapes spilling off a cake stand. Or I'll pour crackers onto the table itself. These informal arrangements excite people. You can see it in their faces. That's what I like to do.

I always line trays, but I hate paper doilies, except for under petit fours; I think they're just terrible. But especially if you're using silver trays, which can react with certain foods, it's important to line trays with kale or other deep green leafy vegetables.

Are there certain foods you stay away from because they just don't present well?
I don't like to do tenderloin if it has to be sliced ahead. It bleeds and by the time the last guest gets it on his plate it will be an awful gray. You have to slice and serve this meat for

each diner. And I stay away from stir-fried vegetables because they lose their color and get soggy really fast.

What about flowers?

I like simple flowers. I'll go buy a bunch of gladiola and put them in a tall ginger jar. Danny and I had a party a couple of years back, a pig roast in the backyard. We did mason jars of wildflowers. Flowers don't have to be expensive. Nor do the arrangements have to be formal. I have a collection of funky water pitchers—all left over from wedding presents—and I like to use those. I'm not much good at arranging flowers myself, but if you give me a bunch of those little colored marbles, I can throw them into the bottom of something and make it look pretty decent.

You're a professional. How do you deal with food safety?

Very important. Don't do more than you can refrigerate. Put food in your neighbor's refrigerator or freezer. Keep everything covered. Just remember the safe zone. Under 40° or over 140°.

What does that mean?

It means keep foods either over 140° or under 40° so that bacteria won't grow. And keep airborne bacteria off foods by keeping them covered. Never leave foods out on a buffet for more than two hours except for a cheese course warming up. And even that should be covered.

We've talked about almost everything except the most important item: the guests. Should you mix 'em up? How do you decide who to invite?

I think it's good to mix your guests so you get a diversified conversation, but on the other hand, you've got to be careful. Last year, I had a disaster on my hands. For Danny's birthday—a surprise party—I invited his high school friends and college fraternity brothers—the party hearty crowd—and his business associates, and political pals—he's deep into Democratic politics here in Lexington. It just never worked out. That party did not jell. I'd hired a band and nobody would dance. I was just sick about it.

You never know, Suzy. Those people might have had a better time than you did.

Yeah, but if I don't have a good time at a party I'm throwing, then I think it's failed.

So this brings up the question of open houses.

I like them. Mother's given a few that I've done for her. It's a good way to repay a lot of social obligations and have a good time. You can usually get away with not having to feed them a whole meal. People will come for a short time. You can stagger the invitations. Invite the business and social obligations for the first couple of hours, then your close friends to close the party down. That way you get to have your formal acquaintances over early, then relax and have a good time with your close friends before the evening's over.

When is your favorite season for parties?
February and summer. People get too partied out at holiday time. But by late February or early March—at least around here—we get lots of snow and people are housebound and we all get a little stir crazy.

But summer's the best. Here, on our street, three of us have backyards that connect by gates. Next door is a sous chef and his wife, and across the way is our friend who just likes to party. So we often do a casual summer party, with hors d'oeuvre and drinks in my backyard, then dinner next door, and finish up with swimming and conversation across the way. All our kids just cycle back and forth among the yards. It's not too much work for any one family and we all have a good time. Makes us feel like we've got a real community going on here. We look after each other's kids. We have fun.

Any last words of advice to potential party givers?
Absolutely. Get as much done ahead of time as possible. Give yourself enough time, say an hour or an hour and a half, to take a bath, get dressed, get your husband dressed. Be ready so that when you open the door for the first guests, you've got a glass of wine in your hand and you're relaxed. Your guests will feel welcome immediately. That's the secret to success. Organization is the key to avoiding stress. That's what makes a party fun for you and for your guests.

You're singing our song, Suzy. We want to come to your house.
You're always invited!

Some Like It Hot Summer Menus

Memorial Day Italian Grill Summer Kickoff

The first ingredient in a successful summer picnic is smoke. Plan your meal around something cooked on the grill and you will have attracted the attention of the neighborhood. Think about street fairs. They have their own traditional cuisines lovingly remembered. The smell of charcoal and the sounds of pickup bands quicken the scene.

Although we personally cannot give you a recipe for making cotton candy (what we were never permitted to eat and what looked sooooo good because it was forbidden), we can help you turn a Memorial Day celebration into your own private street fair. And this is idiot-proof entertaining. Throw some Italian sausage on the barbecue, crank open a few cans of beans for salad, set out prepared antipasti, and it's nearly done.

You can re-create the street fair scene in your own backyard, or at a neighborhood block party. Get out the charcoal grill and turn up the boom box for your friends and neighbors. What a perfect event to make into a potluck. Assign someone to the grill and another to ice down the drinks.

This is paper-plate food. Don't even consider using anything you have to put in the dishwasher.

The Menu

COLD ANTIPASTI (SEE PAGE 304)

ITALIAN SAUSAGE SANDWICHES WITH GRILLED ONIONS AND SWEET PEPPERS

THREE-BEAN SALAD

WATERMELON ASTI

COOKIES AND LEMONADE

Wine Suggestions

Appetizer and Main Course—We would definitely serve either an Italian Sangiovese or a Barbaresco; they are fruity and high in acid and will be the perfect foil to the fatty spicy sausage. Beer is always welcome as well.

Cooking Tip

Grilling vegetables outdoors is easy. Just buy an expanded metal vegetable-seafood grill to put over the regular grill surface and you are in business. This type of grill has smaller

openings so that the vegetables won't fall through. Vegetables such as bell peppers, onions, eggplants, and squash make the best candidates. You can even grill firm or green tomatoes. Marinate the vegetables in oil and vinegar with your choice of spices for about an hour, then throw them on the hot grill until they cook to your taste.

When cooking over charcoal, avoid petroleum starters. Remove the grill rack. Make a charcoal starter chimney from a 5-gallon can with both ends removed. Fashion a loose wire handle by punching two holes near the top of the can and stringing a coat hanger or wire to make a loop so that you can lift the chimney up, off the hot coals. Place the can in the bottom of your grill. Stuff the chimney with wadded-up newspaper, top it off with charcoal, then light it. Once the charcoal is white, lift off the chimney, spread the hot coals, and set the grill rack on top to preheat. Always preheat the squeaky clean grill thoroughly, or food will stick to it. Rub a raw potato over the hot grill and you've made organic Teflon. Nothing will stick to the grill now. Trust us. Nothing.

Pointers for Easy Outings

- **Pack it in, pack it out.** *Bring plastic garbage bags and a roll of paper towels to make cleanup easy.*

- **Water, water everywhere and not a drop to drink.** *Or to wash up with either. Carry along a gallon of water for washups and drinks.*

- **Keep hot food hot and cold foods cold.** *Food safety dictates that you keep foods above 140° or below 40° to prevent bacterial growth. Use those new soft-sided carry-alls to preserve hot and cold foods— separately of course. Don't forget a sack of ice for drinks, as well as to nestle bowls of cold food in at the picnic site.*

- **Discourage pesky pests.** *Set the legs of your portable table in paper cups of water so ants can't march up to join you for dinner. Stick sprigs of basil in fruits and salads to discourage fruit flies. Rub vanilla extract on everybody to control the gnats. If you picnic in swampy country, Avon Skin-So-Soft, Off, or Deep-Woods insect repellent may be necessary to keep you from being on the insects' banquet menu. Just try to keep it off your hands, or you'll make the food taste icky.*

Suggestions for Potluck Additions to the Party

Here's a list of Italian picnic foods you could ask people to pick up at a gourmet grocery store or Italian deli. Remember that if you have a potluck, you only have to ask each person to bring a bowl of *something* and there's always plenty of food. All you have to do then is provide enough plates, forks, napkins, and drinks.

Biscotti

Italian dry sausage

Marinated mushrooms

Fresh mozzarella with beefsteak tomatoes and basil

Olive salad

Caponata

Stuffed peppers

Calimari salad

ITALIAN SAUSAGE SANDWICHES WITH GRILLED ONIONS AND SWEET PEPPERS

3 tablespoons extra virgin olive oil

2 very large sweet yellow onions, thinly sliced

3 green or red Italian sweet frying peppers, seeded and cut lengthwise into strips

3 red, orange, or green bell peppers, seeded and cut lengthwise into strips

18 cloves garlic, chopped (3 tablespoons), to taste

Salt and freshly ground black pepper, to taste

8 (6-inch) sweet or hot Italian sausage links

8 (7-inch) hero or Italian rolls, sliced lengthwise

Brown mustard

In Brooklyn, as well as the other New York boroughs, the sight of vendors making these sandwiches on portable grills is as common to summer as the cacophonic music of the street. Sweet Italian frying peppers are best in these sandwiches, but green, red, and yellow bells taste great too, so we recommend a mix of the two for optimum taste. Use sweet summer onions—Vidalia, Walla Walla, or Texas 1015—for the best flavor. You can expand this recipe to fit the limits of your party list. The cooking time remains the same, it's only limited by the square footage of your grill surface. Make these sandwiches at home in the backyard on the big Weber gas grill, or carry along a little portable grill and set it up on a park table and grill away. No matter where you are, it's easy and it's satisfying. Summer is, hallelujah, here at last.

PREPARATION TIME: 15 MINUTES
GRILLING TIME: 10 MINUTES
MAKES 8 SERVINGS

Sauté the vegetables beforehand in the kitchen, then transfer the pan to the outside grill and reheat them while you grill the sausages and toast the rolls.

Heat the oil in a large skillet over medium-high heat, then sauté the onions and peppers with the garlic until the vegetables are limp and beginning to brown, about 5 minutes. Season to taste with salt and pepper, and set aside until serving time.

Preheat a gas or charcoal grill and grill the sausages, turning them with tongs, until hot and browned on all sides, about 5 to 10 minutes. Toast the split rolls on the grill for a moment or two, then add a hot sausage and top with a spoonful of peppers and onions. Pass the mustard, please.

Borrow a trick from the street vendors and wrap each sandwich in foil before handing it to the waiting diner. That way it's less messy to eat and holds the heat well.

Three-Bean Salad

1 (16-ounce) can cut green beans, drained	1 teaspoon salt
1 (16-ounce) can garbanzo beans, drained	$^1/_2$ teaspoon freshly ground black pepper
1 (16-ounce) can red kidney beans, drained	$^1/_2$ cup salad oil
1 medium red onion, chopped	$^2/_3$ cup malt vinegar
$^1/_3$ cup sugar	

Remember that a 1-pound can of beans makes three servings, and you can multiply this potluck dish to feed the multitudes. You could even go so far as to double all the beans in the dish and still use the dressing as listed. The recipe is as flexible as it is reliable.

PREPARATION TIME: 1 0 MINUTES

MARINATING TIME: AT LEAST 30 MINUTES

MAKES 8 TO 1 0 SERVINGS (MAY BE DOUBLED, TRIPLED, OR WHATEVER)

Can be made up to 1 week in advance.

Stir the beans and onion together into a large salad bowl. Combine the sugar, salt, pepper, oil, and vinegar in a jar and shake to mix. Pour the dressing over the bean mixture and toss. Cover and refrigerate at least 30 minutes until serving time.

Watermelon Asti

1 (6-pound) chilled watermelon (the long torpedo shape with one flat side works best because it won't roll off the table)

²/₃ cup sugar (or to taste)

2 lemons, 1 juiced and zested, the other thinly sliced

¹/₂ cup white rum

2 pounds white seedless grapes, washed and stemmed, chilled

1 bottle Moscato d'Asti or Asti Spumante, chilled*

Fresh mint sprigs for garnish

One of those oh-so-easy desserts that lets the diners do most of the work. All you do is scoop out the pulp and discard the seeds of the watermelon, fill the melon with rum, sparkling wine, and fruit, then chill and serve. Guests scoop their own servings into plastic glasses. It's dessert you both eat and drink.

PREPARATION TIME:	10 MINUTES
CHILLING TIME:	Overnight for the watermelon plus 30 minutes for the filling
MAKES 12 SERVINGS	

In a hurry? Freeze the filled watermelon for an hour or so. Otherwise, chill the watermelon overnight, then add the chilled fruit, rum, and sugar 30 minutes before serving.

Set the cold watermelon, flat side down, on the counter and cut off the top (the hat). Scoop out and place the seeds and pulp in a colander. Let the juice drain back into the melon, then pick out and discard the seeds. Stir the sugar into the melon. Add the pulp, lemon juice and zest, and rum. Add the grapes. Replace the top of the watermelon and chill at least 30 minutes or until serving time. When ready to serve, uncork the cold Asti and pour it into the cavity. Garnish with fresh mint leaves. Scoop the filling into short barrel plastic glasses and serve, giving each diner some melon, along with the other fruit, sparkling wine, garnished with a lemon slice and a sprig of mint.

*Note: Ask your wine merchant for a soft, low-alcohol Asti Spumante if Moscato is not available.

Rainy Summer Weekend Paella Supper

We had the beach house and houseguests on the weekend it rained. People showed up with beach balls and long faces. Kids and grown-ups both threatened to storm. It was time for Sylvia's Paella. Serious comfort food made with fresh shellfish, chicken, and good chorizo, it's a one-pot dinner that goes together in about an hour. It can stand around for up to an hour, is appealing to children and adults, and doesn't even have to be served piping hot. Now that will cheer up any cook!

All that is needed to accompany it is a baguette and a simple salad. Set the table with daisies and a bright tablecloth. We even played the Ventures and the Beach Boys.

Meet your guests at the door with a sure smile-maker, a glass of Sangria. This is such a great menu, you might not even want to wait for a rainy weekend!

The Menu

SANGRIA

SYLVIA'S PAELLA

BAGUETTE

ORANGE SLICES WITH RED PEPPER FLAKES AND GRAND MARNIER

TOSSED ROMAINE SALAD

SUNSHINE SECRET CAKE

Wine Suggestions

Main Course—If you want to have a white alternative to the sangria, try the Spanish albariño grape. It is our favorite Spanish white from the Galicia region. The grapes are grown on the hills near the Atlantic Ocean, and you can almost get that sea breeze flavor from them. Alternatively, try manzanilla Fino Sherry, made in the seaside town of Sanlúcar, is also a great complement to paella. Both wines are really great with all seafood.

Cooking Tip

To speed up the paella preparation, buy peeled shrimp, fresh or frozen. If you can only find them precooked, just add them at the last minute.

All the Trimmings

Set the table and decorate it with seashells and small beach toys. Display the cake in the dining room to entice your guests. For a dramatic presentation, serve the paella on a large platter in the middle of the table. If you have a paella pan, definitely use that. The shellfish and orange shrimp against the yellow rice, topped with chopped fresh parsley and basil, are beautiful. Pass the oranges and serve the salad as a separate course before dessert.

Sangria

2 large seedless oranges

2 bottles light, dry red wine

2 green apples, seeded, peeled, and sliced

1 (8 1/4-ounce) can crushed pineapple, with juice

10 strawberries, sliced

1 1/2 liters Sprite

1 cup brandy (optional)

Mint sprigs

Jay, Katherine's brother, spent a semester in Seville, Spain, and what he learned best, besides the fact that Spanish girls are hard to pick up, was how to make a good sangria. Make and refrigerate this Spanish punch in a large serving pitcher, or use two pitchers if you don't have one large enough to hold all the wine and fruit. Just divide the ingredients in half and put one part in each smaller pitcher. Serve the punch in tall, narrow glasses, garnished with a sprig of mint and an orange slice.

Stir together everything except the Sprite at your convenience. Marinate the mixture at room temperature for about an hour, then refrigerate it until serving time. Add the bubbly soda at the last moment. To keep the sangria cold while serving, fill a jar with ice cubes, secure the lid, and place the jar in the pitcher. This way the sangria will not get watery.

Cut the entire peel from the oranges in one long spiral, beginning at the stem end. Add orange peels to the pitcher(s). Chop the orange fruit, discarding the seeds and membrane, and add it to the pitcher(s). Pour in the wine. Add chopped apples, pineapple, and strawberries. Stir thoroughly, then cover and set the mixture aside to marinate at room temperature for an hour or so. Refrigerate until serving time. Just before serving, add Sprite and brandy and pour into glasses, garnishing each glass with a sprig of mint and an orange slice.

SYLVIA'S PAELLA

6 chicken thighs

$^1/_4$ cup extra virgin olive oil

$^1/_2$ pound chorizo sausage, removed from casings and crumbled

1 large yellow onion, coarsely chopped

2 cloves garlic, chopped

1 yellow Hungarian wax pepper, seeded and chopped

2 tablespoons paprika

$^1/_2$ teaspoon crushed saffron threads

1 (13-ounce) can chicken broth

1 (6-ounce) bottle clam broth

$^3/_4$ cup water

$1^1/_2$ cups long-grain rice

1 large ripe tomato, chopped

$^1/_2$ pound medium peeled shrimp

12 large sea scallops

12 clams, tightly shut

$^1/_2$ cup frozen green peas

Freshly ground black pepper, to taste

$^1/_2$ cup coarsely chopped flat-leaf parsley

$^1/_4$ cup freshly chopped basil

Sylvia Kristal learned how to make this wonderful dish growing up in Lima, Peru. Of course, she says the seafood available to Americans is not as good as what she could get in Lima, but we'll have to make do. She also says you shouldn't be limited by the list of seafood here. Add whatever you like. Sylvia starts with peanut oil, but we suggest olive oil for added flavor and Spanish authenticity.

The word paella *refers to the Spanish pan that looks most like the large flat-bottomed gold mining pans sold in hardware stores in California's gold country. Use a wok, a Dutch oven, or any large, deep cooking pot you may have around. And don't be distressed if your memory of this rice dish is different from Sylvia's. Paella is a peasant dish and makes use of whatever the cook has on hand.*

People from Spain to Puerto Rico, from Cuba to New Orleans, all have their versions of this one-dish rice and something dinner. In Louisiana they call it jambalaya. In the Caribbean, cooks toss in spiny lobsters and maybe some stone-crab claws; and in Puerto Rico, where it is sometimes called arroz con pollo, *they add canned Spanish pimentos, peas, and asparagus. When you're making paella, let your imagination rule. Add ham, snails, mussels, lobster, crab, monkfish, squid, rabbit, little game birds, asparagus, or green beans, if you wish. It's your party.*

PREPARATION TIME:	10 MINUTES
SAUTÉ TIME:	20 MINUTES
COOKING TIME:	30 MINUTES
MAKES 6 SERVINGS	

The first seven ingredients may be sautéed and stored in the refrigerator the day before though you will have to allow 10 minutes more cooking time at the end.

In a paella pan or a large Dutch oven set over medium-high heat, brown the chicken thighs in the oil for 2 to 3 minutes on each side. Remove from the pan and set aside. They will finish cooking in the broth. In the same pan, sauté the chorizo, onion, garlic, yellow Hungarian wax pepper, and paprika for about 5 minutes or until the onion is translucent. Remove from the pan. Add the saffron threads, chicken broth, clam broth, water, rice, and tomato, and stir. Add the sautéed ingredients, cover, and cook on medium-low heat for 20 minutes, or until the rice is fluffy and the chicken is cooked through. Add the shrimp, scallops, clams, peas, and black pepper to taste. Cover and cook until the shrimp turns pink and clams open, about 10 more minutes. Discard any clams that do not open, and serve on a platter or in the paella pan, with the parsley and basil sprinkled on top.

ORANGE SLICES WITH RED PEPPER FLAKES AND GRAND MARNIER

3 oranges, seeded, peeled, and pith removed $^1/_2$ cup Grand Marnier

$^1/_8$ teaspoon cayenne, or to taste

Almost too easy to be called a recipe, this can be done with many variations, including coconut and rum instead of the pepper and Grand Marnier. Fresh mint leaves make a good-looking garnish.

PREPARATION TIME: 10 MINUTES

MARINATING TIME: 30 MINUTES TO ALL DAY

MAKES 6 SERVINGS

Can be made the morning of the party, covered and refrigerated.

Slice the oranges into $^1/_2$-inch-thick rings and place them on a large serving platter. Mix the cayenne with the Grand Marnier and pour it over the slices. Cover, chill, and marinate until ready to serve.

Tossed Romaine Salad

¹/₄ cup extra virgin olive oil

¹/₈ cup balsamic vinegar

1 clove garlic, crushed

1 scallion, thinly sliced

¹/₂ teaspoon salt

Freshly ground black pepper, to taste

1 large ripe tomato, chopped

1 head romaine lettuce, washed, dried and cut into 2-inch strips

For maximum taste and best texture, wash and thoroughly dry the cut lettuce. Mix the dressing in the serving bowl. Layer on the greens, then the tomato. Do not toss until just before serving. The dressing will marinate while the greens and the tomato patiently wait.

PREPARATION TIME: 1 0 MINUTES

MAKES 6 SERVINGS

May be made the morning before, covered, and refrigerated. Always toss at the last minute.

In the salad serving bowl, mix the olive oil, vinegar, crushed garlic, scallion, and salt and pepper. Layer the prepared greens over the dressing, then layer the tomatoes. Cover with plastic wrap and refrigerate until ready to serve. Toss just before serving.

Sunshine Secret Cake

Cake:

1 (17-ounce) box plain yellow cake mix plus other ingredients listed on the box

Juice and zest of 4 to 6 lemons

Glaze:

1 cup powdered sugar

2 tablespoons milk

The zest and juice of a lemon can turn an ordinary cake mix into your secret weapon. Always use plain yellow cake with no artificial flavoring. We have a debate over a pudding cake mix or a light cake mix. The pudding makes a denser, moister cake. The plain or light mix is lower in fat and makes a lighter cake. You should try both and decide what works for you.

PREPARATION TIME: 10 MINUTES

COOKING TIME: 35 MINUTES

COOLING TIME: 1 HOUR

MAKES 12 SERVINGS

This can be made a day in advance, and stored in a cake server.

Grease and flour a Bundt pan. Make the cake according to the instructions on the box, substituting the lemon juice and zest for part of the liquid. If the lemons yield 1 cup of juice, substitute the lemon juice for the same amount of liquid. Make up the rest with water. Bake in the prepared pan for the time and temperature designated on the box. Cool on a rack.

For the glaze, mix the powdered sugar and milk. Drizzle the glaze on the cooled cake and let it run down the sides.

Cooking Tip

Hunt for Baker's Joy, an oil and flour mix in an aerosol can, at the supermarket. Then you will be able to grease and flour a pan with one quick spray.

June Garden Party of Scallops with Lemon-Vodka Sauce

Eating in the garden is a wonderful, casual way to entertain. The long June evenings, summer flowers, candlelight, and mild weather contribute to a relaxed mood, and the anticipation of many more evenings outdoors. Arrange enough citronella candles on the table to provide adequate light and turn off the electricity. This menu is designed to be prepared quickly on a weeknight to entertain lovers, friends, or clients.

The Menu

GAZPACHO (SEE PAGE 259)

SEARED SCALLOPS WITH LEMON-VODKA SAUCE OVER
ANGEL-HAIR PASTA

ZUCCHINI GRATINÉE

ANGEL FOOD CAKE WITH THREE-BERRY FOOL

Wine Suggestions

Main Course—Try a dry muscadet from the Loire Valley in France. This dry, highly acidic wine will work well with the lemony scallops.

Cooking Tip

Deep sea or diver scallops are always best. You can figure four per person, five for big eaters. Scallops should never smell fishy or of ammonia when you buy them. If they do, return them immediately.

For perfect angel-hair pasta, use a large pot and add 3 tablespoons of salt and no oil to the water. Oil in the water just increases the calories and keeps the sauce from sticking to the pasta. Give the pasta a good stir from time to time while it's cooking. To keep the pasta from sticking, just before you drain the angel hair, reserve 1 cup of the cooking water. Drain the pasta and quickly return it to the pot. Do not rinse. Slowly add back the cup of water, stirring constantly. The pasta will continue to absorb water. Stop when the pasta does not appear to be absorbing any more water. As a result of adding back the extra hot liquid, your pasta should never stick.

All the Trimmings

An early summer dinner party is all about light. Use brightly colored tablecloths and napkins, and put fresh flowers on the table. Because the bugs may be out, burn plenty of citronella candles or torches. The menu is designed to minimize trips to the kitchen, but for convenience, use a large tray to maximize each load. Draped with colorful dish towels or napkins, the tray can be placed right in the center of the table. Serve the gazpacho and gratinée from lidded dishes to keep the bugs out and the heat in. The pasta will look great on a large platter with the scallops and sauce in a well in the middle. Chives and lemon zest are used as a colorful garnish for the scallops.

You're Invited!

Press some pansies in a book and include them in a plain note envelope with a nice handwritten invitation to your friends.

SEARED SCALLOPS WITH LEMON-VODKA SAUCE OVER ANGEL-HAIR PASTA

3 quarts water + 3 tablespoons salt

1/4 cup extra virgin olive oil

1/4 cup unsalted butter

2 pounds large sea scallops

2 tablespoons freshly snipped chives or 2 teaspoons dried, plus 4 or 5 3-inch pieces of fresh chive, for garnish

1 1/2 cups heavy cream combined with 1/2 cup vodka

Grated zest and juice of 3 lemons (about 1 1/2 cups juice), reserve a few julienned zest strips for garnish

Salt and freshly ground black pepper, to taste

1 1/2 pounds fresh angel-hair pasta

PREPARATION TIME: 10 MINUTES

COOKING TIME: 10 MINUTES (20 MINUTES IF USING DRIED PASTA)

MAKES 6 SERVINGS

Sear the scallops and make the sauce within an hour of serving, then plunge the pasta into boiling water just moments before you're ready to serve. Enjoy this dish promptly for best flavor and texture.

Start a large pot of water boiling for the pasta. Add 3 tablespoons of salt. Then, preheat a 12-inch skillet over medium-high heat.

Add the oil and butter to the skillet and swirl the pan while it foams, then add the scallops. Allow them to sear without moving until the edges are golden, about 2 to 3 minutes. Turn them only once, sprinkle the skillet with the chives, and sear the second side. Remove scallops and chives to a warmed plate, cover, and set aside. Deglaze the pan by pouring the combined cream and vodka in the skillet and bringing it to a boil. Boil hard 3 minutes, then add the lemon juice and zest and boil until thickened, about another 3 minutes. Taste and adjust seasonings with salt and pepper. Right before topping the pasta, add scallops to the sauce and toss to mix.

Cook the angel hair in boiling water for 2 minutes, or according to package directions. (See Cooking Tip, pages 211–12.)

To serve, mound the pasta on a serving platter leaving a well in the center. Top with the scallops and sauce, and garnish with the julienned lemon zest and fresh chives. If you want to go for that vertical New York garnish look, stand five or six whole chives upright in the sauce and pasta. Very dramatic.

Zucchini Gratinée

1 tablespoon butter

1 cup coarsely chopped onion (1 medium)

$1/4$ teaspoon sugar

$1^1/_2$ pounds green zucchini, cut into chunks

$1/4$ teaspoon freshly ground black pepper

$1/4$ teaspoon cayenne (optional)

$1/2$ teaspoon salt (or to taste)

1 cup seasoned Italian bread crumbs

2 large eggs

1 cup milk

Instead of a deep casserole dish, we prefer to make this in a 2-inch-deep × 12-inch-oval gratin dish. This gives a lot of crisp brown crust and makes it easy to cut into squares or festive diamonds to serve.

PREPARATION TIME:	5 MINUTES
ZUCCHINI COOKING TIME:	15 TO 18 MINUTES
BAKING TIME:	25 TO 30 MINUTES
MAKES 6 SERVINGS	

May be made a day in advance, covered, and refrigerated, then reheated at serving time, 10 to 15 minutes in a 350° oven.

Preheat the oven to 350°. Spritz a 12-inch gratin dish with vegetable cooking spray. Melt the butter in a large saucepan over medium-high heat. Add the onion and sauté for 1 to 2 minutes. Stir in the sugar and sauté another minute. Add the zucchini, two types of pepper, and salt. Stir well and heat to a simmer, then reduce the heat to medium low, cover, and cook until the squash is soft, stirring from time to time. (No liquid is needed if the heat is kept low and the mixture is stirred often.) Allow 15 to 18 minutes to cook.

Mash the squash in the pan with a fork or potato masher. Do *not* puree it. Stir in the crumbs. Taste and adjust the seasonings. Beat the eggs with the milk until blended and stir into the squash.

Pour the mixture into the gratin dish and bake 25 to 30 minutes, or until the mixture is puffed and golden brown on top. Cut into 2-inch squares or diamonds and serve.

Angel Food Cake with Three-Berry Fool

1 (10-inch) angel food cake

1 pint ripe strawberries

1 cup fresh raspberries

1 cup fresh blueberries

1 pint heavy cream

2 tablespoons confectioners' sugar

Start with a bought angel food cake and all you have to do is mix the berries and whip the cream.

PREPARATION TIME: 10 MINUTES

REFRIGERATION TIME: 30 MINUTES

MAKES 8 TO 10 SERVINGS

Assemble the cake before you serve dinner and hold it in the refrigerator until time for dessert.

Place the cake on a platter or a footed cake stand. Stem the strawberries, then wash and pat them dry. Gently wash and dry the raspberries and blueberries. Toss the berries together. Whip the cream with the confectioners' sugar until it forms soft peaks. Mix half the berries with the whipped cream and fill the center of the cake, then dab the remaining mixture over and around the cake. Use the remaining berries on and around the cake. Cover and refrigerate until serving time. Slice in thick wedges and serve on dessert plates.

Fourth of July Fancies for Six

Fourth of July is a time to celebrate tradition and revolution—"the rockets' red glare, the bombs bursting in air"—barbecue, backyards, and fireworks, you know the drill. This menu has a little of both. A grilled salmon steak with barbecue sauce on a bed of fresh baby greens in a light mustard vinaigrette. The flavors of salmon and barbecue sauce, surprisingly enough, are perfect together—revolutionary in fact! Okay, for tradition you can have your friends bring over the potato salad and other accompaniments. Or you can make a trip to your favorite deli and pick up the conventional. It is important to *not* be slaving in the kitchen on the Fourth. Better to be with your friends.

The Menu

MARINATED RED PEPPERS WITH ARUGULA ON BAGUETTE ROUNDS

MARINATED VIDALIA ONIONS

GRILLED SALMON WITH BARBECUE SAUCE

PERFECT CORN ON THE COB WITH JALAPEÑO-LIME BUTTER

STORE-BOUGHT POTATO SALAD

RED AND ORANGE WATERMELON

TWO-BERRY FLAG CAKE

ICED TEA WITH LEMON AND MINT

COLD BEER AND WINE

Wine Suggestions

Main Course—Grilled Salmon with Barbecue sauce is a perfect opportunity to serve a great American wine—Oregon Pinot Noir. Watch the alcohol content (it should be below 12.5 percent). The fruity Northwestern wine is a natural for salmon made sweet with grill marks!

Cooking Tip

If you are using charcoal, and must resort to starter fluid, be sure to let it burn off so your fish does not taste as if it were cooked at a gas station. (See Cooking Tip page 199 for alternate suggestions.) The fish should be thoroughly dry, then brushed with a little bit of oil before placing it on a thoroughly preheated grill so it won't stick, will get great grill marks, and will achieve maximum flavor and texture. The biggest crime when cooking fish is to overcook it. Fish is one of the cleanest types of meats you can eat. Err on the side of underdone for the juiciest, most mouthwatering taste.

All the Trimmings

A red-checked tablecloth with a bunch of daisies in an old mason jar sets the right festive tone. You can add a few bottle rockets and fire crackers to the bouquet to capture the spirit. This is a great opportunity for patriotic paper napkins.

Serve the salmon steaks on a bed of greens, with a ring of marinated cold Vidalia onions around the edge of the plate. The beauty of the pink salmon and red barbecue sauce on a bed of greens surrounded with delicate onions! Serve the corn on a side plate. The combination of flavors, colors, and textures really works and is luscious to look at. Buy a red and an orange watermelon. Cut them into wedges and alternate the colors on the plate for a dramatic presentation. Finally, decorate the sheet cake with berries in a stars-and-stripes design! What a feast for the eyes!

Marinated Red Peppers with Arugula on Baguette Rounds

1 (28-ounce) can roasted red peppers, drained and chopped

¹/₄ cup extra virgin olive oil

¹/₄ cup balsamic vinegar

Salt and freshly ground black pepper, to taste

1 bunch arugula, (about 2 cups) washed thoroughly, dried, and chopped

1 baguette, cut into thick rounds

The peppery taste of arugula is the perfect foil for the sweet roasted peppers. The colors and textures also go wonderfully together.

Preparation time: 10 minutes

Marinating time: at least 30 minutes

Makes 6 servings

May be made up to 1 day in advance, though the arugula will wilt. If you want the arugula to be crisp, simply add it at the last minute.

In a bowl, combine the peppers with the olive oil, vinegar, salt, and pepper. Stir in the arugula. Cover and refrigerate for 30 minutes. Serve on slices of a fresh baguette.

Marinated Vidalia Onions

4 Vidalia, Walla Walla, or Texas 1015 sweet onions, sliced paper-thin

1 cup rice wine vinegar

¹/₄ cup sugar

We love this recipe. Definitely a standby and good with almost anything. Vidalia, Walla Walla, or Texas 1015 onions are sweet and mild and available all summer. If you can't find these varieties, use red onions. If we find great Kirby cucumbers at the farmer's market, we sometimes slice a cucumber in with the onion.

Here is a great opportunity to get out your food processor slicer attachment, if you have one. Otherwise get ready to slice very thin by hand using your sharpest knife. It really makes a difference.

PREPARATION TIME:	10 MINUTES
MARINATING TIME:	AT LEAST 30 MINUTES
MAKES 6 SERVINGS	

Can be made up to 2 days in advance.

Toss the onions in the vinegar and sugar. Cover and refrigerate for 30 minutes. Lift out of the liquid and serve. Remember, you can add new onions and/or cucumbers to the vinegar-sugar mixture for the next day. We have been known to keep one of these marinated onion bowls going for weeks during high summer.

GRILLED SALMON WITH BARBECUE SAUCE

6 Chinook salmon steaks

Oil to brush on the salmon

6 cups baby greens

Three-Citrus Dressing (see page 93)

12 teaspoons best-quality barbecue sauce (we prefer Bull's-Eye)

A truly revolutionary idea, the distinct taste of salmon really goes very nicely with barbecue sauce. And for those who prefer other firm-fleshed fish, we have tried and recommend halibut, shark, and rockfish. If you are having a large group, why not cook a variety of fish steaks?

PREPARATION TIME:	10 MINUTES
GRILLING TIME:	10 MINUTES MAXIMUM
MAKES 6 SERVINGS	

Preheat and oil a squeaky-clean grill. Thoroughly dry the salmon steaks. Brush them with a little bit of oil to keep them from sticking and falling apart on the grill. Grill salmon 3 inches above the heat, turning the steaks only once when you see the fish is beginning to brown on the edge—about 3 to 4 minutes per side—and has developed nice grill marks on the cooked side.

While the fish is cooking, toss the greens with the salad dressing and divide them among six dinner plates.

After you turn the fish, brush a little barbecue sauce on the cooked side. It's best to add the sauce after the meat has been seared. This prevents the fish from steaming, which will leave it dry and tough. Turn steaks once more and brush the second side with a little barbecue sauce. Serve over a bed of baby greens, surrounded with the marinated onions.

Perfect Corn on the Cob with Jalapeño-Lime Butter

6 ears of corn* (husked just before you are about to cook them)

1 large pot of rapidly boiling water sweetened with ¼ cup sugar

Jalapeño-Lime Butter (recipe follows)

Salt and freshly ground black pepper, to taste

PREPARATION TIME: 10 MINUTES

COOKING TIME: 3 TO 5 MINUTES TO BOIL (OR 15 MINUTES ON THE GRILL)

* If you'd prefer genuine "roasted ears," soak the ears of corn in their husks in water for a few minutes, then line them up on the grill surface while you're preheating it. Cook, covered, turning a couple of times, until the husks are well grill marked and dry, about 15 minutes. Remove from the grill and let them stand 5 minutes or so to steam while you grill the fish.

Slip the corn into the sugared water. Cook for 3 to 5 minutes after the water comes back to the boil. Be careful not to overcook. Serve with the flavored butter, and salt and pepper to taste.

To serve, whack both ends off the ears, remove the cooked husks and silks, and serve heaped on a platter with the flavored butter and salt and pepper.

JALAPEÑO-LIME BUTTER

1 stick butter ($^1/_2$ cup)

$^1/_2$ fresh jalapeño pepper, seeded and minced

$^1/_2$ clove garlic, peeled

Juice and zest of 1 lime

Flavored butters are great with corn on the cob.

PREPARATION TIME: 5 MINUTES

The butter can be formulated several days in advance.

In a food processor, pulse together the butter, jalapeño, garlic, and lime juice and zest to mix. Place on a sheet of waxed paper and roll into a log. Cover and refrigerate until ready to serve.

Hint: When zesting a lime use a lemon-lime zester and be careful not to let any of the white pith get into the mix. That is the bitter part of the lime. The thin strings of colored rind will impart the oil of the citrus to whatever dish you're making and will always pump up the flavor in a desirable way. We couldn't live without our zester and think of it as part of our secret kitchen arsenal for creating dynamite dinners.

Other flavored butter ideas:

To each stick of soft butter, add a pinch of any of these flavor enhancers

basil	mint
chili powder	nutmeg
cilantro	sage
cumin	thyme
lemon	

Two-Berry Flag Cake

Cake:

1 (18-ounce) box plain yellow cake mix   Juice and zest of 4 lemons

Icing:

1 pint heavy cream   2 pints raspberries

$1/4$ cup sugar   1 pint blueberries

The zest and juice of a lemon can turn an ordinary cake mix into a secret weapon. We have a debate over a pudding cake mix or a light cake mix. Katherine prefers the pudding cake version, which makes a denser, moister cake. Linda prefers the plain or light mix because it is lower in fat and makes a lighter cake. You should try both and decide what works for you. The juxtaposition of the tart lemon with the sweet whipped cream icing and fruit is delicious! If you prefer chocolate cake, by all means buy your favorite devil's food cake mix and try that too. The dark chocolate enrobed in whipped cream with fresh berries is heaven.

PREPARATION TIME:	10 minutes
COOKING TIME:	about 35 minutes or by package directions
COOLING TIME:	1 hour
DECORATING TIME:	10 minutes

MAKES 12 SERVINGS

Make the cake according to the instructions on the box, substituting the lemon juice and zest for part of the liquid. (If the lemons yield 1 cup of juice, substitute it for an equal amount of the liquid called for in the mix.) Bake in a greased and floured 13 × 9 × 2-inch baking pan or an 11 × 16 × 1¼-inch sheet cake pan, following the box directions for cooking times and temperature. Cook on a rack.

For the icing, whip the cream for at least 4 minutes to a very dense consistency, adding the sugar 1 teaspoon at a time. Ice the top and sides of the completely cooled cake. Make a United States flag by arranging the raspberries for the bars and the blueberries for the stars. Cover and refrigerate until serving time. You will have a work of art that would make Martha you-know-who proud.

Born in the U.S.A. Backyard Grilled Pizza Birthday Party

For lucky birthday boys and girls who were born in the heart of the summer, the weather's great for a party. Friends seem to be more relaxed and have more time for fun. How about a participatory birthday party that starts with that staple that got us all through college—pizza. And this pizza's made outside on the grill.

Remember the last time you had a piece of thin-crusted pizza cooked in a wood-fired oven? Didn't you wish you could make that at home? With a covered charcoal or gas grill, wood chips for that great smoked flavor, and an easy made-in-the-processor pizza dough (or one bought at the pizzeria), you can do everything but throw the pizza in the air. That, you'll have to figure out for yourself.

Flavorful thin pizza crusts can be topped with everything from traditional Italian pizzeria toppings to Asian ingredients to All-American barbecued chicken. And for summertime entertaining? Nothing could be easier than a do-it-yourself pizza party in the backyard: A quick trip to the deli and market for some toppings, lots of icy cold beer and wine, and cakes baked in ice-cream cones for dessert, and you're all set. It's a birthday party sure to please children of all ages. Let your adult guests do the grilling. Cleanup is minimal. You'll be wishing all the birthdays in your family fell in the summer months.

Using our easy technique, you can make pizza crust in your food processor, then precook it on the wood-smoky grill. If you're flat out too stressed to make your own, buy prepared pizza dough from your local pizzeria.

Set up an assembly line pizzeria around your backyard barbecue. Arrange ingredients in "groups," then just get out of the way. Guests can top their own, then grill and eat them, sharing slices so that everybody gets a taste of everybody else's pizza.

The Menu

ICY COLD MICROBREWED BEER AND WINE

MAKE-IT-YOURSELF GRILLED PIZZAS

GRILLED SUMMER SALAD WITH THREE-CITRUS DRESSING
(SEE PAGE 93)

CUPCAKES IN ICE-CREAM CONES

Wine Suggestions

Main Course—Prosecco from the Veneto region of Italy is nice for an outdoor meal like this. Of course, you can always serve microbrewed beer or a Chanti, Barolo, or Barbaresco with pizza.

Cooking Tip

Using a gas grill is as simple as using your kitchen range, and getting that spectacular wood-smoke flavor into pizza and other foods couldn't be simpler. Buy or cut fruitwoods, hickory, or other aromatic wood chips. Place them in a clean tuna can or a cup you make from aluminum foil, and nestle it on top of the firebox. Light your fire, close the lid, and soon you'll have a hot, smoky oven in which to make the best-tasting pizza you ever had.

The secret to knock 'em dead grilled pizza is simple: great crust, never more than three or four thin-sliced toppings, and dough rolled as thin as possible so that it will cook quickly. Brush the best-quality extra virgin olive oil on the flavorful dough before you add the first topping, and don't slop too much sauce on—$^{1}/_{4}$ cup per 9-inch pizza is about right. In Italy, extra virgin olive oil is often drizzled onto the pizza after it comes out of the oven. The Italians frequently add 1 or 2 cups of loosely packed fresh green garnish such as arugula, flat-leaf parsley, or a few tablespoons of fresh oregano. We like to top sizzling hot pizzas with fresh uncooked vegetables before serving so that you get hot and cold, cooked and raw flavors for an all-in-one make-it-yourself meal.

All the Trimmings

The success of this meal is in the staging, and because your "kitchen" is outside, you will be on stage, so read the pizza recipes carefully to memorize all your cues. Set up a couple of buffet stations in the backyard—one for the pizza makings and another for the salad, side dishes, and dessert. Chill the beer and wine in a washtub brimming with ice. Serve the cupcakes from a flat lug basket, lined with snowy white paper doilies for an easy-to-pass dessert. Since the cooking process is complicated, don't feel bad about using paper plates and plastic utensils. After all, it *is* a barbecue of sorts.

MAKE-IT-YOURSELF GRILLED PIZZAS

Look over these choices and choose three or four combinations. Don't expect your guests to conform to your ideas of the ideal pizza, however. Let them do their own thing. If you wish, roll the pizza dough into 6-inch rounds for individual pizzas.

PREPARATION AND RISING TIME: 45 MINUTES TO 1 HOUR 15 MINUTES

BAKING TIME: 10 TO 15 MINUTES

MAKES 4 (9-INCH) PIZZAS TO SERVE FROM 4 TO 8 PEOPLE

An alternative to preparing your own dough is to buy ready-made pizza dough from the local pizzeria. You can also prebake the pizza crust on the grill before the party. It's best to top and grill the whole pizza when you're ready to serve.

GENERAL DIRECTIONS

Preheat the covered gas or charcoal grill at least 30 minutes, until the internal temperature reaches 500°. (If your covered grill doesn't have a thermometer, place an oven thermometer on the grill and check it after 15 minutes or so.) Create hot and cool grill surfaces either by raking the charcoal to one side, or by turning off one of the burners. Start cooking the pizzas on the *off* side, or cooler part of the grill. Rotate the pizzas as they cook, from the cool part to the hot part so that they cook evenly. Use a pizza peel or a cookie sheet with no sides to shovel the pizzas on and off the grill.

HOMEMADE PIZZA DOUGH

2 cups bread flour

1 teaspoon salt

$^{1}/_{2}$ teaspoon sugar

$2^{1}/_{2}$ teaspoons (1 [$1^{1}/_{4}$-ounce] packet) instant yeast

2 tablespoons extra virgin olive oil

$^{7}/_{8}$ cup lukewarm water

$^{1}/_{4}$ cup coarse yellow cornmeal

Combine the flour, salt, sugar, and yeast in the bowl of a food processor fitted with the steel blade. Pulse to mix, then pour in the oil and water. Process until the dough forms a ball that rides the blade around, then process 1 minute. Remove the dough and blade from the bowl. Form the dough into a doughnut shape and replace it in the processor bowl. Cover and set it aside for 30 minutes to 1 hour, or until doubled in bulk.

Alternatively, stir the dry ingredients together in a large bowl, then make a well in the middle and pour in the liquid. Stir with a wooden spoon to moisten the flour, then knead, about 15 minutes in a lightly floured bowl, until the dough is supple and soft. Form it into a ball, replace it in the bowl, cover with a piece of plastic wrap, and let it rise to double in bulk, 30 minutes to 1 hour.

Punch the dough down and separate it into four equal-size balls. Let the dough rest about 10 minutes. Spritz a work surface with water, then add a thin coating of flour. On this lightly floured surface, roll each ball into a 10-inch circle, $^1/_8$ inch thick. (Actually, we prefer free forms to circles. Amoebas, maps of Africa, and Greenland are all good shapes. Ellipses are exciting. All are welcome.) Transfer each circle of dough to a piece of plastic wrap and cover it with more plastic. Stack the pizzas until you have all four made and covered with plastic wrap.

You may, if you wish, refrigerate the rolled dough for up to 4 hours, then bake it at serving time.

Preheat the grill to 500°. Rake the coals to one side, or turn off one burner. To precook the pizza crusts, sprinkle a pizza peel with cornmeal and transfer one pizza circle to it, discarding the plastic wrap. Shovel the pizza onto the cool side of the grill, close the top, and grill for 2 to 3 minutes, or until the pizza is puffed and the underside is well marked with grill marks. Remove the half-cooked pizza crust with a pizza peel and tongs to a baking sheet, then precook the first side of the remaining pizzas.

You may precook the pizza crusts up to this point, stack them to cool and dry, and set them aside for as long as 4 hours before topping and grilling them for serving.

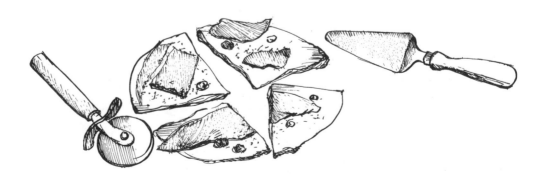

To finish the pizzas, turn the grill-marked side up, cover with the toppings of your choice, then replace on the pizza peel and shovel the pizza back onto the 500° grill. Cook pizzas, beginning on the cool part of the grill, away from the flame, rotating them at least once after a minute or so, and moving them over to the hotter part of the grill to guarantee even cooking. Grill until the tops are bubbly and brown and the sauces and cheeses are boiling, usually from 5 to 10 minutes, depending on the toppings you have chosen. Lift the pizza off the grill, using the pizza peel, to a waiting serving platter. Top with cold ingredients, if you wish, and cut into wedges with a pizza wheel.

#1 Pizza Margherita with or without Arugula

1 (9-inch) prepared pizza crust

1 teaspoon extra virgin olive oil, plus 1 teaspoon more for drizzling

4 thinly sliced plum tomatoes

8 thin slices fresh mozzarella cheese (about 3 ounces)

2 tablespoons fresh oregano leaves or 1 tablespoon dried

Fresh basil or arugula leaves, for garnish (optional)

After brushing the dough lightly with 1 teaspoon oil, make concentric circles of tomatoes and mozzarella, overlapping and alternating the two. Drizzle with 1 more teaspoon oil and sprinkle with oregano. Bake as directed. Top with fresh raw basil or arugula leaves if desired at serving time.

#2 Pizza Bianca

1 (9-inch) prepared pizza crust

1 tablespoon extra virgin olive oil, plus 1 teaspoon more oil for drizzling

1/2 cup freshly grated Parmesan cheese

1 (5-ounce) jar marinated artichoke hearts, drained and cut in wedges

After brushing the crust lightly with oil, sprinkle with cheese, then arrange artichoke wedges over the top. Cook as directed.

#3 BARBECUED CHICKEN PIZZA

1 (9-inch) prepared crust

¼ cup spicy sweet barbecue sauce (your favorite; we like Bull's Eye)

¼ cup grated smoked Gouda cheese

½ cup grated mozzarella cheese

1 cup sliced roast chicken

6 green onions with tops, chopped

2 tablespoons chopped cilantro

Coat the pizza crust with a thin layer of barbecue sauce, then sprinkle with the Gouda and half the mozzarella. Mix the chicken with the remaining barbecue sauce and arrange it over the cheese. Top with the green onions and the remaining mozzarella. Grill as directed, covered, until the cheese is bubbly and the crust is brown, about 8 to 10 minutes. Top with the cilantro and serve.

#4 Summer Pizza with Grilled Eggplant, Tomatoes, and Mozzarella

1 medium eggplant, cut into thin slices

1 teaspoon extra virgin olive oil, plus additional for coating the eggplant

Salt and pepper

1 (9-inch) prepared pizza crust

4 medium plum (Roma) tomatoes, cut into thin slices

8 thin slices mozzarella cheese (3 ounces)

2 tablespoons oregano leaves or 1 tablespoon dried

1/2 cup fresh spinach leaves, cut into chiffonade

1 tablespoon balsamic vinegar

Coat the eggplant slices lightly with extra virgin olive oil. Salt and pepper the slices, then grill them, 2 to 3 minutes per side, until soft and well marked on both sides by the grill. Remove to a plate and reserve.

Coat the pizza crust with 1 teaspoon of the oil, then top with concentric circles of grilled eggplant, tomato, and mozzarella. Sprinkle with the oregano and grill as directed. Add a handful of spinach, tossed with the balsamic vinegar, to the plate for garnish.

To cut green leafy vegetables into chiffonade, stack leaves, then roll up like a fat cigar. Holding the cigar with your left hand on the cutting board, cut thin strips off, using a chef's knife in your other hand.

#5 Real American Pizza

1 (9-inch) prepared pizza crust

1 tablespoon extra virgin olive oil

1/4 cup marinara sauce

1 cup shredded mozzarella cheese

1 Italian sweet sausage with fennel (2 ounces), cooked and crumbled

10 thin slices pepperoni

1/2 cup thinly sliced white mushrooms

1/2 cup freshly grated Parmesan cheese

After coating the pizza with a thin film of oil, spread marinara sauce over it and sprinkle about ³/₄ cup of the shredded mozzarella on top. Scatter with the crumbled sausage, followed by the pepperoni and mushrooms. Sprinkle remaining ¹/₄ cup mozzarella and all the Parmesan cheese on top and bake as directed.

Other Good Pizza Combos to Select From

#1—Goat cheese, green, red, and yellow bell peppers with plum tomatoes.

#2—Shrimp, roasted garlic, red onion, and mozzarella with flat-leaf parsley.

#3—Shrimp and pesto, Parmesan cheese, plum tomatoes, and Kalamata olives.

#4—Smoked salmon with red onion, capers, dill, and low-fat sour cream stirred with a few drops of lemon juice

#5—Grilled eggplant, red onion, mushrooms, broccoli florets, and sun-dried tomato slivers.

#6—Prosciutto, mushrooms, marinated artichokes, and Kalamata olives on marinara sauce.

#7—Capers, Kalamata olives, anchovies, sea salt and pepper on marinara sauce.

#8—Grilled corn, red bell pepper, poblano chilies, and Fontina cheese, with green onions and cilantro.

#9—Black beans, grilled chicken breast, and sharp Cheddar cheese, grilled and topped with chopped lettuce, tomato, and onions, with salsa on the side.

#10—Thai chicken with commercial spicy peanut-ginger and sesame sauce, and green onions, grilled and topped with bean sprouts, carrots, cilantro, and roasted peanuts.

GRILLED SUMMER SALAD
WITH THREE-CITRUS DRESSING

4 plum tomatoes, cored and cut in half, lengthwise

1 red bell pepper, seeded and quartered

1 medium Vidalia or other sweet onion, peeled and quartered

1 small eggplant, cut into ¹/₂-inch-thick rounds

2 yellow summer squash, cut into ¹/₂-inch-thick rounds or lengthwise planks

2 tablespoons extra virgin olive oil

Salt and freshly ground black pepper, to taste

2 tablespoons balsamic vinegar

¹/₂ cup pitted Kalamata olives

Three-Citrus Dressing (see page 93) or your own favorite dressing

8 cups bite-size pieces romaine lettuce

2 cups seasoned croutons

PREPARATION TIME: 10 MINUTES

GRILLING TIME: 10 MINUTES

MARINATING TIME: 10 MINUTES TO HALF A DAY

MAKES 6 SERVINGS

If it's convenient, grill the vegetables, cover, and set them aside early in the day, then simply toss them with the romaine at serving time.

Place the prepared tomatoes, bell pepper, onion, eggplant, and squash in a large bowl and toss with the olive oil. Season to taste with salt and pepper and set aside to marinate at least 10 minutes or for up to half a day.

Prepare a charcoal fire or preheat a gas grill. Place the vegetables in a grill basket spritzed with cooking spray and place them on the grill to cook. Grill the vegetables until softened and browned, about 5 minutes per side. Remove them as they're ready and put them in the salad bowl. Toss with the vinegar and olives, cover, and set aside.

Make the Three-Citrus Dressing, and toss with the romaine at serving time. Mound the grilled vegetables on the lettuce and top with the croutons.

CUPCAKES IN ICE-CREAM CONES

24 flat-bottomed cake ice-cream cones

1 box yellow cake mix

1 cup water

$1/3$ cup fresh lemon juice

$1/3$ cup canola oil

3 large eggs

Confectioners' sugar, for dusting the tops

Ice cream of your choice

Nothing could be easier than baking cupcakes in flat-bottomed ice-cream cones. There's nothing to clean up except the mixing bowl. They're easy to serve and easy to eat. Sure to please kids from four to forty-five years of age.

PREPARATION TIME: 10 MINUTES

BAKING TIME: 30 MINUTES

MAKES 24 CUPCAKES

May be prepared 1 day in advance and stored in an airtight container.

Preheat the oven to 350°. Arrange the cones on a baking sheet, sides not touching, and set aside.

Combine the cake mix with the remaining ingredients, except the sugar and ice cream, in a large bowl and beat with an electric mixer for 2 minutes. Fill each cone half full. Bake 30 minutes or until the tops are browned and domed above the tops of the cones. While warm, dust the tops with confectioners' sugar shaken through a tea strainer. Cool on a rack. To serve, top each cone with a scoop of ice cream.

Dog Days of Summer
Middle Eastern Grilled Supper

Light and fresh Middle Eastern cuisine, with its bold flavors, is perfect for summer. After all, the cuisine originates in one of the hottest parts of the world. Eat this wonderful, casual food with your fingers, using a torn piece of pita bread to pick it up. Who wouldn't relax immediately?

The olives, nuts, dried fruit, baba ganoush, hummus, and baklava on this menu can be purchased ready-made from a deli. When Katherine has out-of-town guests, she always takes them to Brooklyn. The tour includes stops along Atlantic Avenue, at Sahadi Importing Company, El Asmar International Delights (our favorite), and around the corner, Fatoosh Bakery. Because many American cities have significant Middle Eastern populations complete with Middle Eastern grocery stores, there's no reason to make these exotic side dishes at home.

We get most of our spices from El Asmar in bulk, always fresh and inexpensive. Believe us. This is a no-sweat dinner, no matter what the thermometer on the patio says.

The friendly proprietor at El Asmar gave us very precise instructions for making this Fatoosh salad, which we hereby pass along to you. Don't you love the way recipes travel around the world and over the counter from culture to culture?

The Menu

SELECTION OF OLIVES, DRIED FRUITS, NUTS

BABA GANOUSH AND HUMMUS

PITA BREAD

GRILLED LAMB KEBABS WITH GARLIC YOGURT MARINADE

COLD CHICKPEAS, PARSLEY, RED PEPPER, AND LEMON

FATOOSH TOASTED PITA BREAD SALAD

BAKLAVA

Wine Suggestions

Main Course—Try a sauvignon blanc from Sancerre or Pouilly (Pouilly-Fumé). The lemony, high-acid tanginess of this summer wine will complement the tangy garlic-yogurt flavor of the lamb and will also work well with the baba ganoush and hummus.

Dessert—The Greek favorite, baklava, longs for a Greek muscat dessert wine. The honey flavor of the dessert will pick up the honey note in the wine.

Cooking Tip

When grilling, always be patient with the charcoal and make sure all the coals are nice and gray. Don't start your charcoal fire with starter fluid, or your food will taste as if it were made at a gas station. Invest in one of those electric coil starters, or a newspaper and charcoal firestarting chimney (see page 199.) We love our gas grill. So convenient. Just turn it on and go.

Always use freshly squeezed lemon juice and fresh mint. Bottled lemon juice is bitter, and dried mint might as well be lawn clippings—practically no taste at all!

When cutting mint or parsley, don't chop it on a cutting board. After washing the herbs, simply use clean, sharp scissors to trim the bunch over the salad bowl. The finely cut leaves will appear to have been chopped.

All the Trimmings

Serve the baba ganoush, hummus, and chickpea salad on one plate. Make a well in the baba ganoush and the hummus and put a little olive oil in it, then sprinkle paprika over everything. Traditionally, this Middle Eastern food is eaten with your fingers using pita bread to pick up the food. Put the platter in the middle of the table, with the warmed pita in a basket.

Grilled Lamb Kebabs with Garlic Yogurt Marinade

1 cup plain low-fat yogurt

1 teaspoon crushed garlic (2 cloves)

1 teaspoon salt

Freshly ground black pepper

2 pounds boneless leg or shoulder of lamb, cubed

PREPARATION TIME: 5 MINUTES

MARINATING TIME: AT LEAST 1 HOUR OR OVERNIGHT

COOKING TIME: 10 TO 15 MINUTES

MAKES 6 SERVINGS

May be marinated overnight.

Stir together the yogurt, garlic, salt, and pepper to taste. Toss the lamb cubes in the mixture, cover, and marinate for at least 1 hour. If you plan to marinate the meat longer than 1 hour, cover and refrigerate it. Preheat the grill 30 minutes before dinner.

Skewer the meat. Though we prefer metal skewers, if you are using wood, soak them in water until cooking time to prevent burning. Place the skewers over the hot coals for 10 to 15 minutes or until kebabs are golden brown, turning frequently.

Cold Chickpeas, Parsley, Red Pepper, and Lemon

1 (15-ounce) can chickpeas, drained

1/2 yellow onion, finely chopped (about 3/4 cup)

1 clove garlic, chopped (1/2 teaspoon)

1 red bell pepper, peeled, seeded, and chopped

1/2 cup pitted black olives, coarsely chopped

1/2 cup chopped flat-leaf parsley

1/4 cup extra virgin olive oil

1/2 cup freshly squeezed lemon juice

1/2 teaspoon salt and freshly ground black pepper, to taste

PREPARATION TIME: 1 0 MINUTES

MARINATING TIME: AT LEAST 1 5 MINUTES

MAKES 6 SERVINGS

Start early on the chickpea salad and the Fatoosh because they require lots of chopping. Everything in this salad may be prepared 1 day in advance, then covered and refrigerated.

Toss all ingredients together; cover, chill, and marinate for at least 15 minutes.

Fatoosh Toasted Pita Bread Salad

3 (8-inch) pitas, each cut into 6 triangles

Dressing

1 clove garlic, crushed ($^1/_2$ teaspoon)

$^1/_2$ cup freshly squeezed lemon juice

$^1/_2$ cup extra virgin olive oil

1 teaspoon salt

Freshly ground black pepper, to taste

Salad

1 head romaine lettuce, coarsely chopped

1 seedless cucumber, sliced

2 medium ripe tomatoes, sliced

$^1/_2$ cup chopped scallions

$^1/_2$ cup freshly chopped stemmed mint leaves

The mint makes the flavor of this salad light and original. It is sure to wow your company even on the hottest of days.

PREPARATION TIME: 25 MINUTES

Everything except the pita triangles may be prepared 1 day in advance, then covered and refrigerated. Start early on the chickpea salad and the Fatoosh because they both require lots of chopping. The results are worth the planning and preparation.

Toast the pita bread triangles in the toaster oven until brown. In the salad serving bowl, stir together the crushed garlic, lemon juice, olive oil, salt, and pepper. Layer the romaine, cucumber, tomato slices, scallions, mint, and toasted pita bread in the bowl. Just before serving, toss thoroughly. Serve immediately.

Elegant Picnic for a Concert in the Park

One of our finest summer traditions is a concert in the park. From Mozart to jazz, from John Philip Sousa to blues, a great concert is complemented by a beautiful picnic. When planning a picnic, remember that you don't want to have much to clean up, and finger foods are best. But there are some things you should not forgo in the name of convenience. A good bottle of wine and glass wine goblets are a must. The flavor of wine is compromised by plastic. Wrap the glasses in the same cloth napkins you are going to use to prevent breakage. It is worth the extra care. This menu is simple and delicious, and the variety of flavors offered by the three sandwich choices is great fun.

You could just put your stereo speakers out your back windows, spread out a blanket and have your own backyard concert, music selected by *you*. In Brooklyn in the summer, you'll see the neighbors sitting in chrome kitchen chairs in front of the stoops of their brownstones, well guarded by plaster Madonnas, listening to opera from their stereos, speakers aimed out the windows.

The Menu

SELECTION OF SANDWICHES ON SLICED BAGUETTES

ROAST BEEF SANDWICHES WITH HORSERADISH SAUCE AND
ROMAINE LETTUCE

SMOKED TURKEY, CREAM CHEESE, AND CRANBERRY SAUCE SANDWICHES

HAM AND MANGO CHUTNEY

STUFFED MUSHROOMS

CUCUMBERS AND ONIONS IN TARRAGON VINEGAR

MIXED BERRIES AND SHORTBREAD COOKIES

Wine Suggestions

Main Course and Dessert—From Australia, a Shiraz, with its slightly sweet, spicy flavor will complement this menu. Some wine experts claim that Shiraz wines from this part of the world are so great that you can take your vitamins with them. Alternatively, on a picnic, another great Australian choice would be the Yalumba Valley Brut Rosé. The tiny bubbles and flavor will put you in a wonderful mood and really complement most foods.

All the Trimmings

Of course a picnic is best served buffet-style! Spread a big blanket or tablecloth. Use cheerful, brightly colored cloth napkins, which can double as wraps for the wine glasses. A medium-size cooler serves well as a side serving table, and since Mother Nature provides most of the beauty for this setting, you don't have to worry about decor. Just in case "Mother" is too much with you, however, remember to include insect repellent and citronella candles. Damp washcloths in Ziploc bags help to wipe up sticky hands.

You're Invited!

Though many summer concerts are free, if you purchased concert tickets in advance and want to meet your guests at the picnic site, a quick note sent with their tickets can prevent the inconvenience of waiting at the gate. Give your guests landmarks to help find you and get there early to stake out the picnic site. A bunch of helium-filled balloons, purchased at most party or card stores, makes an excellent marker for your friends.

Roast Beef Sandwiches with Horseradish Sauce and Romaine Lettuce

Horseradish Sauce

$^1/_4$ cup prepared white horseradish

$^1/_4$ cup mayonnaise

$^1/_4$ cup sour cream

$^1/_2$ teaspoon salt

1 baguette, cut in half lengthwise

$^1/_2$ pound deli roast beef, thinly sliced

4 to 5 leaves romaine lettuce

Choose low-fat mayo and sour cream and you'll never know the difference.

Preparation time: 10 minutes

Makes 6 sandwiches

Make and wrap these sandwiches in plastic wrap at home, and carry them to the park. The horseradish sauce may be made 1 day in advance.

Stir together the horseradish, mayonnaise, sour cream, and salt. Spread the mixture on both sides of the baguette halves. Layer roast beef and romaine lettuce on the bread. Put the bread together and cut the baguette into 3-inch sandwiches. Wrap in plastic and keep cool until serving time.

Smoked Turkey, Cream Cheese, and Cranberry Sauce Sandwiches

$^1/_2$ pound cream cheese

1 (15-ounce) can cranberry sauce

$^1/_2$ pound smoked turkey

1 baguette, cut in half lengthwise

Turkey isn't just for Thanksgiving. At the Reading Terminal Market in Philadelphia, you can order a fresh roasted turkey sandwich any day of the year. Make these a time or two and you'll be thankful. Too easy! Use light cream cheese if you wish to slash the fat grams.

Make and wrap these sandwiches just before you plan to transport them to the park. Keep them chilled for best results.

Spread one side of bread with cream cheese and one side with cranberry sauce, layer smoked turkey on one half, put the bread halves together, and slice into 3-inch sandwiches. Wrap each sandwich in a plastic bag or plastic wrap and chill until serving time.

HAM AND MANGO CHUTNEY

1 baguette, cut in half lengthwise   **1/2 pound thin-sliced deli ham**

1 (8-ounce) jar mango chutney

We like Major Grey's Chutney, but there are so many choices now on the market that you should try a few until you find one you adore.

PREPARATION TIME: 5 MINUTES

MAKES 6 SANDWICHES

Make, wrap, and chill the sandwiches right before you plan to travel to the picnic site.

Slather the chutney on both halves of the bread, layer ham on one side, close up and cut the bread into 3-inch-long sandwiches. Wrap in plastic bags or plastic wrap and chill until serving time.

OTHER SANDWICH SUGGESTIONS

L'Explorateur or St. André cheese and thinly sliced Granny Smith apple

Avocado, Monterey Jack cheese, and tomatoes

Peppered goat cheese, pesto, and sun-dried tomato paste

Swiss cheese, roasted red peppers, and arugula

Turkey and olive pesto

Cream cheese, duck sauce, and watercress

Mango and avocado with lump crabmeat

Mascarpone cheese with raspberries

Grilled vegetables with honey mustard

STUFFED MUSHROOMS

2 (8-ounce) boxes fresh brown (Crimini) mushrooms, stems removed and reserved, bottoms cut off

1 cup plain dry bread crumbs

1/2 cup freshly grated Parmesan cheese

1/8 cup extra virgin olive oil

1/2 teaspoon salt

1 teaspoon freshly ground black pepper

PREPARATION TIME: 10 MINUTES

BAKING TIME: 20 MINUTES

MAKES 6 SERVINGS

Prepare these mushrooms early in the day, then transfer them to an unbreakable tray, wrap tightly with plastic wrap, and refrigerate until it's time to go. Transport them to the picnic to be eaten at room temperature.

Preheat the oven to 375°. Spritz a 10 × 13-inch baking dish with cooking spray or olive oil. Wash and drain the mushrooms in a colander. Separate the stems from the caps. Place the mushroom stems, bread crumbs, Parmesan cheese, olive oil, salt, and pepper in the food processor and pulse until blended. Arrange the caps upside-down in a baking dish, sides touching, and stuff each cap with the processed mixture. Bake for 20 minutes or until the tops are bubbly and brown. Serve warm or at room temperature.

Some Like It Hot West Indian
Picnic on the Beach

Although the notion of hot foods for hot weather seems like an anachronism, it's one of life's truths, so if you're planning to entertain at the shore, think spicy. Trinidadian French Creole Sauce Chien is a Caribbean-style salsa: a fresh, hot sauce that works well with this menu. Icy cold pineapple juice with a splash of rum and store-bought shortbread cookies are, of course, a good ending to this spicy menu.

The Menu

BLUE TORTILLA AND PLANTAIN CHIPS

COLD BOILED SHRIMP AND CRUDITÉS WITH SAUCE CHIEN

SPICY CHICKEN WINGS

PIGEON PEAS AND RICE

JICAMA MANGO SALAD

SHORTBREAD COOKIES

ICED PINEAPPLE JUICE AND/OR RED STRIPE BEER

Cooking Tip

Buy your crudités ready-made or, better yet, ask a friend to bring them. Now *that* is a real time-saver.

Picnic Tip

Get foods to the picnic site safely, so that you, your family, and friends are protected from uninvited microscopic guests known as pathogens.

Remember the 2-hour rule. Fresh-cooked foods shouldn't sit at room temperature for more than 2 hours. Keep hot foods hot, and cold foods cold. The window of opportunity for germs to grow and multiply is between 40° and 140°. Use an ice chest with ice or gel ice to hold cold foods under 40°. Wrap hot foods in layers of newspaper and place them in a second insulated chest to keep them hot until you reach the picnic area. When you set out the food, and if it's a hot day, place cold foods in a nested bowl of ice to keep them icy fresh.

Always carry along a good supply of water to wash up with, since one of the cardinal rules of picnics is that the best place to set up the buffet will be at least five miles from the nearest source of running water. Be prepared. And don't forget to bring a bar of soap.

You know the drill. Big umbrella if you're out in the sun. Folding chairs and blankets to sit on. Heaps of paper napkins. Since all camping-out comes down to keeping the sand out of the food, Linda is a firm believer in off-the-ground buffets, whether this means from the ice chest or on a folding table. Katherine thinks a large blanket or tablecloth is just fine and easier to transport. Ask the kids to gather shells to decorate and don't hesitate to call to service the kids' favorite sand-castle-making pail to hold a bouquet of flowers you gather in the dunes. Citronella candles help to keep the flying friends out of your airspace. A boom box will give you music to order, and sunscreen will ensure that the lobster is on the plate and not one of the guests.

Cold Boiled Shrimp and Crudités with Sauce Chien

2 tablespoons shrimp boil (mixed spices)
3 pounds medium-large shrimp,* in the shell
or 2 pounds shelled

Sauce Chien

1 small red onion

1 orange bell pepper, peeled (see page 55)

1 Scotch bonnet pepper, seeded

1/4 cup cilantro leaves

1 cup rice wine vinegar

Juice and zest of 1 lime

1/2 teaspoon sugar

Salt and freshly ground black pepper, to taste

1 pound mixed crudités: carrots, celery, cauliflower, broccoli

If you can find banana leaves, line a platter with them, then compose the cold boiled shrimp and various cru-dités—both vegetables and fruit—around a bowl of this classic Trinidadian French Creole Sauce Chien. It's easy to whiz up, and hot as the devil. This is probably the original "hot dog." To tell you the truth, Sauce Chien is ad-dicting. We dipped everything into it and just kept asking for more. Katherine's husband, Gordon, even ate it over rice and dipped his chicken in the sauce. As for peeling the shrimp, we bought them precooked and already peeled—although, at the beach, we could have just peeled the cooked shrimp and thrown the shells over our shoulders.

PREPARATION TIME:	20 MINUTES
COOKING TIME:	10 MINUTES
REFRIGERATION TIME:	30 MINUTES
MAKES 8 SERVINGS	

The sauce is best when made the day before.

Fill a medium saucepan with barely salted water and bring to a boil. Add the shrimp boil spices. Add the uncooked shrimp and boil until the color changes to opaque pink, about 5 minutes. Turn off the heat and let the shrimp cool in the water. Drain and transfer to a bowl. Cover and chill until serving time.

* You can buy the shrimp precooked and shelled at most fine grocery stores. If you don't have shrimp boil spices, make up an ad-lib mixture using a few cloves, some peppercorns, a couple of bay leaves, and a pinch of thyme and cayenne. Works the same way.

To make the sauce, process the onion, peppers, and cilantro in a food processor or blender until finely chopped. Pour in the vinegar, lime juice and zest, sugar, salt, and pepper and stir to mix. Cover and refrigerate. Serve the sauce in a bowl surrounded by crudités and shrimp.

Spicy Chicken Wings

2 pounds chicken wing drumettes (wing tips discarded)

Marinade

2 tablespoons extra virgin olive oil

2 tablespoons light or dark brown sugar

2 tablespoons grated fresh ginger

1/2 teaspoon hot red pepper flakes

1 teaspoon chopped garlic (2 cloves)

1/2 teaspoon Tabasco sauce

1/2 teaspoon salt and freshly ground black pepper, to taste

If you can find the time, bathe the chicken wings in the spicy marinade for 4 hours or so, then bake and pack them for the trip to the beach. But you can also get away with a 30-minute marinating time. Kids of all ages love these things.

PREPARATION TIME:	10 MINUTES
MARINATING TIME:	30 MINUTES TO 4 HOURS
BAKING TIME:	40 MINUTES
MAKES 8 SERVINGS	

May be prepared up to a day in advance, chilled, and served cold.

Put the chicken wings in a large Ziploc bag. Combine the olive oil, brown sugar, grated ginger, red pepper flakes, garlic, Tabasco, salt, and pepper in a small jar or bowl, then pour the mixture over the chicken. Cover and refrigerate a minimum of 30 minutes or a maximum of 4 hours. Preheat the oven to 350°. Drain the excess marinade, and arrange the chicken wings in a single layer on a large, flat baking dish. Bake until the chicken is golden on one side, about 20 minutes, then turn and cook until golden and done through, about 20 minutes more. Cool in the dish, then transfer to a serving platter or Ziploc bag to carry to the picnic.

PIGEON PEAS AND RICE

1 cup long-grain rice

1 green onion with top, finely chopped

1 clove garlic, chopped ($^1/_2$ teaspoon)

$^1/_2$ teaspoon ground allspice

$2^1/_2$ cups chicken broth

1 (15-ounce) can pigeon peas, rinsed and drained

2 tablespoons extra virgin olive oil

2 sprigs of cilantro, chopped

Salt and freshly ground black pepper, to taste

*Pigeon peas are a cousin to split peas and are available in cans wherever Caribbean populations exist. If you can't find them, substitute kidney beans or black-eyed peas. The use of allspice is traditional with Caribbean cooks. And yes, it is one spice, not a mixture. Travel to the Islands and you'll see big allspice nuts sold in every tourist trap. Do remind your guests to slosh a little of the Sauce Chien into the peas and rice to pep them up. Soon they'll be doing the wild **merengue**.*

PREPARATION TIME: 5 MINUTES

COOKING TIME: 20 MINUTES

MAKES 8 SERVINGS

Can be made up to half a day in advance, covered, and refrigerated. Serve at room temperature or hot.

In a medium saucepan, combine the rice, onion, garlic, allspice, and broth. Bring to a boil, cover, and lower the temperature to a simmer. Cook until the rice is tender and all the liquid is absorbed, about 20 minutes. Stir in the peas, oil, and cilantro, and adjust the seasonings with salt and pepper. Serve hot or at room temperature.

Jicama Mango Salad

1 medium jicama, peeled and cut into matchstick julienne (about 2 cups)

2 ripe mangoes, peeled, seeded, and chopped (about 2 cups)

1/2 cup chopped cilantro

Juice and zest of 1 lime (about 2 tablespoons juice)

2 tablespoons extra virgin olive oil

PREPARATION TIME: 10 MINUTES

MAKES 8 SERVINGS

May be made the day before, covered, and refrigerated until serving time.

Combine the jicama, mangoes, and cilantro in a medium bowl. Toss with the lime juice, zest, and oil. Cover and chill until serving time.

It Was the Best of Times
Bastille Day Brasserie Dinner

According to the French—who don't count the Magna Carta but do remember Marie Antoinette's admonition to the poor—"Let them eat cake"—Bastille Day is a great celebration of the first true revolt against tyranny, and warrants its own party if for no other reason than that the food is so good.

We've created a perfectly French menu from our fond remembrance of Paris, with its loud, well-lit brasseries spilling over with food and spirited conversation. Re-create the brasserie in your dining room and pay tribute to freedom with great wines and good food.

Our good friends Sandra Mounier and Andrew Jack in Paris introduced us to brasseries. Showier than bistros, they are also open all the time, unlike bistros and restaurants. When Andrew (a *Financial Times* journalist who, being British, had not been known for his culinary standards) suggested a brasserie on Rue St. Paul, we were slightly disappointed, thinking he was taking us to a diner. It was not the intimate little bistro we imagined. Unbeknownst to us, Andrew's Parisian girlfriend, Sandra, had imposed culinary standards in his life, and not a minute too soon. He, in turn, opened our minds beyond the view of France informed by the book *A Year in Provence*.

In fact, according to Andrew, the French virtually invented the concept of the restaurant after the revolution, when their best chefs found themselves without wealthy houses to cook in. Most of their masters had found their way to the guillotine. In desperation, these chefs began cooking for the public and created what we know of as the modern restaurant. *Vive la France!*

Brasseries originated as breweries, as a *brasseur* is a brewer. In contrast to a bistro, in a brasserie friends can indulge in loud political argument—a great French pastime—and not feel self-conscious. A slab of pâté, rabbit in mustard sauce, a cheese course, and chocolate mousse for dessert—no diner we'd ever heard of in the States served such delicacies. The French definitely have standards when it comes to food.

The Menu

PÂTÉ DE CAMPAGNE AND CRUSTY FRENCH BREAD

MUSTARD CHICKEN WITH BUTTERED EGG NOODLES

SLICED BEEFSTEAK TOMATOES

TOSSED ROMAINE SALAD (SEE PAGE 209)

CHEESE COURSE (SEE CREATING A CHEESE COURSE PAGE 287)

CHOCOLATE MOUSSE

COFFEE

Wine Suggestions

This is a great chance to show off several great wines. How appropriate for the French holiday!

Appetizer—While a French jurançon from the Bergerac region, a sweet wine, will nicely complement the pâté, the classic pâté wine is a Bordeaux Barsac. Sauternes—Sauternes gets its flavor from botrytis, also known as the noble rot. This gives the wine a very exotic rich flavor that parallels the rich pâté. It's a French celebration. Try them both! We guarantee that the noble rot will give you some great dreams as a bonus.

Main Course—For mustard chicken, food from the heart of France, try a good French Côte d'Or Burgundy (red or white). This rich meal will be complemented by the buttery vanilla flavor of a white Burgundy, or the tart mustard will offset the tart fruitiness of the red Burgundy.

Dessert—A French Banyuls from the Languedoc region fits the bill. A seamless match for a chocolate mousse.

Always buy good-quality mustard (preferably whole grain) and never use cooking wine with a screw top from the grocery store. A good dry wine under $6.00 is better. A variety of cheeses and a good pâté make this dinner spectacular.

All the Trimmings

Arrange the bottles of wine at the head of the table, next to the host. Serve the mustard chicken on a large platter, with a heaping amount of coarsely chopped fresh flat-leaf parsley spread loosely on top. Serve the salad with the cheese course and the Chocolate Mousse in *très elegant* balloon wine goblets. Make a great centerpiece from red, white, and blue carnations, with a few small French flags sticking out.

MUSTARD CHICKEN WITH BUTTERED EGG NOODLES

12 chicken thighs, thoroughly dried

1 cup Dijon-style mustard (preferably whole grain)

1 tablespoon canola oil

2 tablespoons butter, divided

1 large yellow onion or 2 medium onions, coarsely chopped

1 tablespoon flour

1 litre bottle dry white wine

Several bunches fresh thyme or 1 teaspoon dried

1 bay leaf

$1/2$ teaspoon salt and freshly ground pepper, to taste

Buttered Egg Noodles (recipe follows)

Coarsely chopped fresh flat-leaf parsley

Adapted from a rabbit with mustard sauce recipe, this one uses chicken thighs, which most closely resemble the moist quality of rabbit. You may want to throw in some extra thighs, since some people will no doubt want seconds. If you are feeling bold, go to a good butcher and order a couple rabbits, then use this recipe to prepare it. Be sure to have it cut up for you. Rabbit is a lean and moist meat not to be missed, but for those with less time, the thighs are really good.

PREPARATION TIME: 20 MINUTES

COOKING TIME: ABOUT 1 HOUR

MAKES 6 SERVINGS

May be made 1 day in advance, covered, and refrigerated until serving time, then reheated in the oven just until piping hot.

Toss the chicken thighs with ¹/₂ cup of the mustard until they are thoroughly coated. Heat the oil and 1 tablespoon butter in a large Dutch oven, preferably Le Creuset, over high heat. Brown the chicken (skin side down first) in three batches, for 3 minutes on each side to sear skin. It will finish cooking in the sauce. Be careful not to crowd the chicken in the pan.

Remove the chicken thighs from the pan as they are cooked and set them aside on a plate. Add the onions and remaining butter and cook 3 or 4 minutes, until translucent. Add the flour and cook 1 to 2 minutes more. Deglaze the pan with half the bottle of wine, scraping the bottom to loosen all of the brown bits. Add the other ¹/₂ cup of mustard and the remaining half bottle of wine, the thyme, bay leaf, salt, and pepper to taste. Return the chicken to the pan and simmer, uncovered, on low heat for 45 minutes, stirring occasionally, until the chicken is done and the sauce is slightly thickened. Taste and adjust the seasonings. Remove and discard bay leaf before serving. Serve the sauce and chicken over egg noodles, topped with a bunch of coarsely chopped fresh parsley.

Buttered Egg Noodles

1 (1-pound) package dry egg noodles

3 to 4 tablespoons salt

¹/₄ cup butter (¹/₂ stick)

COOKING TIME: 15 MINUTES

MAKES 6 SERVINGS

Best if made and served immediately

Bring a large pot of water to a boil. Add the salt and noodles, stirring very well at first, and cook to desired doneness. Remove 1 cup of the cooking liquid, then drain the noodles but do not rinse them. Return the noodles to the pot and stir in butter. If the noodles start to stick together, add some of the cooking liquid, as needed.

Cheese Course

Most brasseries offer a choice of either the cheese course or a dessert. However, since this dinner is not being served in a brasserie, why not offer the cheese course and a dessert? The cheese course serves as a palate cleanser, and to showcase wines. For a satisfactory cheese course, we suggest the following: one or two goat cheeses, a sheep's milk cheese, a hard cheese (such as Gruyère), a blue cheese, and a triple crème (such as Brie or Explorateur). Go to a gourmet grocery that has a good cheese selection and try a few types. It's the only way you will learn what you like. Serve the cheese with crusty French bread and good wine just before dessert. See our Creating a Cheese Course interview with Lea Batzold, the cheese buyer and day manager at Chanterelle Restaurant in New York.

CHOCOLATE MOUSSE

6 ounces best-quality semisweet chocolate
(chips or squares)

6 large eggs, separated

1/4 cup liqueur (Grand Marnier, Crème de
Cassis, or your choice)

Whipped cream, for garnish (optional)
Shaved chocolate curls, for garnish (optional)

PREPARATION TIME: 10 MINUTES
COOLING TIME: 1 HOUR
MAKES 6 SERVINGS

The chocolate mousse can be made up to 2 days in advance. That is, no doubt, what the brasserie does.

Melt the chocolate in the microwave on high (100 percent power) for 1 minute or until melted. Whisk the egg yolks until ropey, then fold them into the chocolate mixture. Cook in the microwave on high (100 percent power) for 30 seconds more. Alternatively: stovetop, melt chocolate over simmering water in a double boiler, about 5 minutes, then fold in egg yolks and cook until thick, about 5 minutes. Stir the liqueur into the egg yolk mixture. Beat the egg whites to the stiff peak stage. Mix 1 cup of the stiff egg whites with the chocolate and egg yolk mixture, then gently fold the chocolate mixture into the egg whites. Be careful not to overmix. Divide the mousse among six dessert dishes, or balloon wine-glasses, cover, and refrigerate for a minimum of 1 hour.

Garnish with whipped cream and/or shaved chocolate or both.

A Cool Saturday Supper for Four

You will be one cool host when you serve this simple dinner with its Iberian flair. A brightly flavored saffron-colored mayonnaise sauce is simple to stir together and makes the plate look like a Miró painting. Much of this menu can be made in advance. Make it your little secret that the chicken was roasted down the street at the deli. Who's to know if you don't tell? We certainly won't let on. Take the compliments. You are, after all, a very good shopper and dinner composer.

The Menu

GAZPACHO

COLD ROAST CHICKEN WITH SAFFRON GARLIC SAUCE

CHOPPED CELERY AND BLACK OLIVE SALAD

RUSTIC BREAD

COUSCOUS

FLAN ALMENDRA

Wine Suggestions

Appetizer and Main Course—Serve a chilled Spanish Albariño. Made from the Albariño grape, this wine is light and dry and complements the assertive taste of the gazpacho and the garlicky saffron sauce.

Dessert—A muscat from Greece, California, or the Rhone region of France will pick up the caramel note from the flan.

Cooking Tip

Couscous is about the most convenient starch course in the world. Although it resembles a grain, it is a semolina flour pasta that originated in Morocco and is widely consumed in France. Traditionally, the preparation of couscous is a labor-intensive process that requires hand rolling and two heatings. However, here in the United States couscous is generally sold in a "quick" form. All you have to do is add butter and hot water, then cover and let it sit—no stirring or anything. Purists may scoff, but soon it is ready. The results are generally perfect if you can follow box instructions. It just goes to show that some things *can* be improved with technology.

All the Trimmings

Start by serving the Gazpacho in rimmed soup plates. For the main course, chicken, two of the plates get a leg and thigh and two of the plates get a breast. Arrange the bird slightly overlapping the couscous, with the Chopped Celery and Black Olive Salad to the side. Spoon the saffron sauce into either a pastry bag or a plastic catsup bottle. We prefer the latter. Make a swirling design, reminiscent of Miró, on the chicken pieces, the couscous, and the plate. The bright yellow contrasted with the black olives and light green celery is dramatic.

GAZPACHO

2 thick slices bread (white or French preferred)

1 (28-ounce) can whole plum tomatoes and their juice

¼ cup extra virgin olive oil

1 tablespoon white or red wine vinegar (thyme or tarragon vinegar adds additional flavor)

1 to 2 cloves garlic (cut back on the garlic if you are garlic-averse)

Pinch of cayenne

Freshly ground black pepper, to taste

1 teaspoon salt

4 ice cubes

½ green or red bell pepper or flat-leaf parsley, finely chopped, for garnish

This soup is incredibly simple to prepare—with a blender, it can be done in about 10 minutes.

PREPARATION TIME: 10 MINUTES

REFRIGERATION TIME: 1 HOUR

MAKES 4 TO 6 SERVINGS

Cold soup is a perfect candidate for advance preparation. Make it the night or even a few hours before the meal so the flavors will have time to release and blend.

In a shallow bowl, soak the bread in water 5 minutes or until mushy. Place the tomatoes, olive oil, soaked bread, vinegar, garlic, cayenne, black pepper, and salt in a blender and puree for 3 to 5 minutes, or until the consistency is smooth. Pour into a serving bowl, add four ice cubes, and chill for an hour in the refrigerator. Serve cold, garnished with chopped green pepper or parsley.

Saffron Garlic Sauce

7 cloves garlic, peeled

1 cup water

2 teaspoons freshly squeezed lemon juice
(about $^1/_2$ lemon)

$^1/_4$ teaspoon saffron threads

$^1/_2$ teaspoon salt

$^1/_4$ teaspoon cayenne

1 cup mayonnaise

Preparation time: 5 minutes
Cooking time: 5 minutes
Makes 4 servings

May be made up to 3 days in advance, covered, and refrigerated.

Place the whole cloves of garlic and the water in a medium saucepan or in a medium ceramic bowl for cooking in the microwave. Boil either way for 5 minutes. Drain the garlic cloves and add them to a food processor or blender, along with the lemon juice, saffron, salt, cayenne, and mayonnaise. Blend for a few seconds. The sauce may be chilled or served immediately.

Here is a list of the other great sauces, good for cold roasted chicken, beef, pork, or fish, that you can make beginning with 1 cup of best-quality mayonnaise.

Aioli: 1 cup mayonnaise; juice of $^1/_2$ lemon; 4 cloves garlic, crushed.

Andalusian-Style: 1 cup mayonnaise; $^1/_4$ cup tomato paste; 1 tablespoon each: red pepper, and chopped chives.

Chantilly: 1 cup mayonnaise; $^1/_2$ cup heavy cream, whipped.

Curry: 1 cup mayonnaise; 1 tablespoon toasted* curry powder.

Dijon-Style: 1 cup mayonnaise; $^1/_2$ cup Dijon-style mustard.

* To toast curry powder, place powder in a dry, preheated skillet over medium-high heat for 30 seconds or until it begins to turn a deeper color and becomes aromatic. Transfer immediately to the preparation bowl so you don't burn it.

Gribiche: I cup mayonnaise; $^1/_2$ hard-cooked egg, chopped; 2 teaspoons each: minced capers, fresh thyme, shallots.

Red Aioli: I cup mayonnaise; $^1/_2$ cup lemon juice; $^1/_2$ red bell pepper, pureed; pinch of cayenne.

Rémoulade: I cup mayonnaise; 2 teaspoons each: cornichons, capers, fresh thyme, anchovy paste.

Suedoise: I cup mayonnaise; I cup applesauce; I tablespoon horseradish.

Tartar Sauce: I cup mayonnaise; 2 teaspoons each: minced chives, parsley, cornichons, capers; $^1/_2$ hard-cooked egg, chopped.

Chopped Celery and Black Olive Salad

2 tablespoons extra virgin olive oil

2 tablespoons red wine vinegar

$^1/_2$ teaspoon freshly ground black pepper

1 cup coarsely chopped celery

1 cup coarsely chopped pitted black olives

Preparation time: 5 minutes

Makes 4 servings

May be made as much as a day in advance, covered, and refrigerated until serving time.

In the serving bowl, mix the olive oil, red wine vinegar, and pepper. Toss in the celery and olives. Cover and chill until serving time.

Couscous

1 (14-ounce) can chicken broth

1/2 cup water

Finely chopped fresh flat-leaf parsley

1 (10-ounce) box couscous (1 cup)

Preparation time: 2 minutes

Cooking time: 5 minutes to boil liquid

Standing time: 10 minutes

Makes 4 servings

This, too, may be made an hour or 2 in advance, held at room temperature, and reheated at mealtime in the microwave or on the stovetop over medium heat.

To make a highly flavored chicken stock base for the couscous, stir the chopped parsley into the boiling chicken broth before stirring in the couscous.

Follow the directions on the box for cooking the couscous, substituting the chicken broth for most of the water. Fluff up with a fork before serving.

Flan Almendra

1/2 cup sugar

1 (14-ounce) can sweetened condensed milk

1 1/2 cups fresh whole milk

3 eggs

3 egg yolks

1 teaspoon vanilla extract or seeds from a vanilla bean

1 cup slivered almonds

This recipe originated in a restaurant kitchen that made a week's worth of flans at a time, then covered them with foil and refrigerated them in their cake pans until needed. The caramelized sugar runs out over the top when you turn the flan out onto a serving dish. You can learn an easy restaurant technique for caramelizing sugar with this recipe. No need to add water to the sugar before heating it. Simply heat it in a metal pan, swirling the sugar around with tongs while watching it melt and turn a lovely caramel color. Take care not to leave it on the heat too long or it will carbonize—a polite word for burn.

Preparation time: 1 0 minutes

Cooking time: 60 minutes

Refrigeration time: 30 minutes to 1 week

Makes 4 servings

May be made up to a week in advance, then covered and refrigerated.

Spread the sugar evenly in a 9-inch metal cake pan and place it directly over medium heat. Caramelize the sugar by shaking the pan occasionally and lifting it off the heat with metal tongs, until the sugar is melted and light brown in color. Remove from the heat using the tongs and tipping the pan to complete the melting of the sugar. Set it aside to cool; the mixture may crack slightly.

Preheat the oven to 350°. Stir together the sweetened condensed milk, whole milk, eggs, egg yolks, vanilla, and slivered almonds. Pour over the caramelized sugar. Cover the pan with aluminum foil and place it in a Pyrex baking dish containing 1 to $1^1/_2$ inches of hot water. Bake on the middle rack of the oven for 1 hour, or until a knife or toothpick comes out clean. Cool on a rack. You may refrigerate the flan at this point until ready to serve. To serve, run a knife around the edge and invert the flan onto a serving plate. It may also be served warm or cold.

A Summer Supper from the Farmer's Market

Linda's garden grows abundant tomatoes and squash as well as herbs that are completely out of control. Katherine relies on New York's abundant farmer's markets, which burst forth with the bounty of summer.

Because Oregon mountain summers are cool and peaceful, we love to eat out under the grape arbor, where the perfume of the ripening Concord grapes can be absolutely staggering. We never put a tablecloth on the old marble-topped table out there, and we try to make meals that can be put together in a hurry because our list of activities is long. This menu is a winner with us. We swing through the farmer's market for the ripest produce and rainbow trout, and make a huge pitcher of peach iced tea. The menu is great for the arbor or a city rooftop or terrace at dusk.

The Menu

CUCUMBERS AND ONIONS IN TARRAGON VINEGAR (SEE PAGE 169)

PANFRIED TROUT WITH ALMONDS AND FRESH THYME

JEANNE VOLTZ'S OLD-FASHIONED YELLOW CROOKNECK SQUASH CASSEROLE

FRENCH COUNTRY BREAD AND FRESH BUTTER

PEACH ICED TEA

ROASTED PEACHES WITH CASSIS AND VANILLA ICE CREAM

Wine Suggestions

Main Course—A great moment for a French Chardonnay such as Pouilly-Fuissé. The almonds and butter that give the trout flavor show off these bigger French wines.

Arrange the oven racks in the bottom third and the top third of the oven and you'll have plenty of room, even in a 30-inch oven, to cook the squash and the peaches at once.

Since the squash start on the stovetop, they need to bake only long enough to blend the flavors and brown the top, 20 minutes or so. The hot oven will work just fine for everything and will guarantee luscious, caramelized flavors from the beginning of the meal to the end.

All the Trimmings

Serve this menu buffet-style. A bunch of daisies or flowers from the farmers' market will brighten up the table! Relax . . . it's summer.

Panfried Trout with Almonds and Fresh Thyme

$^{1}/_{2}$ cup all-purpose flour

$^{1}/_{2}$ cup toasted almonds*

3 tablespoons fresh thyme leaves, stripped off the stem

2 teaspoons salt

Freshly ground black pepper, to taste

4 to 6 rainbow trout, cleaned, heads and tails intact

2 tablespoons peanut or extra virgin olive oil

Lemon wedges, to serve

This simple summer dish harks back to a time when wild trout were abundant in our streams. Nowadays, trout are abundant at the hatchery, but they have not lost their characteristic delicate taste, despite a much more comfortable, but arguably shorter life. Now we catch them at the farmers' market.

PREPARATION TIME:	15 MINUTES
COOKING TIME:	15 MINUTES

MAKES 4 TO 6 SERVINGS (EQUAL TO THE NUMBER OF FISH)

If you really want to economize on time, pulse up the flour mixture hours in advance. Then all you have to do at the last minute is dredge and fry.

Combine the flour, almonds, thyme, 2 teaspoons of salt, and pepper to taste in a food processor and pulse until the almonds are pulverized. Salt and pepper the cavities of the trout. Put the flour mixture in a wide bowl, and dredge the outside of the trout in it.

Heat the oil in a skillet over medium heat for 3 minutes. Place the trout in the skillet for 3 to 5 minutes per side, or until the flour browns crisp and golden. Serve with the lemon wedges.

JEANNE VOLTZ'S OLD-FASHIONED YELLOW CROOKNECK SQUASH CASSEROLE

2 tablespoons butter, plus additional for the baking dish

1/2 cup coarsely chopped yellow onion (1 medium)

1 1/2 pounds small, tender crookneck or other yellow summer squash, cut into chunks

1/4 teaspoon freshly ground black pepper

1/2 teaspoon salt

1 cup crumbled saltine crackers

2 large eggs

1 cup milk

We're totally addicted to the farmers' market and every week we hunt for the first squash of the season. One Southern friend, Jeanne Voltz, agrees that the old-fashioned yellow crookneck is one of the best things about summer. Squash casserole, made with the smallest, tenderest crooknecks, is a standby in the South. Of course, you can also make it with zucchini, yellow or green, but Jeanne reminds us that the flavor will never compare to that of an old-fashioned crookneck. It isn't high summer until you've had your first crookneck squash for supper.

* To toast almonds: Arrange them in a single layer on a baking sheet and place in a 350° oven (or toaster oven) for 3 to 6 minutes, or until golden.

PREPARATION TIME: 15 MINUTES

COOKING TIME: 15 MINUTES

BAKING TIME: 20 TO 30 MINUTES

MAKES 4 TO 6 SERVINGS (CAN BE DOUBLED EASILY; JUST USE A LARGER CASSEROLE DISH)

Wash and slice the squash upon return from the market and refrigerate it. Then it will be ready when you need it an hour before dinner.

Preheat the oven to 450°. Butter a $1^1/_2$-quart baking dish and set it aside. Melt the 2 tablespoons of butter in a large saucepan over medium heat. Add the onion and sauté for 1 to 2 minutes. Add the squash, pepper, and salt. Stir well and heat to a simmer, then reduce the heat to medium low and cook, stirring frequently, until the squash is soft. (No liquid is needed if the heat is kept low and the mixture is stirred often.) Allow 15 to 18 minutes to cook.

Mash the squash in the pan with a fork, a potato masher, or a handheld blender, but do not puree the squash smooth. Stir in the cracker crumbs. Taste and add more salt or pepper if needed. Beat the eggs with the milk until blended and stir into the squash mixture.

Turn into the buttered baking dish and bake for 20 to 30 minutes, or until the top is brown, the mixture is firm near the center and has a hissing sound to it.

ROASTED PEACHES WITH CASSIS AND VANILLA ICE CREAM

6 freestone peaches

1½ cups raspberry jelly

¼ cup Crème de Cassis liqueur

6 tablespoons butter

1 pint good-quality vanilla ice cream

This quick recipe piggybacks in the hot oven for the squash casserole. Put the peaches in with the casserole for the last 10 to 15 minutes before dinner, and let them rest during the meal.

PREPARATION TIME: 10 MINUTES

COOKING TIME: 15 MINUTES

MAKES 4 TO 6 SERVINGS

Tastes best if cooked and eaten right away, but there's no need to waste time peeling the peaches. Just wash and dry them, rubbing off the fuzz under running water.

Cut the peaches in half and remove the stones. In a bowl, stir together the jelly and the Crème de Cassis. Place 1 tablespoon of butter in the cavity of each peach, and fill each cavity with the jelly mixture. Place on a lightly greased cookie sheet and roast in the 450° oven for 15 minutes or just until they are bubbly and hot through. May be served hot or at room temperature, with vanilla ice cream.

Summer Tapas for Twenty

As fortune would have it, Katherine's first New York roommate was Alicia Villamarin, an Andalusian woman from Seville (where tapas were invented). Most of these recipes are compliments of Alicia and her mother, Carmine. Alicia never let the fact that she was getting a Ph.D. in cellular molecular biology stop her from throwing as many parties as was humanly possible. She is proof that a stylish party can come together without days of preparation. Tapas fit the bill. Alicia explained that tapas means top (referring to the little plates they are served on). "Originally, bar owners in the south of Spain invented tapas as a way to keep the flies out of the beer," she said. "You know . . . you put your little plate over your glass of beer. Since flies are no longer an issue, tapas are now used to attract the customers to the bar." Bar owners compete to see who can originate the best, most unusual tapas. The result is hundreds of tapas recipes throughout Spain and, now, the world. Olé.

We have devoted this menu to tapas, bite-size appetizers served on little plates or bowls, most often requiring a toothpick or fork to eat. They are perfect for a summer stand-up party because they are easy to make and to eat. While the initial preparation is somewhat time consuming, tapas are, after all, Spanish bar food and can be made in advance and served cold or at room temperature. Those that need warming can usually go into the microwave on high (100 percent power) for a minute. The predominant flavors are extra virgin olive oil, garlic, oregano, lemon, cilantro, and puckery vinegars: white, red wine, and sherry. They are served with crusty bread to soak up the juices. You can definitely get creative and invent your own.

The Menu

OLIVES AND TOASTED SALTY ALMONDS

CARMINE'S MARINATED CARROTS (*ZANAHORIAS À LA CARMINE*)

GARLIC SHRIMP (*GAMBAS AL AJILLO*)

CHORIZOS ALICIA À LA MICROWAVE

PORK KEBABS (*PINCHO MORUNO*)

WRINKLED POTATOES FROM THE CANARY ISLANDS *(PAPAS ARRUGADAS)*

MOJO PICÓN DIP AND *MOJO DE CILANTRO* DIP

SLICED BLOOD RED TOMATOES *(TOMATES ALIÑADOS)*

MUSHROOMS WITH PROSCIUTTO AND GARLIC

CRUSTY BAGUETTE

SANGRIA (SEE PAGE 205)

GRAPES AND COOKIES

Wine Suggestions

All tapas—As an alternative to the sangria, try Spain's wonderful red Rioja wines or the Galician white Albariños.

All the Trimmings

As with many meals, the colors and textures of the food are the stars of this party. Decorate with bunches of flowers, candles, and fruit in baskets. We usually stuff the bottom of the basket with newspaper then cover the paper with a brightly colored napkin and arrange the fruit so it looks more bountiful. Set up the food buffet-style. Little plates, cocktail napkins, and forks are a must. Tapas are really not finger food.

CARMINE'S MARINATED CARROTS
(ZANAHORIAS À LA CARMINE)

1 (1-pound) bag baby carrots

2 cloves garlic, peeled

1 teaspoon oregano

1/4 cup finely chopped cilantro

1/4 cup extra virgin olive oil

1/4 cup white wine vinegar

1 teaspoon salt

Freshly ground black pepper, to taste

PREPARATION TIME: 5 MINUTES

COOKING TIME: ABOUT 10 MINUTES

REFRIGERATOR MARINATION TIME: AT LEAST 30 MINUTES

MAKES 20 TAPAS SERVINGS

May be made up to 2 days in advance.

Boil the carrots in water to cover for 8 to 12 minutes, just until they are slightly soft. Meanwhile, in a food processor or blender, process the garlic, oregano, cilantro, olive oil, vinegar, salt, and pepper. Drain the carrots and toss with the dressing. Marinate in the refrigerator until serving time.

GARLIC SHRIMP (GAMBAS AL AJILLO)

1/2 cup extra virgin olive oil

4 cloves garlic, finely chopped (2 teaspoons)

1/4 to 1/2 teaspoon hot red pepper flakes

2 pounds medium shrimp, peeled*

PREPARATION TIME: 5 MINUTES

COOKING TIME: 4 MINUTES

MAKES 20 TAPAS SERVINGS

* We like peeled raw shrimp. It may cost a bit more but the time saved is worth it.

Can be made several hours in advance (but no sooner) if stored in the refrigerator and rewarmed slightly in a skillet or in the microwave on high (100 percent power)—no more than a minute or so. If you are going to reheat it, you might want to slightly undercook the shrimp.

In a large skillet, heat the olive oil, garlic, and red pepper flakes for 1 minute. Add half the shrimp and cook for 2 minutes, or until the shrimp turns orange. Remove and add the other half of the shrimp. Cook for 2 more minutes. Be careful not to overcook the shrimp or it will taste like rubber. Toss all the cooked shrimp with the flavored oil from the pan and serve warm or at room temperature, with toothpicks or small skewers.

Chorizos Alicia à la Microwave

2 pounds chorizo link sausages   Lots of toothpicks

This is definitely in the category of recipes that are so easy it's an embarrassment. Slice the sausage in advance, but wait to cook it until you're ready to eat. Serve with toothpicks. That's our kind of preparation.

PREPARATION TIME: 5 MINUTES

COOKING TIME: 2 MINUTES IN MICROWAVE

                           8 TO 10 MINUTES STOVETOP

MAKES 20 TAPAS SERVINGS

Slice the chorizos into $1/2$-inch-thick slices. Stick a toothpick in each one and arrange one layer deep on a microwavable plate. (This will make more than one plate full.) Cook, uncovered, in the microwave on high (100 percent power) for 2 minutes. Alternatively, fry in a skillet over medium-high heat until golden brown, turning once, about 8 to 10 minutes. Serve immediately.

PORK KEBABS (PINCHO MORUNO)

2 tablespoons extra virgin olive oil

2 tablespoons freshly squeezed lemon juice

8 cloves garlic, minced (4 teaspoons)

1 teaspoon grated fresh ginger

1 1/2 teaspoons cumin

1 teaspoon coriander

1/4 teaspoon turmeric

1 teaspoon sweet paprika

1/4 teaspoon hot red pepper flakes

1/2 teaspoon saffron threads

1/2 teaspoon salt

1 pound boneless pork loin cut into cubes

PREPARATION TIME: 5 MINUTES

MARINATING TIME: 3 TO 24 HOURS

COOKING TIME: 10 MINUTES

MAKES 20 TAPAS SERVINGS

The pork may be mixed with the marinade up to 24 hours in advance. It may be cooked 2 hours in advance and reheated a minute or so in the microwave or in a 350° oven.

In a bowl, combine the olive oil, lemon juice, garlic, ginger, cumin, coriander, turmeric, sweet paprika, red pepper flakes, garlic, saffron threads, and salt. Toss in the pork cubes and mix thoroughly. Marinate for at least 3 hours—it's even better if marinated for 24 hours or overnight. At grilling time, soak wooden skewers in water to prevent them from burning while you preheat the grill. Remove the pork from the marinade. Thread 3 or 4 cubes on a skewer and grill for 5 to 10 minutes, until the pork is cooked through, turning as it browns. Alternatively, sauté the pork in batches in a large black skillet for 5 minutes or until golden red. Be careful not to crowd the pan or the meat will steam. When done, skewer the cooked cubes and serve either hot or at room temperature. These may also be reheated in a minute in the microwave on high (100 percent power) or in a 350° oven for 5 minutes or so.

WRINKLED POTATOES FROM THE CANARY ISLANDS
(PAPAS ARRUGADAS)

2 pounds small new potatoes   1¹/₂ tablespoons kosher salt

PREPARATION TIME: 5 MINUTES
COOKING TIME: 1 0 MINUTES
MAKES 20 TAPAS SERVINGS

May be made up to 2 hours in advance.

Place the potatoes and the salt in a saucepan with cold water to cover. Boil for 10 minutes, or until barely tender. Drain off the water and continue to cook in the dry pan for 5 more minutes, until the potato skins start to wrinkle. Slice into ¹/₂-inch-thick medallions and insert a toothpick through the skin like a lollipop. Serve at room temperature, with the *picón* and *cilantro* dips below.

Mojo Picón Dip

1 red bell pepper, peeled (see page 55)

1 (1-inch) piece dried red chili pepper or $1/2$ teaspoon hot red pepper flakes

$1/4$ cup red wine vinegar

$1/2$ teaspoon (1 clove) chopped garlic

$1/4$ teaspoon kosher salt

$1/2$ teaspoon cumin

$3/4$ teaspoon dried thyme

$3/4$ teaspoon dried oregano

1 teaspoon paprika

$1/4$ cup fresh flat-leaf parsley

$1/2$ cup extra virgin olive oil

1 piece white bread

This dip is good for just about anything: bread, potatoes, kebabs, cardboard.

PREPARATION TIME: 5 MINUTES

REFRIGERATION TIME: 30 MINUTES (OPTIONAL)

MAKES 20 TAPAS SERVINGS

May be made up to 2 days in advance.

In a food processor, blend all the ingredients together for 30 seconds. Do not overblend. Refrigerate, covered, until ready to serve. We have served this many times immediately after it is made. Of course, it gets better with time.

Mojo de Cilantro Dip

6 cloves garlic, chopped (3 teaspoons)

1 green bell pepper, peeled (see page 55)

1 cup fresh cilantro

$^3/_4$ cup extra virgin olive oil

3 tablespoons white wine vinegar

1 teaspoon salt (or to taste)

Freshly ground black pepper, to taste

This dip is also good for bread, potatoes, kebabs, or just about anything.

PREPARATION TIME: 5 MINUTES

REFRIGERATION TIME: 30 MINUTES (OPTIONAL)

MAKES 20 TAPAS SERVINGS

May be made up to 2 days in advance.

Blend all the ingredients together for 30 seconds. Do not overblend. Refrigerate until ready to serve. We have served this many times immediately after it is made. Of course, it gets better with time.

Sliced Blood Red Tomatoes *(Tomates Aliñados)*

$^1/_4$ cup extra virgin olive oil

1 teaspoon fresh oregano leaves

$^1/_4$ cup white wine or sherry wine vinegar

$^1/_2$ teaspoon salt

5 very ripe beefsteak tomatoes, sliced $^1/_4$ inch thick

PREPARATION TIME: 5 MINUTES

REFRIGERATION TIME: 30 MINUTES (OPTIONAL)

MAKES 20 TAPAS SERVINGS

May be made up to 30 minutes in advance.

In a small bowl, combine the olive oil, oregano, vinegar, and salt. Arrange tomatoes on a platter and drizzle them with the dressing. Refrigerate up to 30 minutes before serving, if you wish, or serve immediately at room temperature.

Mushrooms with Prosciutto and Garlic

2 cloves garlic, chopped (1 teaspoon)

1/4 cup extra virgin olive oil

2 pints mushrooms, cleaned and quartered

1/4 pound thin-sliced prosciutto

3 tablespoons red wine vinegar

1/4 cup freshly squeezed lemon juice

1 teaspoon salt

Freshly ground black pepper, to taste

A loaf of crusty bread

Alicia says they use Spanish Serrano ham in her hometown, but in the States, prosciutto works just fine.

PREPARATION TIME:	5 MINUTES
COOKING TIME:	10 MINUTES

MAKES 20 TAPAS SERVINGS

May be made up to 1 day in advance. Bring back to room temperature before serving.

Sauté the garlic in the olive oil for 30 seconds; add the mushrooms and prosciutto and sauté another 2 minutes. Add the vinegar, lemon juice, salt, and pepper, and cook about 5 minutes or until the liquid evaporates. Serve hot or at room temperature, with crusty bread.

An Easy Summer Lunch of Panfried Oysters

The thing about summer is, you don't want to spend too much time on lunch. Whether you are at a beach house, a country house, or a city apartment, time is somehow more precious during these three months. This menu takes that into account, yet the flavors are bright and delicious, to say the least. Summer tomatoes, corn on the cob, corn bread (which may be made from a mix or bought at a bakery), and fresh oysters! After all, they're quick to cook, easy to serve, and they'll hold the memory of summer long into the winter, when the snow blows and the office seems to close in around us.

The Menu

SLICED BEEFSTEAK TOMATOES AND BASIL

PANFRIED OYSTERS

CORN ON THE COB WITH LIME AND CUMIN BUTTER (SEE PAGES 221–22)

BLACK SKILLET CORN BREAD (SEE PAGE 59)

MIXED FRESH FRUIT AND COOKIES

Wine Suggestions

Main Course—Because oysters have the same texture as a muscadet from France or a California sauvignon blanc, they are a perfect match for these wines.

Cooking Tip

Corn on the cob can be cooked in a number of ways. We usually steam it unshucked in the microwave on high (100 percent power) for 4 minutes per ear, but you can also cook it the same way outside on the grill. Soak the corn—shucks and all—in water, while the grill heats up, then throw the corn, unshucked, onto the grill. Cook and turn until the shucks have blackened. Remove to a cutting board, slice off both ends to remove the shucks and silks, and serve. It doesn't take long to cook corn; about all you're trying to do—regardless of the cooking method—is to heat it thoroughly and firm up the starch molecules inside the kernels.

All the Trimmings

The colors of corn, tomatoes, and basil will carry the message—even if served on paper plates. The dishes in this meal are best served family-style and passed around the table. Arrange the tomatoes on a platter, slices overlapping, in a fan or circle shape. The corn should be served in half cobs from a large bowl, as directed in the recipe. Arrange the fried oysters on a bed of lettuce, interspersed with lemon wedges and around a small bowl of red cocktail sauce in the center.

SLICED BEEFSTEAK TOMATOES AND BASIL

1 pound ripe beefsteak or large tomatoes, sliced 1/2 inch thick

1/3 cup fresh basil leaves, chopped coarsely (reserve a few whole for garnish)

Salt and freshly ground black pepper, to taste

2 tablespoons extra virgin olive oil

1 1/2 teaspoons balsamic vinegar

Once considered a fruit, but reclassified as a vegetable to avoid taxation in the last century, wonderful beefsteak tomatoes are the joy of late summer. This dish takes no time, and the taste is synonymous with August.

PREPARATION TIME: 5 MINUTES

MAKES 6 SERVINGS

Can be made up to 2 hours in advance of time and refrigerated. May be served cold or at room temperature.

Overlap the tomato slices on a nonreactive platter, and sprinkle the chopped basil on and around them. Sprinkle with salt and pepper, and drizzle with olive oil and balsamic vinegar. Cover and refrigerate. At serving time, spoon the juice that has accumulated at the bottom of the platter over the tomatoes.

PANFRIED OYSTERS

36 medium oysters, shucked and drained	Canola or peanut oil, for frying
Yellow cornmeal, for dredging the oysters	1 lemon, cut into wedges
Salt and freshly ground black pepper, to taste	Lettuce leaves, for serving

Before marine biology and fisheries science subverted the rhythm of nature, oysters were available only in months with an "r" in their name. Now, oysters are farmed, shucked by someone in a processing plant, and you can buy them in a jar all year round. This dish is quick, which is useful if you are rushing around trying to close the summerhouse. However, you could still be delayed by the legendary amorous qualities these shellfish are said to endow on those who consume them.

PREPARATION TIME: 10 MINUTES
COOKING TIME: 10 MINUTES
MAKES 6 SERVINGS

Dredge the oysters in cornmeal, then season them generously with salt and pepper. Set aside. Pour the oil 1 inch deep in a large skillet and heat over medium-high heat. Fry the oysters until golden brown in batches, taking care not to overcrowd the skillet. Cook on the first side, about 3 minutes, then turn only once and finish cooking on the second side, no more than 2 minutes. Transfer to a warmed plate. They are best served immediately, but if you wish, you can also place the cooked oysters in a warmed oven, for an hour or so until serving time. Put the oven on the lowest setting. With gas, I warm it up to 200° and then turn it off. To serve them, intersperse the lemon wedges on a bed of lettuce.

A Caribbean Mini-Vacation for Labor Day

For fifty years the Caribbean people of New York have claimed Labor Day for their own. They gather in Brooklyn for a Mardi Gras–style parade and street fair. Caribbean foods are everywhere. Roasted goat. Sorrel drinks. Roti bread. Grilled fish and fantastic curries. The air is filled with the aroma of grilled foods. The light reflects off the dazzling costumes that people have been making all year. The reggae beat keeps everybody's bootie shakin'. It's one event that brings together all the people of the Caribbean, both English- and French-speakers, and New York's mayor leads the parade.

Perhaps you're too far away to join in come Labor Day. But you can bring the Caribbean flavors home and have your own celebration. All you have to do is put a little reggae on the CD player, pull on your shorts, and make this brightly flavored Caribbean dinner for six on the back patio. Can't find Roti or Cuban bread? Substitute any soft, white bread that's slightly sweet. Some markets sell "Hawaiian" bread that's an Island cousin to Cuban bread. It's a feast that's really fast. You could double or even triple any or all of these recipes with no change in cooking or marinating time.

The Menu

TROPIGRILL CODFISH WITH MANGO-ORANGE SALSA

PIGEON PEAS AND RICE (SEE PAGE 249)

GREEN PAPAYA SLAW

FRUIT ICED TEA

CUBAN BREAD AND ROTI

STEAMED CINNAMON SHERRY CUSTARD

Cooking Tip

You can grill in your kitchen regardless of the weather, using an indoor grill skillet. We love our Le Creuset. Make sure it's squeaky clean, then preheat it over medium-high heat. A quick wipe with oil (don't ever spritz it with cooking spray—it will never come clean), then add the fish, turn the heat down to medium, and grill that fish carefully, turning it only once.

Remember the *10-minutes-to-the-inch rule* for cooking fish (see page 337). Cook skin side *down* no more than 5 minutes, then turn and cook only until the translucent middle looks barely opaque, no more than 3 to 5 minutes. Serve at once.

All the Trimmings

Decorate the table with a basketful of tropical fruits from the market: plantains, starfruit, mangoes, papayas, and bananas. You may want to fill the bottom of the basket with tissue paper and cover the paper with a bright napkin. Now your fruit will really look abundant. Bathe the room in gentle Caribbean music. Use straw place mats with brightly colored aqua, hot pink, and yellow napkins. Greet your guests at the door with a tall cool guava soda or an exotic rum drink decorated with a paper umbrella. Divide the cooked fish into portions about the size of the palm of your hand, about 4 ounces each, and then arrange on dinner plates, along with a dollop of Mango-Orange Salsa, a side of papaya slaw, and a serving of cooked rice. Garnish the plates with sprigs of cilantro.

Tropigrill Codfish

1 1/2 pounds cod (or other firm-fleshed white fish, such as snapper, haddock, or halibut) fillets

Chinese hot pepper oil (available in supermarkets)

1/2 cup cilantro sprigs, plus additional for garnish

1/2 cup fresh mint leaves

1/2 teaspoon salt

1/2 teaspoon freshly ground black pepper

Marinating fish fillets in a few drops of hot pepper oil and fresh herbs gives them a new tropical taste. If you grill outside, scent the fire with a few dried herbs to further intensify the flavor.

PREPARATION TIME: 5 MINUTES

MARINATING TIME: 20 MINUTES MAXIMUM

GRILLING TIME: 10 MINUTES

MAKES 6 SERVINGS

Place fish fillets in a Ziploc bag and sprinkle them with a few drops of hot pepper oil. Add the fresh herb leaves, zip the bag shut, and let it rest on the counter for no longer than 20 minutes.

Just before cooking, preheat the grill—inside or out—and wipe it with oil. Sprinkle salt and pepper on the fish and place the fillets, skin side down, on the grill. Grill about 5 minutes over medium heat, then turn the fish and continue to grill the second side until cooked through, about 3 to 5 minutes. Stab fish with a fork and twist. If the center looks opaque and *not* opalescent, the fish is done. Watch carefully so you don't overcook it. Divide fish into pieces the size of your palm and arrange on plates with salsa.

MANGO-ORANGE SALSA

2 large navel oranges

2 ripe mangoes

1 small red onion, finely chopped

Zest and juice of 2 limes (about ¼ cup juice)

¼ cup finely chopped cilantro

1 to 2 seeded and chopped jalapeño peppers (or to taste)

2 cloves garlic, chopped (1 teaspoon)

Salt and freshly ground black pepper, to taste

PREPARATION TIME: 10 MINUTES

MAKES 2 CUPS

For best flavor development, make the salsa early in the day, cover, and refrigerate it until serving time. Serve at room temperature.

Use a sharp knife to cut away and discard the skin and white pith of the oranges. Hold each orange over a medium bowl to catch the juice and cut the segments from their surrounding membrane, letting the segments fall into the bowl.

Peel and pit the mangoes. Coarsely chop them into the bowl and toss with the oranges. Add the onion, lime zest and juice, cilantro, jalapeños, garlic, and salt and pepper. Toss to mix. Taste and adjust the seasonings. Cover and refrigerate until serving time. For best flavor bring back to room temperature before serving.

Green Papaya Slaw

1$^1/_2$ cups green papaya, peeled and seeded

$^1/_2$ medium red bell pepper, seeded

1 small carrot, scraped

1 small white onion

1 (1$^1/_2$-inch) piece fresh ginger, peeled

Juice and grated zest of 1 lime (about $^1/_8$ cup juice)

$^1/_2$ teaspoon salt

$^1/_2$ teaspoon freshly ground black pepper

The green unripe papaya is useful since that's about all Americans get in the grocery store anyway. The skin color is green, the flesh is pale cream to slightly rosy, and the texture is firm and slightly starchy. Grated with the other ingredients in this slaw it makes a brightly flavored, crunchy salad.

Preparation time: 1 0 minutes

Makes 6 servings

Tastes best if made early in the day, covered, and refrigerated until serving time. Use your food processor for speed grating.

Using a mandoline, box grater, or food processor fitted with the grater blade, grate the papaya, pepper, carrot, onion, and ginger into a bowl, catching all the juice, then toss with lime juice and zest, and seasonings. Cover and refrigerate until serving time.

Steamed Cinnamon Sherry Custard

1¹/₄ cups cream sherry

¹/₄ cup fragrant flower honey

Zest of ¹/₂ lemon

1 (2-inch) piece cinnamon stick

3 large eggs

Whipped cream, sprigs of mint, and/or fresh starfruit slices, for garnish

A pale cream-colored custard brightly flavored with sherry. Quick to fix because it's steamed, it will cool in the refrigerator in 20 minutes.

Preparation time: 5 minutes

Cooking time: 20 minutes

Refrigeration time: 30 minutes

Makes 6 servings

Make this at your convenience in the morning, or even the day before, then cover and refrigerate it until serving time. Serve cold.

Combine the sherry, honey, lemon zest, and cinnamon in a saucepan and heat to boiling over high heat. Reduce the heat and simmer over medium-low heat, uncovered, 10 minutes. Discard the zest and cinnamon.

Meanwhile, whisk the eggs lightly in a medium heatproof bowl. Pour the sherry mixture into the eggs in a stream, whisking constantly. Divide the mixture equally among six custard cups or ramekins.

Place the cups on a steamer rack over simmering water in a large saucepan and lay a piece of waxed paper or foil over the tops of the cups. Cover the pan and steam the custard about 10 minutes, or until it is just set but still jiggles in the middle when shaken gently.

Cool the custards on a rack, then cover and refrigerate until serving time. Top with whipped cream, if you wish, and garnish with a sprig of mint and/or fresh starfruit slices.

Creating a Cheese Course

Chanterelle, one of New York's preeminent haute cuisine French restaurants, located in the TriBeca section of Manhattan, is noted for its outstanding cheese course. Chanterelle offers the widest variety of cheese and is committed to having a cheese course that is equivalent to that of any four-star restaurant in Paris. Taking a seat on a stool in the basement kitchen, we spoke with Lea Batzold, the day manager, who has been tasting, buying, and arranging the cheese course for five years. She shared her experience with us.

Lea, tell us. What makes a good cheese course?
Basically, it starts with the different milks that cheese comes from. There's cow's milk, sheep's milk, and goat's. There's also buffalo, but we don't get into serving that. So, if you're going to do a cheese course, you want at least one or two of each.

What about flavor variety? What kinds of flavors are you after?
The key is that it's almost like wine. The cheeses in a cheese course should have complex flavors. For example, there's this type of cheese from Spain called Cabrol. There's a whole list of tastes you can get from it—you can taste nuts, tobacco, hamburger, cream, fruit, wine—so much just from this one cheese. So there is no particular flavor combination, but you always want interesting cheeses with various flavors.

Does the cheese need to go with what you're serving?

I don't really think so. It's sort of a whole thing of its own, with many flavors on the board itself. On the other hand some people say all you need is just one perfect cheese to serve at a party—which I go along with, too. They do it both ways in France.

When, during the meal, should you serve cheese?

Americans, a lot of times, will have it at the beginning, but that's not the traditional place to serve cheese. The traditional place is after the main course but before the sweets. Or even in place of the sweets. Cheese can get your palate ready for dessert or it can end the meal.

Why?

Well, cheese has a very strong, lingering taste. I mean, if you have a really strong cheese before you start the meal, you're not going to be able to taste anything else. It is also too filling. You don't want your guests to be full before dinner even starts.

How much cheese should a person be served?

We don't give a whole lot in each serving. We just give a little slice that is equal to maybe three or four bites of each type of cheese per person. That way they can have a greater variety of cheeses. You really just want to get the taste to set up the palate for dessert.

One thing we noticed is that Americans tend to serve cheese with bread or crackers. Do you think that's absolutely necessary, or do you think that for a cheese course you can serve just the cheese?

A person can just eat the cheese with a knife and fork without bread, but I don't think Americans will enjoy it as much. The French will be happy with a piece of cheese and a knife and fork. But Americans aren't really like that. At Chanterelle, we make a special kind of bread to go with the cheese, a raisin walnut bread.

Would you recommend something like that for most diners?

Yes. There's a little bit of sweetness in the raisins that complements the cheese. If I were doing a party, I'd have both bread and crackers for people who have to have it.

What do you think is the most wonderful way to present cheese? On what sort of surface?

Well, I can show you pictures of cheese boards in France where there's absolutely no garnish at all—just beautiful cheeses laid out on pristine white marble. A complete minimalist approach to presentation. That can be really beautiful. But we go to great lengths to get these grape leaves to go underneath the cheeses, and lots of grapes for a full and bountiful look. We do always serve on a smooth surface. Wooden mats, like Chinese mats, work too.

Do you only serve your cheese with grapes or do you ever serve it with other fruits?
We pretty much always use grapes, or figs, and sometimes pears or apples.

Do you cut the figs in half when you put them out or do you just let people cut their own?
A beautiful fig looks so great whole. I like to have the waiters pick it up with a fork and put it on a plate in all its glory. But that's just my preference.

Okay. This is sort of an elementary question, but what about serving utensils? How should you serve the cheese to your guests? With a butcher knife?
We serve it with two small sharp knives. The diner's fork is never supposed to touch the serving block of cheese. There are cheese knives that have a prong on the end. A Stilton spoon is used for the gooey Stilton and other blue cheeses.

How would you serve a cheese course at home? Would you pass the cheese board with the two knives or would you serve your guests?
I'd probably serve the guests and pass little plates so that you could encourage everyone to try everything and serve the right small-sized servings. People tend to serve themselves too large a slice when they are unfamiliar with a cheese course. Then, for seconds, I would just pass around the board. That, of course, depends on the size of the board. I would pass the bread in a basket.

Now, let's get down to the composition of the cheese board itself. What cheeses are most popular at Chanterelle?
Well, there are a couple. There's one called Morbier, a washed cheese that's not only delicious, but has a great story behind it. It has ash down the middle of it that separates the morning milk from the evening milk of the cows. They first make the morning milk, then put the ash down—that actually comes off the kettle they cook the stuff in. They take the ash off the kettle and just sort of pat it around the cheese so it makes a line. Then the evening milk goes on top. People really get into that. So our waiters say, "Can you taste the difference?" Some people say they can.

There's also a Spanish cheese that's really terrific called Torta del Casar, which translates as "wedding cake." It's really nice. They make it in a little doily thing so it looks lacy. You cut off the whole top—the rind—and it's so luscious and gloopie you have to serve it with a spoon. It's amazing. That's a 100 percent raw sheep's milk cheese.

What is your favorite cheese-producing region?
Right now, it is Spain. The cheeses are made on farms by artisans, who still make it by hand. They are really great, outstanding in fact. Hard to find but really worth it. Request them from your cheese merchant. There is only one American producer I like. Otherwise I prefer European cheeses.

Are there different cheeses available at different times of year?
Definitely. There's a cheese we have all summer long, actually, that is a Bashram; the Swiss name for it is Monste'or, and it has a whole long story to go along with it. The Swiss were making it, then the French started making it as well, and they got into a huge battle over the rights to the name—you know, that whole *appellation* thing. It's only made from cow's *winter* milk. It only lasts one season, then it's gone. You won't see it again until the next year.

How do you select the cheeses that you serve?
The main thing is to smell it. If it smells like ammonia, you have to sort of think twice. If you get a first whiff of ammonia, you have to wait and see if it's going to dissipate when it's cut. If you smell it again, and the ammonia's gone, then it's okay. But if it keeps on smelling like ammonia, you don't want it.

On the other hand, I heard this lecture by Steve Jenkins, who is the "cheese god" of Manhattan, and he said that if you see a cheese in the market and it's beautiful, the color is uniform, gorgeous and pristine, you don't want it. Cheese has got to be funky, it's got to have mold on it. It's gotta have some character to it.

Unfortunately, most Americans would look at a moldy lumpy cheese and go, "I don't think so." But you really have to educate yourself and your guests. Develop standards and a taste for cheese with character.

How can Americans educate themselves about cheeses?
Go to a place that lets you taste, basically. In France, if you go into a cheese store, you can poke, prod, and pick it up. Smell it. Americans are not really into that, but that's the best way to learn.

Do you go for different varieties and textures on each cheese board?

Definitely. You have a luscious smooth cheese, then you go to a sort of crumbly one, like a blue, then you could go to a pressed cheese, like a good aged Gouda that's really dry, or maybe a Parmesan. So you go from a goopy, really runny cheese that you actually eat with a spoon to a crumbly dry one.

We brought along this list of cheeses that we got out of Ed Edelman's good guidebook, The Ideal Cheese Book. We like this book because it describes a lot of different cheeses and tells us what we need to know about different varieties. Could you point out which of these cheeses you serve at Chanterelle?

Sure, let's see. We find that we can always get people to eat cheese by giving them the facts. We don't serve fresh cheese on the board. But we start with soft ripened cheeses. Camembert. Toma de Carmagnola. Then, in the double and triple crèmes, we always have Explorateur, Gratte Paille. In washed cheeses, we serve Pont l'Evêque, Livarot, Chaumes, Maroilles.

Let's see. The most flavorful, strongest cheeses are really great. In the semisoft cheese category, we offer Reblochon, Fontina, Morbier, Taleggio. Then in the goat cheeses, we buy Ste. Maure, Crottins. The history behind Crottins is that it means gum. They're packed in their tiny gum baskets and they can be all the way from fresh, pure white to so nasty-looking that you would think nobody's going to eat it, yet they're wonderful, really intense. And here—this is my new favorite cheese: Pouligny St. Pierre. I think this is wonderful.

In sheep's milk cheeses, we sell Brin d'Amour, Spanish Manchego de la Sirena, and Torta del Casar—that's the wedding cake one. If you ever see that, you have to have some. Perail de Brebes, and there's this really cool one, Gamomedo. As you can see, we like the Spanish cheeses a lot at Chanterelle. Those last three are all smoked over apple wood.

We overnight-in one American sheep's milk cheese, Sally Jackson from Washington state. It's wrapped in chestnut leaves—so nice.

Then in the blue cheeses, we offer Stilton and Bleu d'Auvergne.

How long do you leave the cheese out of the refrigerator before you serve it?

At least three hours. It definitely has to be at room temperature. There's nothing worse than having cheese right out of the refrigerator. Cold cheese has no subtlety of taste.

Why is that?

Because, like wines that reach their full flavor at room temperature, you don't want to drink them ice cold. The flavor just doesn't come out when it's cold. It's the same with cheese.

The deal is cheese can get older and older . . . as long as it doesn't smell like ammonia.

So, you can buy a bunch and bring it home?
Yes. Just keep it clean, well wrapped, and refrigerated.

And keep a little journal?
Yes, you need to know what kind of things you like. Besides the cheeses I have mentioned,
I will give you a list. (See chart)

Lea's list of Cheeses

type of cheese	name
Soft Ripened	Camembert, Brie, Toma de Carmagnola
Double and Triple Crème Cheeses	Explorateur, St. André Gratte Paille
Washed Cheeses	Pont l' Evêque, Livarot, Chaumes, Maroilles
Semisoft Cheeses	Roblochon, Beaumont, Fontina, Morbier, Tilsit, Monterey Jack, Cream Havarti, String Cheese
Goat Cheeses	Montrachet, Ste-Maure, Crottins, Chèvre
Sheep's Milk Cheeses	Brin d'Amour, Manchego, Torta del Casar, de la Sirena, Perail de Brebis Sally Jackson
Blue Cheeses	Stilton, Bleu

Lea, how long did it take you to become an expert?

I'm nowhere near an expert. The thing that's great about working here is that the customers want the best, so it's easy, you know, a pleasure. We need brilliant cheeses so that we can spoil our customers. Just as you want to serve your guests at home.

You are too modest!

WHERE TO BUY GREAT CHEESES BY MAIL ORDER.

- *Ideal Cheese Shop (imports everything), 1205 Second Avenue, New York, NY 10021, 800-382-0109.*

- *Sally Jackson Cheese Co. (sheep's), Star Route Box 106, Oroville, WA 98844; mail orders only.*

- *Mozzarella Company, 2944 Elm Street, Dallas, TX 75226, 800-798-2954.*

- *Mousehouse Cheeshaus (excellent aged Cheddars), Junction 190—94 and Highway 19, P.O. Box 527, Windsor, WI 53598, 800-526-6873.*

- *Shelburne Farms (farmhouse Cheddar), Shelburne, VT 05482, 802-985-8686.*

- *Sadie Kendall Cheese (goat), P.O. Box 686, Atascadero, CA 93423, 805-466-7252.*

- *Gethsemani Farms, Inc. (washed semisoft), 3642 Monks Road, Trappist, KY 40051, 502-549-3117.*

- *Monastery Country Cheese (Gouda), Our Lady of Angels Monastery, 3365 Monastery Drive, Crozet, VA 68730, 804-823-1452.*

The Bounty of Autumn

Tailgate Hibachi

The day of a big game, tradition dictates that we carry along a hot picnic for a tailgate party. Years ago, we bought a cast-iron double hibachi known as "The Son of Hibachi," which folds into one neat carry-all container. This year, we decided the Son was too rusty to be revived, so we grabbed a disposable portable grill from the supermarket and took that with us to cook the tailgate picnic.

Because this is lawn chair cuisine, we've discovered that pita pockets provide a handy holder for all sorts of foods: the grilled kebabs, the shrimp slaw, and Aunt Helen's beans. For those who are too excited to sit down and eat their lunch from a plate, remember to bring along plenty of pitas so you can open them and fill them with both hot and cold foods.

The Menu

CHIPS AND DIPS

AUNT HELEN'S MEMORIAL BEANS

SPICY SLAW WITH SHRIMP

NORMANDY PORK BROCHETTES

HOT PITA BREAD POCKETS

ICY COLD BEER AND HOT APPLE CIDER

FANCY S'MORES

Cooking Tip

Bring as much of the food as you can already warmed or hot, ready to eat. Just heat it up at home and pack it wrapped in dish towels and foil for makeshift insulation. Carry along a thermos of hot apple cider. Don't try to warm the bulk of the food on the hibachi or the game will be over by the time the cider is ready to drink. Lace the grown-ups' cider with applejack, if you wish.

All the Trimmings

Make a checklist for yourself, so that you don't end up stranded on the asphalt without some necessary item. Remember to bring charcoal, matches, soap, water, paper towels, napkins, plates, cups, ice, lawn chairs, and a stadium blanket or checked tablecloth to throw over a portable table or tailgate. Sunscreen or woolly mittens, depending upon the weather. Parking lot parties are usually stand-up events, so just serve the food buffet-style. The simpler the better. Definitely a paper-plate opportunity.

AUNT HELEN'S MEMORIAL BEANS

1 (1-pound, 12-ounce) can pork and beans

2 thick slices bacon, chopped

1 large green bell pepper, peeled (see page 55), seeded, and chopped

1 small yellow onion, chopped

1 tablespoon light or dark brown sugar

1 tablespoon chili powder

$^1/_2$ cup ketchup

$^1/_2$ cup water

1 small jalapeño pepper, seeded and finely chopped

This recipe has come down in our family through divorce, remarriage, stepchildren, and dowries. We might wish to change partners, but we insist on hanging on to the best recipe for beans this side of Galveston.

PREPARATION TIME: 10 MINUTES

BAKING TIME: 3 HOURS

MAKES 6 SERVINGS

May be cooked a day in advance, covered, and refrigerated overnight. Reheat in a 350° oven for 15 minutes or serve at room temperature.

Preheat the oven to 325°. Stir all the ingredients together in a large ovenproof casserole dish. Bake in the slow oven for 3 hours, stirring from time to time. That's it. Just stand back when your guests dig in. It's that good.

For a large group, say 12 or more, here's a bigger recipe.

2 (1-pound, 12-ounce) cans pork and beans plus 1 (1-pound) can

6 slices bacon, chopped

2 chopped bell peppers—1 red and 1 green

2 large yellow onions, chopped

3 tablespoons brown sugar

2 tablespoons chili powder

1$^1/_2$ cups ketchup

1$^1/_2$ cups water

2 jalapeño peppers, seeded and finely chopped

Preheat the oven to 325°. Mix all the ingredients in a large ovenproof casserole dish and bake 4$^1/_2$ to 5 hours, stirring frequently.

Spicy Slaw with Shrimp

1 head cabbage, red or green, shaved into thin slices (about 6 cups)

$^1/_2$ small red onion (about 1 cup), finely diced

1 small fresh jalapeño pepper, seeded and diced

$^1/_4$ cup chopped cilantro leaves

Juice and zest of 1 lime

$^1/_4$ cup sherry or cider vinegar

1 tablespoon sugar

$^1/_2$ cup extra virgin olive oil

Salt and freshly ground black pepper, to taste

$^1/_2$ cup cooked rock or bay shrimp*

Pita bread

Gulf Coast cooks add shrimp to everything.

* To cook shrimp, film the bottom of a heavy saucepan with oil, add a touch of chopped garlic and the shrimp, and cook over medium-low heat, until the shrimp become opaque, 3 to 5 minutes. Set aside. Alternatively, purchase cooked bay shrimp and toss them in.

May be made a day in advance, covered, and refrigerated. Bring back to room temperature before serving. Add the shrimp at the last minute.

Combine the vegetables and the cilantro in a large bowl and toss with the lime juice and zest. Whisk together the vinegar, sugar, oil, salt, and pepper and toss with the salad. Cover and marinate in the refrigerator for at least 30 minutes or up to 24 hours before serving. Add the shrimp at the last minute. Best served at room temperature in a pita pocket.

NORMANDY PORK BROCHETTES

2 pounds boneless pork tenderloin, cut into
rough $1^{1}/_{2}$-inch pieces

Brandy Marinade

$^{1}/_{3}$ cup extra virgin olive oil

$^{1}/_{3}$ cup pear or apple brandy

1 teaspoon sherry wine vinegar

$^{1}/_{2}$ teaspoon salt

$^{1}/_{8}$ teaspoon ground cloves

4 medium yellow onions, cut into chunks

8 large brown Crimini mushrooms, cut in half

2 large red or green tart apples such as
Granny Smiths, cored and cut into chunks

Sweet hot mustard, commercial or homemade
(see page 302)

Pita breads

These tender, delicate shish kebabs taste great cooked and served from the tailgate. The addition of tart first-of-the-season apples, mushrooms, and sweet onions reminds us that fall is in the air.

PREPARATION TIME: 15 MINUTES

MARINATING TIME: 4 TO 24 HOURS

GRILLING TIME: 15 TO 20 MINUTES

MAKES 6 SERVINGS

Marinate as long as overnight in a Ziploc bag, then transport to the party site, string the cubes onto skewers, and grill just before you're ready to serve.

Place the pork pieces in a large Ziploc bag. Add the marinade ingredients and zip shut. Refrigerate for 4 to 24 hours, turning the bag from time to time.

If you're using bamboo skewers, soak them in water for 30 minutes before skewering the meat. At serving time, preheat a hibachi or charcoal grill until the coals have developed a thin coating of white ash. String the pork pieces onto skewers alternately with the onion wedges, mushrooms, and apples. Brush them with some of the marinade, and place the skewers, sides touching, on the grill. Cook 2 inches above the coals, turning and basting frequently with the remaining marinade, until done to suit, about 15 minutes for medium-rare. At the last moment, dab the skewers with sweet, hot mustard and heat through on both sides. When done, cut the pita breads in half and fill each pocket with meat and vegetables. Dress with additional mustard.

To make Honey Mustard Sauce, simply stir a tablespoon each of minced shallot, cider vinegar, and honey into a quarter cup Dijon mustard, and season to taste with salt and cayenne.

Fancy S'mores

16 whole cinnamon graham crackers

1 (16-ounce) bag marshmallows

8 Toblerone Swiss or your own favorite chocolate bars

Want to see grown men and women with responsible jobs, mortgages, kids' tuition, and grass to cut revert to Scout camp reveries? All you have to do is announce you're serving s'mores for dessert. We do have better-quality chocolate bars available now, and you can use great grahams or even fancy butter cookies for the sandwich part if you wish.

PREPARATION TIME: 5 MINUTES

COOKING TIME: 5 MINUTES

MAKES GENEROUS 8 SERVINGS

This is a do-it-yourself dessert. Hand out grahams, marshmallows, chocolate bars, and coat hangers or skewers (metal or bamboo) to your guests. Lay chocolate pieces onto the graham crackers, then toast the marshmallows on skewers or bent-out wire coat hangers over the dying embers until the marshmallows are cooked to suit—you know how this goes, the obsessive compulsives of your acquaintance will roast and turn them until they're golden, the impatient children will char them black and may even set them on fire and chase others around the parking lot with flaming marshmallows. Once the marshmallows are cooked, layer them onto the chocolate-covered grahams and slam the other half of the grahams on so the whole thing melts and gushes together before you all eat them.

Columbus Day Italian Feast for Six

Though Columbus's famous trip across the Atlantic Ocean was funded by Queen Isabella of Spain in 1492, Columbus himself was from Genoa, Italy. Italian Americans celebrate their own Christopher Columbus to honor the many great accomplishments of Italians throughout the history of the world—first and foremost, the development of one of the world's most pervasive cuisines.

We believe Christopher Columbus would have welcomed this autumn feast after 42 days at sea. We know your friends will. This menu is best when served in the order listed below. A bitter green salad clears the palate before dessert.

The Menu

COLD ANTIPASTI

CRUSTY ITALIAN BREAD

RISOTTO WITH PORCINI, TOMATOES, AND PROSCIUTTO

ITALIAN CHICKEN CUTLETS

ARUGULA WITH GARLIC VINAIGRETTE

ZABAGLIONE

BISCOTTI AND/OR FRESH FRUIT

Wine Suggestions

Appetizer and Main Course—Italian Barbera. Sangiovese, the grape used in Chianti and Brunello also fits the bill here. Italian wines are always the perfect complement to Italian food. The flavors of the cuisine and of the wine evolved together over time. The high acid quality of the Barbera will cut the creamy risotto and chicken cutlets. On the other hand, the sweet yet spicy Sangiovese will also complement these dishes. Bon appetito!

All the Trimmings

The ingredients for the antipasti are beautiful on their own. For the most dramatic effect, use medium-size plates and put only one ingredient on each. The beauty is in the simplicity of the design. We serve this meal family-style: Mound the risotto on a platter and serve the chicken cutlets on a side dish with a lemon wedge. After all, that is the Italian way. The salad comes last, just before the dessert.

COLD ANTIPASTI

Basic Antipasti for Six

$1/2$ pound prosciutto (thinly sliced at the deli)

$1/2$ pound mortadella (thinly sliced at the deli)

$1/2$ pound Genoa salami (thinly sliced)

$1/2$ pound cappacola (thinly sliced)

2 (6-ounce) cans albacore tuna, drained and dressed with lemon juice, olive oil, and capers (only buy best-quality Italian tuna)

$1/2$ pound provolone cheese, thinly sliced

$1/2$ pound mozzarella cheese, thinly sliced

Hard-cooked eggs, shelled and quartered

2 (12-ounce) jars roasted red peppers drained and tossed in a little red wine vinegar

1 (1-pound jar) pepperoncini, drained

$1/2$ pound Kalamata olives

$1/2$ pint Caponata

1 red onion, thinly sliced

12-ounces olive salad

Antipasti is easy and beautiful. A good deli provides the ingredients, all you have to do is assemble them. Count on $1/2$ pound of food per person, divided among meats, fish, cheeses, and vegetables. So, for six people, you will need a total of 3 pounds, about $1^1/2$ pounds of meat and cheese and an equal quantity of vegetables—give or take. Mix and match ingredients until you have a total of three pounds. For drama, serve each item on its own plate. The bounty will wow your guests.

Risotto with Porcini, Tomatoes, and Prosciutto

2¹/₂ cups water, very hot from the tap

¹/₂ ounce dried porcini mushrooms

3 tablespoons extra virgin olive oil

1 medium onion, chopped

2 cups Arborio rice (or Vialone, Nano, or Carnaroli)

1 (15-ounce) can chicken broth

1 cup dry white wine

6 plum tomatoes, coarsely chopped

¹/₂ cup coarsely chopped prosciutto

¹/₂ cup freshly grated Parmesan cheese

Salt and freshly ground black pepper, to taste

Though there are many variations in the ingredients and broths used in a risotto (see suggestions below), the method for cooking it always stays roughly the same. While cooking the risotto in the microwave doesn't reduce the cooking time, it does eliminate the constant stirring and attention you must give it when made on the stovetop. We know that many Italian mothers disapprove of cooking risotto in the microwave, but just remember that Christopher Columbus would never have found the New World had he not embraced new technologies and gone against conventional wisdom.

Do not substitute long-grain rice for the Arborio or you may end up with rice paste. Arborio is a patented variety of Italian short-grain rice, though there are some producers of an American version of this variety. Most supermarket gourmet sections will have Arborio rice.

PREPARATION TIME: 10 MINUTES

COOKING TIME: ABOUT 30 MINUTES

MAKES 6 SERVINGS

In a ceramic microwavable bowl, combine the water and the porcini mushrooms and microwave on high (100 percent power), uncovered, for 3 minutes. Set aside to soak. Combine the olive oil, onion, and rice in a large ceramic microwavable bowl, and heat, uncovered, in the microwave on high (100 percent power) for 5 minutes stirring once. Stir in the chicken broth and white wine and microwave, uncovered, for 12 minutes. Add the water the mushrooms were soaked in, reserving the mushrooms, and microwave 12 more minutes. Add the mushrooms, tomatoes, prosciutto, Parmesan cheese, salt and pepper to taste, and additional water if needed to maintain a thick, soupy consistency. Microwave for 3 minutes, uncovered, at 100 percent power. If you have a small 400-watt microwave, you may need to cook the risotto longer—a minute or so—at each step.

To cook the risotto conventionally, brown the rice and onion in the oil, stirring, until the rice is golden, about 3 minutes. Add broth, mushroom liquid, and wine in small increments, allowing the rice time to absorb most of the liquid before you stir in more. Once the rice is tender to the bite, add the mushrooms, tomatoes, prosciutto, cheese, and salt and pepper to taste. This process takes about 30 to 45 minutes altogether, with lots of tender, loving stirring from you.

OTHER RISOTTO ADDITIONS:

Stir these in during the last 10 minutes cooking time.

Zucchini, tomatoes, Italian sausage

Olive and eggplant

Shrimp, peas, and saffron

Pesto and breast of chicken

Shredded duck breast and dried cranberries

Asparagus and wild spring mushrooms

Sun-dried tomatoes, basil, and goat cheese

Mussels, oysters, and fish broth

Pumpkin, sausage, and nutmeg

ITALIAN CHICKEN CUTLETS

6 chicken cutlets (a cutlet is half a skinless and boneless breast pounded out for uniform ¹/₂-inch thickness)

³/₄ cup dry Italian bread crumbs

¹/₄ cup freshly grated Parmesan cheese

Salt and freshly ground black pepper, to taste

2 large eggs

¹/₂ cup peanut oil

6 lemon wedges, for garnish

According to one of our Italian authorities, Debra Pucci, Italian American families eat chicken cutlets at least once a week. After trying her mother's recipe we can see why. And she says to try the leftovers cold with ketchup. We can sometimes buy the cutlets cooked at an Italian deli. That saves a step. Try your deli and see. Of course, most Italians claim that their mother makes the best cutlets!

PREPARATION TIME:	10 MINUTES
COOKING TIME:	10 MINUTES
MAKES 6 SERVINGS	

May be made up to 1 day in advance and reheated in the microwave for 30 seconds or so, or uncovered in a 350° oven for 5 to 8 minutes.

If the butcher has not pounded out the cutlets, pound them between sheets of waxed paper with a mallet or the side of a rolling pin so that they are all the same thickness. In a bowl, combine the bread crumbs, Parmesan, salt, and pepper. In another bowl, beat the eggs. Dip the cutlets in the eggs, then in the bread crumb mixture. Preheat the oil over medium-high heat for about 2 minutes. Cook the cutlets about 5 minutes on each side, or until the juices run clear. Serve them with the lemon wedges.

ARUGULA WITH GARLIC VINAIGRETTE

Vinaigrette:

1/8 cup red wine vinegar

1 clove garlic, crushed

1 tablespoon seeded mustard

3/8 cup extra virgin olive oil

Salt and freshly ground black pepper, to taste

2 bunches arugula (about 2 pounds), washed and dried

PREPARATION TIME:	5 MINUTES
MAKES 6 SERVINGS	

The vinaigrette can be made up to 3 days in advance, covered, and refrigerated.

In the serving bowl, combine the vinegar, garlic, and mustard, whisking constantly. Add the oil in a thin stream, then salt and pepper to taste. No more than one hour before serving, rest the arugula leaves on top. Cover and refrigerate until serving time. Toss just before serving.

Zabaglione

6 egg yolks

$^1/_2$ cup sugar

1 cup Marsala wine

Biscotti and/or fresh fruit, for serving

This is one of the easiest custards/sauces you can make. Try substituting Grand Marnier or other liqueurs, and serving it over different fruit combos. Or just have it with biscotti.

PREPARATION TIME: 3 MINUTES

COOKING TIME: 3 TO 4 MINUTES

MAKES 6 SERVINGS

May be made 2 days in advance.

In a metal bowl, whisk together the egg yolks, sugar, and Marsala. Set the bowl over a pan of simmering water and continue to beat for about 3 to 4 minutes (or until an instant thermometer reads 140°). The sauce should be frothy, doubled in bulk, and thick enough that the whisk leaves a path in the bottom of the bowl. Do not overcook it or you will end up with scrambled eggs. Remove from the heat and continue to whisk for 1 minute. Refrigerate until ready to use. Serve in balloon goblets with biscotti or fresh fruit.

Zabaglione Fruit/Liqueur Combinations:

Pear liqueur and pears

Grand Marnier, oranges, and toasted almonds

Cassis and black cherries

Calvados with pears and apples

Sherry with strawberries

White wine with ginger and pineapple

Peach schnapps with mangoes

A Warm Picnic for Leaf Peepers

Whether you live in the Northeast or the West, you must take a Saturday drive in autumn to look at the leaves. We meandered on a lazy loop from southern Oregon down through northern California and back along the Pacific Coast, oohing and ahing at the crimson and golden leaves nestled in the mixed conifer forest in our steep Siskiyou Mountains. Here's a picnic for six that can be made and packed in less than an hour.

The Menu

MARINATED VIDALIA ONIONS (SEE PAGE 218)

NOT! NEW ENGLAND FISH CHOWDER

SAFFRON NASTURTIUM RICE SALAD

STUFFED MUSHROOMS (SEE PAGE 244)

DARK RYE BREAD

CHEESE COURSE (SEE PAGE 287)

FRESH FALL APPLES AND PEARS

SHORTBREAD COOKIES

Wine Suggestions

Appetizer and Main Course—This peppery fish dish cries out for a California Zinfandel. The peppery, spicy, smoky wine is the perfect complement. Ask your wine dealer to recommend a good one. Or you could go with a rich California Chardonnay. This dish is strong enough to stand up to these big wines.

Cooking Tip

Choosing the right fish to cook is an acquired skill. Begin by dealing only with a reputable fishmonger. Take a big whiff of the air. If you get the scent of ammonia, find another store. Once you've picked your market, make friends with the owner. Only buy fish that's displayed on ice, never in the meat section refrigerator case on a Styrofoam tray under plastic. (Fillets should be on an open tray set on the ice, so the flesh isn't "burned.") Take a close look at the fish fillets. The grain of the fish should be tight, not "gaping." The smell of the fish should be fresh, with no fishiness or traces of ammonia. In fish language that's called rot and indicates an appropriate use as lobster bait. When we have a choice of fish to choose from for a recipe, as for the chowder, we ask our fishmonger what was delivered that day and make our pick from those. If you're planning to cut the fish into chunks, you'll find that half-frozen fish is easier to deal with and yields more uniform pieces. The skin should be removed before cooking so that you don't have to fish it out of the stew before serving.

The fish for a stew should be added last and cooked the least amount of time—only until the flesh loses its pearly opalescence and begins to look opaque. Even in liquid, overcooked fish is dry and hard to chew and swallow.

All the Trimmings

Table decorations for al fresco autumn dining could come right from the woods. What's more gorgeous than brilliant crimson and golden leaves gathered by you, right on the spot? It's the best use of these leaves, since their color fades rather quickly anyway. This meal is best served buffet-style. Pour the soup into mugs. Mugs are best for the soup because they help hold the heat. Pack the rice salad down into a bowl when you make it, then unmold it onto a platter at the picnic site. Garnish with a few extra nasturtiums. Surround the molded rice with a ring of stuffed mushrooms. Arrange the apples and pears with wedges of cheese on a disposable tray lined with grape leaves—real or paper—or some red-tipped lettuce. Don't forget a sharp paring knife to cut the fruit, and a cheese knife to pull across the top of these firm cheeses to yield uniform thin slices to serve on the fruit wedges. One of those apple cutters shaped like a circle that cuts five wedges and cores the fruit in one step is always welcome.

To cut down on dishwashing, use colorful throwaway plates and platters. We do, however, draw the line at glassware. For a terrific fall Chardonnay we prefer wineglasses. We also like cloth napkins. Cotton napkins can be used to cushion the glasses in the picnic basket, then to wipe up crumbs and spills.

Not! New England Fish Chowder

3 tablespoons extra virgin olive oil

1 medium yellow onion, finely chopped (about 1 cup)

1 stalk celery, minced

1 teaspoon chili powder

1 (16-ounce) can tomatoes with their juice, cut in bite-size pieces (see Cooking Tip, page 313)

3/4 cup water

1 teaspoon salt

1 teaspoon sugar

1 tablespoon Worcestershire sauce

1 1/2 pounds firm-fleshed fish fillets (such as cod, halibut, bluefish, grouper, salmon, snapper, or rockfish)

1/4 cup minced flat-leaf parsley

A thermos of this hot fish chowder makes a warming lunch in a roadside park and can anchor the menu on a dinner table. While New England chowder is milk-based, and Manhattan chowder is tomato-based, this Gulf Coast tomato-based chowder has the Southern distinction of being perked up with a pinch of chili powder and sugar, which you can't really taste but which makes the flavor sing. The chowder is made quickly—a nod to hot Southern kitchens and the wish to get in and out in a hurry.

Preparation time: 15 minutes

Cooking time: 15 minutes

Makes 6 servings

Best if made and eaten the same day. May be made early and stored in a thermos until ready to serve.

Heat the oil in a heavy soup pot over medium heat. Add the onion, celery, and chili powder, and sauté until the onion is translucent, about 5 minutes. Stir in the tomatoes and their juice, the water, salt, sugar, and Worcestershire sauce, and bring to a rolling boil. Cut the fish into bite-size chunks and add it to the boiling liquid. Reduce the heat and simmer until the fish turns opaque, up to 15 minutes. Sprinkle with the parsley and transfer to a thermos or soup tureen until serving time. Serve in mugs, hot cups, or soup bowls.

Rather than having tomatoes floating around whole in the soup, we prefer to cut them up to bite-size. The easiest way to cut up canned tomatoes is with a pair of scissors right in the can. We keep a few pairs in the kitchen to avoid that frustrating moment when one pair might be misplaced.

SAFFRON NASTURTIUM RICE SALAD

1 cup basmati rice

2 cups water

Salt, to taste

¼ teaspoon saffron threads

1 medium red onion, finely chopped (about 1 cup)

3 tablespoons extra virgin olive oil

1 small fennel bulb, finely chopped (about 1 cup)

1 cup chopped raw almonds

2 tablespoons butter

3 tablespoons sherry vinegar

Freshly ground black pepper, to taste

2 tablespoons pesticide-free nasturtium petals, torn (or substitute marigolds or calendulas), or dried bell pepper flakes

Here's a glorious, fragrant, golden salad that is eminently flexible. Serve it hot, at room temperature, or cold. It looks good. It tastes good. Peppery nasturtium or marigold petals sprinkled on top add not only a saturated ocher color but a surprising tang. If your local market doesn't sell pesticide-free edible flowers, substitute colorful dried bell pepper flakes. Try molding the rice in a Bundt pan overnight. It looks great.

PREPARATION TIME:	15 MINUTES
COOKING TIME:	20 MINUTES
MARINATING TIME:	30 MINUTES TO 24 HOURS

MAKES 6 SERVINGS

Make it a day in advance, or right before serving.

Cook the rice in 2 cups salted water with the saffron, either in a rice cooker or in a covered pot over medium heat—about 20 minutes. Stir a couple of times to distribute the saffron.

Reserve $1/4$ cup of the onion for garnish. While the rice cooks, heat the oil in a large skillet over medium heat and sauté the remaining onion and the fennel until tender and golden, about 10 minutes. Remove to a large salad bowl. Brown the almonds in the butter in the same skillet, stirring, and add them to the onion/fennel mixture.

Add the cooked rice to the bowl and mix with the vinegar. Adjust the seasonings with salt and pepper, and mash the rice down into the bowl. Refrigerate 30 minutes to overnight. You can also mold the rice in a Bundt pan. Unmold it onto a platter and top with the nasturtium petals and reserved chopped red onion. Serve immediately or cover and refrigerate. May be served hot, cold, or at room temperature.

An Ode to Halloween for Kids of All Ages

Halloween is a holiday celebrated not only by kids but by grown-ups as well. Here's an easy party to entertain friends after or *instead of* the traditional trick-or-treat. We start with best-quality premade products: Italian bread, prepared carrot and celery sticks, as well as radishes and a jug of apple cider. We set the mood at the front door with a big jack-o'-lantern on the porch.

The Menu

JACK-O'-LANTERN MOLE IN A PUMPKIN TUREEN WITH
HOT FLOUR TORTILLAS

GRAVEYARD BONES AND SKULLS
(CARROT AND CELERY STICKS)

SQUID INK PASTA WITH ORANGE PEPPERS AND LOX

QUESADILLAS WITH ROASTED GARLIC

SPIDERWEB BROWNIE CAKE

ICY APPLE CIDER WITH OR WITHOUT APPLEJACK

COLD BEER

All the Trimmings

You can decorate the spiderweb cake easily using a plastic mustard dispenser from the dime store instead of a pastry bag. Make frozen ghostly ice "hands" by putting water into plastic gloves the day before and freezing them. Then peel off the gloves and float them in a punch bowl brimming with applejack-laced icy spicy apple cider.

Mark the path to your front door with lunch bag paper luminarias. Luminarias are easily made by putting a little sand in the bottom of lunch sacks. Nestle a candle inside and light it with a match. Voíla. Let there be light. Inside, light black candles from one end of the house to the other. The quesadillas can be served in the living room during the cocktail hour. Serve the soup with a garnish of piped sour cream and a sprig of cilantro. Serve the pasta on a large platter to be passed with another platter of the bones and skulls (celery and carrots)! Clear the table and bring in the cake.

You're Invited!

Whether you're calling people up or sending out written invitations, please, please, make costumes optional. As Joe Eckhardt says, "Gawd, how I hate to be crammed into some monkey suit." Leave it up to the guests to decide what they want to wear.

Jack-o'-Lantern Mole

2 teaspoons extra virgin olive oil

1 large yellow onion, finely chopped

4 cloves garlic, chopped (2 teaspoons)

1 whole chicken breast (about 8 ounces), skinned, boned, and finely chopped

3 tablespoons chili powder (or to taste)

1 jalapeño pepper, seeded and minced

2 chipotle chili peppers (dried smoked) (optional)

1 (15-ounce) can chopped tomatoes and their juice

2 (15-ounce) cans chicken broth plus 2 cans water

2 (15-ounce) cans plain pumpkin puree

1 ounce (1 square) unsweetened chocolate

Salt and freshly ground black pepper, to taste

6 ounces queso fresco (Mexican white cottage-style cheese), crumbled or grated

Fresh cilantro leaves, for garnish, plus whole sprigs for garnish (optional)

Toasted sesame seeds, for garnish

Low-fat sour cream, for garnish

Served in its natural pumpkin tureen, this soup makes a terrific centerpiece for a party sideboard. Dried chipotles are available wherever Hispanic groceries are found, or from Mo Hotta-Mo Betta 1-800-462-3220.

Preparation time:	15 minutes
Cooking time:	40 minutes
Makes 10 to 12 generous servings	

The soup may be made up to 3 days in advance and refrigerated, covered, until serving time. Reheat it on the stovetop or in the microwave, then transfer it to the roasted pumpkin tureen to serve.

In a large stew pot, heat the oil and sauté the onion and garlic with the chicken over medium-low heat until the onion is golden, about 5 minutes. Sprinkle with the chili powder and sauté 1 minute or so. Add the peppers and tomatoes with their juice and cook 5 more minutes. Add the broth, water, pumpkin, and chocolate and simmer over low heat for 30 minutes or so, stirring occasionally. Puree the soup using a wand, a blender, or a food processor. Taste and adjust the seasonings with salt and pepper to taste. Cover and refrigerate until serving time. Reheat in a soup pot over medium heat to boiling, then transfer to the roasted pumpkin serving bowl set on a tray.

To serve, ladle the hot soup into mugs or bowls, add a generous pinch of cheese, then top with cilantro, sesame seeds, and a dollop of sour cream. For a more interesting presentation, pipe the sour cream on in concentric circles, using a ketchup dispenser, then use a toothpick to connect the circles for a spiderweb look. A sprig of cilantro can float in the center.

Pumpkin Tureen

1 (4- to 5-pound) pumpkin (or winter squash)   Salt and freshly ground black pepper, to taste
1 tablespoon milk

Preparation time:	10 minutes
Cooking time:	45 minutes
Makes 1 pumpkin tureen	

May be made 2 hours early.

Preheat the oven to 375°. Cut off the pumpkin top and scrape out the seeds. Rinse out the inside with the milk. Salt and pepper the inside of the pumpkin generously. Replace the top and roast for 45 minutes. Alternatively, microwave the pumpkin on high (100 percent power) for 15 minutes or until tender.

Squid Ink Pasta with Orange Peppers and Lox

5 quarts water

3 tablespoons salt

1/4 cup extra virgin olive oil

9 cloves garlic, chopped (2 tablespoons)

2 pounds dry black squid ink pasta (linguine, fettuccine, or spaghetti)

2 orange bell peppers, peeled, seeded, and cut into thin strips

2 (7-ounce) jars Italian roasted red peppers, drained and cut into thin strips

1/2 pound lox or smoked salmon, cut into thin strips

1/2 cup chopped cilantro, plus whole sprig for garnish

Spooky black pasta tossed with quickly sautéed orange bell peppers and smoked salmon not only maintains a black-and-orange theme, but also provides a complex, rich flavor and a new look at pasta salad. The squid pasta is available at specialty food stores or by mail from Gaston Dupré, 1-800-937-9445. Lox or smoked salmon can be found at specialty food stores or the smoked salmon can be mail ordered from Siletz Tribal Smokehouse, 1-800-828-4269. Serve it on a platter and let your guests help themselves.

PREPARATION TIME: 5 MINUTES

COOKING TIME: 5 TO 8 MINUTES

MAKES 10 TO 12 FIRST-COURSE SERVINGS

Tastes best if made and served immediately.

In a large soup pot, bring 5 quarts of water to a boil with 3 tablespoons of salt. Meanwhile, in a bowl large enough for all of the ingredients to be tossed later, combine the olive oil and chopped garlic. Cook in microwave on high (100 percent power) for 3 to 4 minutes until the garlic is golden brown. (Alternatively, cook the oil and garlic in a small skillet for about 3 minutes, then transfer it to the bowl.) Cook the pasta in the boiling water for 3 to 8 minutes, or to desired doneness. Drain the pasta and toss it with the garlic oil and all the remaining ingredients, except the garnish. Serve on a large platter with a sprig of cilantro in the middle.

QUESADILLAS WITH ROASTED GARLIC

4 large heads garlic

Extra virgin olive oil

Salt and freshly ground black pepper, to taste

1 tablespoon freshly chopped chives

2 tablespoons unsalted butter

12 (8-inch) flour tortillas

$1/2$ pound crumbled queso fresco (Mexican white cottage-style cheese)

Fresh Italian flat-leaf parsley leaves, for garnish

Buy first-quality flour tortillas, a couple heads of good garlic, and you're on your way to an easy hors d'oeuvre.

PREPARATION TIME: 10 MINUTES

COOKING TIME: 45 MINUTES

MAKES 18 TO 20 APPETIZERS

Best if cooked and eaten immediately.

Preheat the oven to 400°. Cut the tops off the garlic heads and place them in an ovenproof bowl. Drizzle olive oil down into each head, then sprinkle them with salt and freshly ground black pepper. Cover with foil and roast until tender, about 45 minutes. Let the garlic cool a few moments, then wrap a paper towel around each head and squeeze out the soft garlic into a bowl. Mix with the chopped chives and butter to spread onto the quesadillas.

Preheat a large skillet and drizzle it with olive oil. Add one large tortilla. Spread the tortilla with the garlic mixture, then top it with a pinch of cheese and flat-leaf parsley leaves. Place a second tortilla on top and cook over medium-high heat until the bottom tortilla is golden, about 4 to 5 minutes. Press down with the back of a spatula to "glue" the two parts together, then flip it and cook the second side until golden, about 3 minutes.

Remove to a cutting board and cut into 8 wedges. Serve warm.

Spiderweb Brownie Cake

3 large egg whites

1 cup sugar

1 teaspoon vanilla extract

$^1/_4$ cup vegetable oil

$^1/_4$ cup plain nonfat yogurt

$^1/_4$ teaspoon salt

$^1/_4$ teaspoon baking powder

$^1/_3$ cup unsweetened cocoa powder

$^1/_2$ cup unbleached all-purpose flour

Frosting

2 cups confectioners' sugar

2 tablespoons skim milk

1 teaspoon unsweetened cocoa powder

The traditional Halloween cake that kids want is called a spiderweb cake. Stir together a low-fat, one-layer brownie cake and frost it with a simple powdered sugar icing, then decorate it with a spiderweb piped from a plastic ketchup dispenser instead of a pastry bag. Use a brownie mix if you're in a hurry, or stir together this easy brownie cake.

PREPARATION TIME:	10 MINUTES
BAKING TIME:	25 MINUTES
MAKES 8 SERVINGS	

Can be made 1 day in advance.

Preheat the oven to 375°. Spritz a 12-inch-round deep-dish pizza pan or a cake pan with cooking spray and set it aside.

In a medium bowl, combine the egg whites, sugar, vanilla, oil, yogurt, salt, baking powder, and cocoa, beating with an electric mixer after each addition. Finally, sprinkle the flour over the mixture and barely beat, just until the flour dissolves.

Pour the mixture into the prepared pan, smoothing the batter evenly. Bake until the center is cooked and a toothpick inserted in the center comes out clean, about 25 minutes, then remove to a rack and cool completely in the pan.

In a medium bowl, combine the sugar and milk and beat until smooth. Spread three quarters of this mixture onto the cooled cake. Beat cocoa into the last portion of frosting and scoop this frosting into a ketchup dispenser. Squeeze the dispenser to pipe a "spider-web" onto the cake, beginning in the middle and piping a continuous circle of brown frosting over the top. Use a wooden skewer to drag lines from row to row, making the "spider-web" pattern.

This cake is dense with flavor and looks great cut into equilateral triangles.

Garnish Suggestions:

How about a big, hairy-legged plastic spider bought at the dime store and placed on top of the cake. Or, twist black pipe cleaners into 8-legged hairy spiders and rest them on the cake.

Navy Beans and Army Greens: A Veterans Day Lunch

This purely American holiday was started to commemorate the Armistice of World War I. Linda's great aunt Esther, who is ninety-five this year, always calls it "Decoration Day." In the past, people decorated the graves of fallen soldiers on this eleventh day of November. You may have seen solemn veterans selling red paper lapel poppies, but you probably never thought—nor did we—about the significance of those red flowers.

Remember the poem "In Flanders fields, the poppies blow, between the crosses, row on row"? France, home to the poppy, became the last resting place for a generation of young men—mostly European, but a number of Americans as well.

Today, you can take this day of rest to have some friends over, decorate with red poppies, and enjoy a simple, peaceful lunch.

The Menu

NEW SENATORS' NAVY BEAN SOUP

FENNEL, RADICCHIO, AND BLOOD ORANGE SALAD

HOTCHA CORN BREAD MUFFINS (SEE PAGE 69)

DEEP-DISH CRUMBLE-TOP APPLE PIE

Wine Suggestions

Main Course—In honor of the role that Alsace played in World War I, the war that started Veterans Day, try an Alsatian Pinot Blanc, Tokay, or Riesling. You will not only be historically correct, but any of these white Alsatians, with their fruity flavors, will marry well with the ham-flavored soup.

Cooking Tip:
Picking the Right Apples to Cook With

Apples for cooking hold their shape and have a tart taste. Depending on the part of the country, different varieties become available as the apple season progresses. You can buy great cooking apples all year long, because they store better than the softer eating apples and are brought to market from cold storage warehouses 12 months a year. Among the good cooking apples are: Stayman-Winesap, Cortland, Jonathan, Rhode Island Greening, McIntosh, Macoun, York Imperial, Northern Spy, Newtown Pippin, Yellow Transparent, Rome Beauty, Baldwin, Wealthy, and Gravenstein—and our all-time favorite for both cooking and eating, the Granny Smith.

All the Trimmings

Red poppies, the fresh kind, may be quite impossible to find in November, but you can suggest the origin of the holiday with paper poppies from the American Legion or the VFW. Locate the flag napkins left over from the Fourth of July and your table is ready. Casual dishes work well. After all, this is meant to be a quiet gathering with close friends. Preset the table with the soup. Pass the corn bread and salad.

New Senators' Navy Bean Soup

3 medium onions, finely chopped

4 cloves garlic, chopped (2 teaspoons)

3 stalks celery, finely chopped

1 tablespoon extra virgin olive oil

2 smoked ham hocks

4 (1-pound, 16-ounce) cans navy beans, rinsed and drained (or 1 pound dry beans soaked and cooked until tender in barely salted water according to package directions)

3 quarts water

1 cup cooked mashed potatoes

1/2 cup finely chopped flat-leaf parsley, plus additional sprigs for garnish

Salt and freshly ground black pepper, to taste

They say you should never watch laws or sausage being made—the process is too slow and cumbersome to be endured—but you can speed up making the U.S. Senate's most famous soup by cranking open cans of navy beans to begin.

PREPARATION TIME: 15 MINUTES

COOKING TIME: 60 MINUTES

MAKES 8 TO 10 SERVINGS

Not only can you make this soup before time, you'll be glad you did. The flavors improve the second day. Store covered in the refrigerator and reheat stovetop over medium heat to boiling, or in the microwave for 3–4 minutes.

In a large stew pot over medium-high heat, sauté the onions, garlic, and celery in the oil with the ham hocks until the onions turn translucent, about 5 minutes. Add the cooked navy beans and the water and simmer about 1 hour. Lift the ham hocks from the soup and debone. Tear the meat into bite-size chunks and return it to the soup. Stir in the mashed potatoes, parsley, and salt and pepper to taste. Serve hot. Garnish each serving with additional sprigs of parsley.

Fennel, Radicchio, and Blood Orange Salad

1 medium bulb fennel, chopped (4 cups plus 1 cup chopped green feathery tops)

1 head radicchio, chopped (2 cups)

2 large sweet blood oranges, peeled, seeded, and chopped, with their juice (or seedless navel oranges)

¼ cup extra virgin olive oil

Be sure you add the orange juice to the mixing bowl. It combines with the olive oil to make a delicate, flavorful dressing.

PREPARATION TIME: 1 0 MINUTES

MAKES 8 SERVINGS

May be prepared 3 hours in advance, covered, and refrigerated.

Combine the fennel, radicchio, oranges and their juice in a large bowl and toss to mix. Pour the oil over all and toss. Cover and refrigerate until serving time.

DEEP-DISH CRUMBLE-TOP APPLE PIE

Pie Filling:

$1/2$ cup each: firmly packed light or dark brown sugar and granulated sugar

$1/4$ teaspoon freshly grated nutmeg

1 teaspoon ground cinnamon

$1/4$ teaspoon salt

3 tablespoons all-purpose flour

8 tart cooking apples (such as Granny Smith or pippin), cored and sliced

Juice and zest of $1/2$ lemon

Crumble Crust:

$1/4$ each: firmly packed light or dark brown sugar and granulated sugar

$3/4$ cup all-purpose flour

$1/4$ cup uncooked oatmeal

$1/4$ cup ($1/2$ stick) soft butter, cut up

1 pint cream, for serving

Nothing is more American, and if you forget about making a piecrust or peeling the apples, and if you use one of those round apple cutters that both cores and segments the apple in one quick motion, you can have this pie ready for the oven in no time flat. Serve it in a dessert dish with a pitcher of cream handy for those who like their lilies gilded.

PREPARATION TIME:	10 MINUTES
BAKING TIME:	45 MINUTES

MAKES 8 SERVINGS

Make this a day in advance if you think you can keep people from eating it until you're ready to serve.

Preheat the oven to 350°. Spritz a 3-quart deep dish pie pan with cooking spray. Combine the sugars, nutmeg, cinnamon, salt, and flour in a small bowl and toss to mix. Add the cut apples to the baking dish. Pour the lemon juice and zest over the apples and toss to mix. Add the sugar-flour mixture and toss to mix. Using the same small bowl, stir together sugars, flour, and oatmeal for the crumble crust. Add the butter and rub the dry ingredients into the butter to form a mixture that resembles coarse crumbs. Sprinkle the crumbs over the apples. Bake until the crumble is brown, about 45 minutes. Cool on a rack.

To serve, spoon the pie into individual dessert dishes and pass the cream.

Laid-Back Thanksgiving Feast for Ten

Of all the holidays that are truly American, Thanksgiving stands out. And while the Pilgrims may have whooped it up with the Indians, who, as we understand it, did most of the bringing in of the sheaves, today things are different.

About all we have time to bring in are our paychecks and our tired, overworked bodies. This should be a day of rest and great food, with maybe a football game thrown in for good measure. The trick is to make it a day of rest for the cook as well.

If you use our easy, trouble-free, laid-back turkey recipe, and ask your guests to kick in on the side dishes and condiments, you won't have to think about the dinner from the time the bird starts roasting until about an hour before serving. Those who can't cook, or have no time at all, get to bring the wine, the bakery bread, and the pies. Thanksgiving inspires our country's best professional bakers. Order a pumpkin pie or your favorite dessert *du jour.* Ask for great rustic breads, maybe some fresh flowers, and you're almost ready to go. And don't fail to solicit volunteers to wash the dishes. After all, what are noncooks good for if not cleaning up?

The Menu

PERSIMMONS AND SALTY GORGONZOLA ON CRUSTY FRENCH BREAD

PUMPKIN TORTELLINI WITH CILANTRO, GARLIC, AND CORN DRESSING

LAID-BACK TURKEY WITH FRAGRANT LILY STUFFING
AND TAWNY PORT GRAVY

ROASTED ROOT VEGETABLES

ROASTED GARLIC MASHED POTATOES

FRESH CRANBERRY CITRUS RELISH

COUNTRY BREAD AND BUTTER

OLD-FASHIONED PUMPKIN PIE AND CRANBERRY TARTS
WITH VANILLA ICE CREAM

Wine Suggestions

Appetizer—In honor of our forebears, try a Verdelho Madeira. Just before the Revolutionary War, as a form of protest against the British, Americans drank Madeira. Unlike sherry, which came through British ports and was therefore taxed, Madeira, imported straight from the island of Madeira, was not taxed. Verdelho Madeira is the best for an appetizer because it is only slightly sweet and will work nicely with the persimmons and Gorgonzola.

Main Course—A fun wine to serve at this time of year is a Beaujolais Nouveau. This partially fermented wine is released on the third Thursday of November and has become an event in and of itself. It is a fruity, amusing wine that is great for Thanksgiving. Just ignore the turkey. Match the wine to the side dishes. They're what makes the dinner great anyway. You don't want a subtle wine with all those classic American sweet side dishes: cranberry sauce, sweet potatoes, jiggly Jell-O salads. You want youth and beauty. The new wine of the season is made to order. But drink it before Christmas. It is not designed to last more than 2 months.

Dessert—From France's Languedoc, a dessert jurançon. The caramel flavors of the wine will complement the pumpkin flavors. You can't go wrong.

Cooking Tip

When buying a turkey, figure about 1 pound per serving, if you want some leftovers for great turkey sandwiches the next day. For a party of ten, choose an 11- to 12-pound bird. If you buy a frozen bird, defrost it in the refrigerator, in the plastic bag it came in for several days, figuring about a day for every 5 pounds of meat. Cook it as soon as it thaws. Although you can skip the trussing of the bird—after all you aren't going to hang him—you will find it cooks better on a rack. If you don't have one, buy it. Throwaway aluminum roasting pans work okay for a smaller bird, if you use two throwaways—one inside the other, they don't wobble as much, but if you're planning to roast a twenty-pounder, spring for a big, sturdy roasting pan. Besides that, you can make the gravy right in the pan.

Arrange the bird on a big platter and nestle the root vegetables all around. Preset the tortellini at each place. Stack the dinner plates next to the designated carver/server. Ask your designated carver to give a helping of turkey and vegetables to each person at the table, along with a scoop of the lovely light stuffing. Pass the mashed potatoes and gravy, cranberry relish and bread and butter.

The theme for Thanksgiving is *bountiful*. Decorate the table with an arrangement of autumn leaves, nuts, acorns, persimmons, pine cones, pumpkins, and squash around a group of candlesticks. If you have a wooden duck decoy or other Americana, put it in the middle of the table. Lighting is important. Light lots of candles. We are convinced it has a soothing effect.

A selection of bought desserts, or desserts made by guests, can be set out in view of the table. A sight like that will certainly move the meal along.

Pumpkin Tortellini with Cilantro, Garlic, and Corn Dressing

2 pounds pumpkin tortellini

6 quarts lightly salted water

1 bunch Italian flat-leaf parsley, washed and stemmed

1 bunch cilantro, washed and stemmed

2 cups frozen corn kernels, thawed

4 cloves garlic, pressed

¼ cup extra virgin olive oil

3 tablespoons balsamic vinegar

1 teaspoon light or dark brown sugar

Salt and freshly ground black pepper, to taste

5 cups torn mixed bitter greens

A lovely beginning to the meal. All you do is boil the tortellini, toss with this easy dressing, and serve about four tortellinis per person on a bed of mixed bitter greens. Arrange salad plates in the kitchen, and place them on the dinner table before seating your guests. It makes this course a breeze for the cook/server. Now all you do is lift the salad plates, get a friend to whisk them into the kitchen, and you're ready to begin the main attraction.

Boil the tortellini in the barely salted water until tender, about 10 to 12 minutes, then drain. Meanwhile, combine the parsley, cilantro, and corn in a large bowl and toss to mix. Stir together the garlic, oil, vinegar, brown sugar, and salt and pepper. Toss with the drained tortellini. Arrange about $^1/_2$ cup bitter greens on each salad plate then top with about $^1/_4$ cup of the corn mixture. Add about four tortellinis with dressing to each plate and serve.

Laid-Back Turkey with Fragrant Lily Stuffing and Tawny Port Gravy

Stuffing:

12 corn muffins (or a 9-inch-square pan of corn bread), crumbled

6 scones or biscuits (with cranberries if possible) plus leftover French or country bread, to make a total of 10 cups including the corn bread crumbled in the food processor

$^1/_4$ cup ($^1/_2$ stick) butter

1 large yellow onion, chopped (about 1 cup)

1 large red onion, chopped (about 1 cup)

6 cloves garlic, chopped (3 teaspoons)

6 stalks celery, chopped

1 large leek, sliced lengthwise, washed carefully, and chopped

1 bunch green onions with tops, chopped

20 frozen pearl onions, thawed

1 cup dried cranberries

2 cups fat-free canned chicken broth

1 large egg, lightly beaten

1 teaspoon dried sage

Salt and freshly ground black pepper, to taste

Salt

1 (12- to 14-pound) turkey

$^1/_4$ cup ($^1/_2$ stick) melted butter

4 cups chicken broth

Tawny Port Gravy (recipe follows)

This version of America's favorite bird is lighter and crisper because it isn't basted. We do recommend, however, that you coat the skin with butter before you begin. Roasting the bird over aromatic broth under a loose foil tent enhances both the taste and the texture. And are those pan drippings delicious? Wow.

The combination of five kinds of sautéed onions plus garlic makes for a succulent stuffing. The mixture of three kinds of bread gives it a complexity of flavor and texture you can never achieve using a bag of Pepperidge Farm. Plus, your stuffing will never have that horrid chemical, stale taste you get when you use stuffing "mix." Now that good bakeries everywhere stock muffins, scones, and terrific country bread, there's no excuse not to start with the very best. You can, if you wish, make your own scones, bread, and muffins up to 3 or 4 days in advance of the big day. But whether homemade or store-bought, begin with the best and you'll have this stuffing made and into the bird in less than half an hour.

PREPARATION TIME: 20 MINUTES
COOKING TIME: 4 TO 5 HOURS
MAKES 10 TO 12 SERVINGS (WITH LEFTOVERS)

Best if made the day it is to be eaten.

In a large bowl, combine the corn muffins, scones, and bread. Melt the butter in a large skillet over medium-high heat and sauté the chopped onions until golden, about 3 minutes. Add the garlic, celery, leek, and green onions, and sauté until tender and limp, about 5 more minutes. Add all the sautéed vegetables to the crumbled bread. Add all the remaining stuffing ingredients to the bowl and toss to mix.

Preheat the oven to 325°. Rub salt in the interior cavity of the bird and lay it on its back on a rack in a large roasting pan. Stuff the cavity of the bird loosely with the dressing. Just grab up handfuls and poke it in. (Cook any leftovers in a separate baking dish at 325° for 30 minutes before serving.) Pour the melted butter over the skin of the turkey, allowing any extra to drip down into the pan. Make a foil tent and lay it loosely over the bird. Pull the oven rack toward you and place the turkey on it, then add the broth to the bottom of the pan. Carefully push the rack back into the oven and begin roasting.

The turkey is done when the juices run clear and a meat thermometer, inserted into the thickest part of the breast but not touching a bone, registers about 165°. See chart page 333 for turkey roasting times. Remove foil tent last few minutes to brown bird. Lift the bird to a warm serving platter, cover it with foil, and allow it to rest about 30 minutes before carving. Serve with the stuffing and the Tawny Port Gravy.

Weight	Cooking Time (Minutes per pound)	Cooking Time (Hours per bird)
6 – 8 pounds	23 – 25	2½ – 3
8 – 10	21 – 23	3 – 4
10 – 14	18 – 20	3½ – 4½
14 – 18	15 – 18	4½ – 5½
18 – 20	14 – 15	5½ – 6
20 – 25	13 – 14	6 – 6½

Turkey Time

These times are for stuffed birds. If you're roasting your bird unstuffed, subtract about 30 minutes from the cooking time. The oven temperature is 325°. Use a meat or instant-read thermometer to check for internal temperature. The breast should be 165°; 175° for the thigh; and 160° to 165° for the stuffing.

TAWNY PORT GRAVY

4 cups defatted turkey pan drippings (add chicken broth if necessary to make up the quantity)

³/₄ cup tawny port

3 tablespoons cornstarch

Salt and freshly ground black pepper, to taste

PREPARATION TIME: 5 MINUTES

COOKING TIME: 10 MINUTES OR SO

Measure the pan juices, then pour them into a large bowl. Remove and discard floating fat.* Add chicken broth if necessary to make 4 cups of liquid. Transfer the defatted pan juices back to roasting pan or to a large saucepan and heat to a boil. Stir together the port and cornstarch until it's lump-free, then stir the port mixture into the boiling juices. Taste and adjust the seasonings with salt and pepper. Cook, stirring, until the gravy is no longer opaque and begins to look shiny and clear, about 5 to 10 minutes. Pour into a gravy boat and serve with the turkey.

* You can also do this easily with a "defatting" measuring pitcher whose spout begins at the bottom. Pour the pan juices into the pitcher, and from the pitcher back into the roasting pan. The fat will remain in the pitcher. Do this in batches if necessary.

Roasted Root Vegetables

2 medium beets, scrubbed and quartered

2 medium parsnips, scrubbed and halved

2 medium carrots, scrubbed and halved

2 medium turnips, scrubbed and quartered

2 medium sweet potatoes, peeled and cut into chunks

1 head garlic, rough outer husk removed

2 leeks, washed and cut in half lengthwise

2 large red onions, quartered

1/2 cup extra virgin olive oil

Sprigs of rosemary

1/2 cup chicken broth

Salt and freshly ground black pepper, to taste

Figure about two pieces of vegetable per person. Pick and choose your favorites from the listed suggestions. This recipe is eminently expandable. All you need is a big pan. Cut the vegetables into big uniform chunks so they'll cook evenly.

PREPARATION TIME: 20 MINUTES

COOKING TIME: 45 MINUTES

MAKES 10 TO 12 SERVINGS

Can be made several hours in advance and served at room temperature or reheated in hot oven while the turkey rests.

Preheat the oven to 400°. Place the prepared vegetables in a large roasting pan. Add the oil and toss to coat. Intersperse sprigs of rosemary among the vegetables, pour in the broth, then salt and pepper well. Roast, uncovered, until the vegetables are tender, about 45 minutes.

Roasted Garlic Mashed Potatoes

1 whole head garlic

2 tablespoons extra virgin olive oil

10 medium potatoes*

1/2 cup milk

1/4 cup (1/2 stick) butter

1 teaspoon salt

Freshly ground black pepper, to taste

Roasted garlic improves on a great American classic. Roasting the garlic mellows its flavor and creates a perfect foil for the potatoes.

PREPARATION TIME:	15 MINUTES
ROASTING TIME:	35 TO 40 MINUTES
BOILING TIME:	20 TO 25 MINUTES

MAKES 10 TO 12 SERVINGS

May be made up to a day in advance and reheated in the microwave, or oven while the turkey rests.

Preheat the oven to 400°. Break up the garlic but do not peel the cloves. Toss the garlic cloves in the olive oil, place them in a Pyrex baking dish, and roast for 35 to 40 minutes, until the cloves are soft. Meanwhile peel and halve the potatoes. Place them in a large pot of cold water, bring to a boil, and boil gently for 20 minutes, or until tender. Drain the potatoes and set them aside. Remove the garlic from the oven and remove the cloves from their skin. Either mash together or mix with an electric mixer the garlic, potatoes, milk, butter, salt, and pepper. Return to the pan to reheat if necessary, and serve hot.

* Yukon gold make the best mashed potatoes. The texture is incredible and the color very rich.
A big improvement over Idahos.

Fresh Cranberry Citrus Relish

1 (12-ounce) bag fresh or frozen cranberries

3 oranges, quartered, seeds removed and discarded, rind left on

3 lemons, quartered, seeds removed and discarded, rind left on

2 cups sugar

You want party favors from your Thanksgiving feast? This almost instant relish makes enough so that you can jar up the leftovers and divide it among your guests as they walk out the door.

PREPARATION TIME: 5 MINUTES

REFRIGERATION TIME: 30 MINUTES TO 2 DAYS

MAKES 10 TO 12 SERVINGS, WITH LEFTOVERS

Can be made 3 to 4 days before serving, covered, and refrigerated.

Combine all ingredients in a food processor and process until you have a coarse puree. Transfer to a glass dish, cover, and refrigerate until serving time.

Warm Autumn Lunch for Friends

A fall Sunday afternoon is a great time to see friends. The sun is still up and often there is a football game to be watched. This menu goes together fast, is not too filling, and is always a hit. More important, the cook gets to enjoy the guests.

We made the tart in the morning, then cooked the salmon and made the salad at the very last minute.

The Menu

WALNUT BREAD WITH TOASTED GRUYÈRE

WARM SALMON AND RED POTATO SALAD

BEETS IN AN ORANGE VINAIGRETTE ON A BED OF BABY GREENS
(SEE PAGE 344)

GARLIC GREEN BEANS

SWISS CHEESE AND FRUIT TART

Wine Suggestions

Main Course—The classic wine for salmon is Oregon Pinot Noir. As an alternative you could try a rich buttery Chardonnay (non-oaked). The richness of the Chardonnay will complement the richness of the salmon, while the fruity Pinot Noir is a nice contrast.

Cooking Tip: How to Cook Delicate Fish Perfectly

For sautéed fish, preheat the skillet *dry* over medium-high heat, then film it with oil just before adding the fish. Dry the fish with paper towels before seasoning with salt and pepper to prevent steaming it when you meant to sauté. The main caveat in cooking fish—no matter what the method—is not to overcook it. To test, use two forks to gently pull the fish apart at the thickest point. The center of the fish should look opaque and milky, not translucent and pearly—as it does when it's raw. If you wish to cut down fat grams, you can steam fish instead.

To steam fish, it's best to place the fish on a heatproof plate or on lettuce leaves, rather than directly on a steamer rack.

Allow about 10 minutes to the inch for cooking fish regardless of method, plus slightly more time if other ingredients are added to the pan. When cooking a mixed batch, take the foods out of the pan and transfer them to a warm bowl as they're cooked through.

All the Trimmings

Serve the pink salmon salad along with a trio of tiny beet jewels, over a bed of greens. The color contrast is great. Serve the green beans on a side salad plate, along with the walnut bread. A few fall leaves on the table will capture the mood of the season. The beauty of this meal is its simplicity.

WALNUT BREAD WITH TOASTED GRUYÈRE

1 (1-pound) loaf walnut whole wheat country bread

1/2 pound Gruyère cheese, coarsely grated

1/4 cup heavy cream

Salt, to taste

Pinch of cayenne

Buy a loaf of best-quality walnut whole wheat country bread the day before and choose the best-quality imported Gruyère you can find for the most delicious results. Mass the toasts in a cloth-lined basket and pass them among your guests.

PREPARATION TIME: 10 MINUTES

BAKING TIME: 10 TO 12 MINUTES

MAKES ABOUT 10 PIECES

Best if made and eaten at once.

Preheat the oven to 375°. Cut thick slices of bread and lay them on an ungreased baking sheet.

In a medium bowl, combine the Gruyère, cream, salt, and cayenne. Heap the cheese mixture onto the bread slices and bake until bubbly, about 10 to 12 minutes. Serve immediately.

Warm Salmon and Red Potato Salad

12 small red new potatoes (about 1¹/₂ pounds), cut in half

2 pounds salmon fillets

Salt and freshly ground black pepper, to taste

Extra virgin olive oil

1 large yellow onion, thinly sliced

1 large red bell pepper, seeded, peeled, and thinly sliced

1 cup chopped cilantro

1 medium fresh jalapeño pepper, seeded and minced

¹/₄ cup white wine vinegar

Zest and juice of ¹/₂ lime (about 2 tablespoons juice)

1 teaspoon dried oregano

A festive lunch that's ready to serve quickly and easily.

PREPARATION TIME: 15 MINUTES

COOKING TIME: 5 MINUTES

MAKES 6 SERVINGS

Best if made and eaten warm, but you can make the salad in advance of your guests' arrival and hold it about 30 minutes, covered, before serving.

Place the potatoes in a medium saucepan with water to cover, and bring to a boil. Reduce the heat and simmer until tender, about 15 to 20 minutes. Drain and set aside. Meanwhile season the salmon fillets generously with salt and pepper. Preheat a large skillet over medium-high heat and film it with oil. Add the fillets and cook until golden brown on the bottom, about 5 minutes. Turn, add the onion, and cook until done, about 5 more minutes. Remove the salmon to a warmed platter and reserve.

Continue cooking the onion another 3 minutes or so, until golden. Add the potatoes to the skillet and sauté them over high heat for about 3 minutes or until browned. Remove from the heat and set aside.

Flake the salmon into bite-size pieces. Toss it with the onion, potatoes, bell pepper, cilantro, and jalapeño in a bowl. Stir together the vinegar, lime zest and juice, the oregano, and a little freshly milled black pepper. Drizzle this mixture over the salmon and toss gently to coat.

Arrange the salad on six dinner plates, next to the beet salad. Serve immediately, while still warm.

Garlic Green Beans

These beans serve as a foil for the salmon salad.

1 pound tender fresh green beans, trimmed	1 clove garlic, crushed (¹/₂ teaspoon)
1 teaspoon extra virgin olive oil	Salt and freshly ground black pepper, to taste

PREPARATION TIME: 1 0 MINUTES

COOKING TIME: 1 2 TO 1 5 MINUTES

MAKES 6 SMALL SERVINGS

If you wish, you can blanch and drain the beans in advance, then sauté them just as you're ready to serve.

Cook the whole beans in a large skillet with a small amount of water until crisp-tender, about 7 to 9 minutes. Drain and add the olive oil, crushed garlic, and salt and pepper to taste. Sauté in medium pan over high heat for 2 or 3 minutes and serve.

SWISS CHEESE AND FRUIT TART

$^1/_4$ pound (1 stick) butter

$^1/_4$ cup sugar

$^1/_4$ teaspoon salt

1 cup coarsely grated Swiss cheese (3 to 4 ounces)

1$^1/_4$ cups flour

2 tablespoons milk

1 cup sweetened shredded coconut

2 cups fruit* of the season (sliced apples, grapes sliced in half, sliced kiwi)

$^3/_4$ cup currant or other red jelly

$^1/_4$ cup brandy, bourbon, or Frangelico liqueur

Don't be taken aback when people ask you for the address of the great bakery where you found this mouthwatering tart. Give them your best Mona Lisa smile and shrug. This fruit and cheese tart is easy, adaptable to the fresh fruits of the season, and looks so good that your guests will think you've just completed a short course in pastry at a cooking school.

PREPARATION TIME: 15 MINUTES

BAKING TIME: 20 MINUTES

MAKES 10 SERVINGS

Best if made and served the same day. May be made the morning of the party.

Preheat the oven to 375°. Combine the butter, sugar, salt, grated cheese, and flour in the bowl of a food processor fitted with the plastic blade. Pulse to mix. Add the milk and process until a dough begins to mass and ride the blade. Stop and form it into a ball. Spread the dough by hand into a 12-inch deep-dish pizza or tart pan, smoothing it with your hands and creating a slight lip around the edge.

Bake 5 minutes, then remove from the oven and sprinkle evenly with the coconut and continue baking 15 minutes more, or until the crust is lightly browned.

While the crust is baking, slice the fruit or combination of fruits. Place sliced fruit in an artful pattern on the crust while it's still warm. Dissolve the jelly in a custard cup in the microwave on high (100 percent power) for about 30 seconds, then stir in the spirits or heat to boiling in a small saucepan, stovetop. Drizzle the jelly glaze over the top of the tart. Serve cut in thin wedges. Good both warm and cold.

* Other fruit combos to use all year long include: nectarines, raspberries, and blueberries for summer; apples, cranberries, and dates in the autumn; mangoes, pineapple, and papaya in the winter; strawberries and cooked rhubarb in the spring.

A Cigars and Scotch
Little Black Dress Dinner

In today's world there aren't enough opportunities for cigars, martinis, scotch, and little black dresses. So we decided to devote this menu to just such an occasion. Meet your guests at the door with a drink, send the cigar aficionados outside to smoke after dinner, and the evening will be complete. We have revived Beef Wellington, a great recipe from the *bon vivant* fifties, when scotch was king and you could serve beef without checking your guests' dietary needs. It was the illusion of life's simplicity that explains the glorification of that era. More important, everyone looks great after a few single-malt scotches.

This is also a great chance to serve a good Burgundy or Bordeaux, along with a port after dessert. The timing is important for this dinner. You must move it along at a slow pace to really enjoy yourself. Cocktails at six-thirty, dinner at eight. Fashionably late was most certainly the rule when people entertained in this style. You should be no less strict with your guests. Of course, this is a perfect night for cameo appearances on the CD player by Mel Torme, Tony Bennett, Bobby Short, or Combustible Edison's lounge music.

The Menu

SINGLE-MALT SCOTCH, BUSHMILLS IRISH WHISKEY, AND PERFECT MARTINIS

SALTED PEANUTS AND PRETZELS

BEETS IN AN ORANGE VINAIGRETTE ON A BED OF BABY GREENS

CORN SOUP

ASSORTED DINNER ROLLS

CARROTS VICHY

INDIVIDUAL BEEF WELLINGTONS

CHEESE COURSE (SEE PAGE 287)

BABAS AUX RUM

TEA AND COFFEE

PORT

Wine Suggestions

Main Course—This is the moment to show off a fine Bordeaux from the Pauillac or Pomerol regions. These wines have been described as hedonistic. They are so rich and opulent, their black fruit flavor is the perfect choice for a rich Beef Wellington. Think how much you would spend in a restaurant, and splurge for these wines. It is worth it. Or, if you want to go the more ordinary route, a California merlot would work nicely.

Cooking Tip

For a winning Beef Wellington, be careful to not overcook the fillets when you sear them in step I. Brown them on each side for *just 1 minute*, as they will finish cooking in the oven. To get this right, preheat a dry black cast-iron or porcelain-clad iron skillet for I or 2 minutes. Add the peanut oil, which can withstand very high heat (higher than corn oil or olive oil). Place the fillets in the pan, and *don't move them* until ready to turn. Pepper the fillets in advance, but *don't* salt them. Salt will draw out the juices.

All the Trimmings

It's white-tablecloth time. However, you don't have to go that formal for elegance. Sometimes we like to use good place mats and show off our beautiful dining table. Candles really set the mood. Serve the beets on top of the greens on individual plates. Stack the soup bowls and place the soup tureen or pot next to the person you appoint to serve it. We like to serve the soup course at the table, while the anticipation is great and the soup is not so hot it burns. Serve the carrots and Beef Wellington on individual plates. Get a volunteer to help you bring in the plates. Remember, for a meal this big, make the servings small so that everyone can enjoy all the courses.

The Perfect Martini

For each perfect martini, combine 4 ounces ($^1/_2$ cup) good-quality Dry Gin and $^1/_2$ ounce (1 tablespoon) dry French vermouth in an ice-filled shaker. Shake gently, then strain into a well-chilled, stemmed martini glass. Garnish with a twist of lemon or an olive and serve. Substitute a cocktail onion and the drink becomes a Gibson. Substitute vodka, and you've made a vodkatini.

Beets in an Orange Vinaigrette on a Bed of Baby Greens

Orange Vinaigrette:

3 tablespoons extra virgin olive oil

2 tablespoons red wine vinegar

2 tablespoons freshly squeezed orange juice

Zest of 1 orange

1 teaspoon sugar

$^1/_2$ teaspoon salt

2 (15-ounce) cans sliced beets, drained

4 cups torn baby greens (mesclun)

PREPARATION TIME:	5 MINUTES
MARINATING TIME:	AT LEAST 5 MINUTES OR OVERNIGHT
MAKES 4 SERVINGS	

The beets may be tossed with the vinaigrette 1 day in advance and refrigerated until serving.

Mix the vinaigrette and toss it with the beets. Marinate in the refrigerator until ready to serve over the greens on individual salad plates.

Corn Soup

1 teaspoon extra virgin olive oil

1 small onion, chopped

4 cloves garlic, chopped (2 teaspoons)

2 cups fresh, frozen, or canned corn kernels

1 large carrot, scraped and chopped

1 stalk celery, chopped

1 quart (4 cups) chicken broth

$1^1/_2$ cups half-and-half

$^1/_2$ teaspoon freshly ground black pepper

$^1/_2$ teaspoon cayenne

$^1/_2$ teaspoon paprika

$^1/_2$ teaspoon salt

$^3/_4$ cup low-fat sour cream, for garnish

1 teaspoon chili powder, for garnish

PREPARATION TIME: 10 MINUTES

COOKING TIME: 20 MINUTES

MAKES 4 SERVINGS

May be made up to 1 day in advance. Reheat in the microwave or stovetop.

In a large pan, heat the oil over medium-high heat, then sauté the onion and garlic until the onion is translucent, about 5 minutes. Add the corn kernels, carrot, and celery and continue cooking 3 or 4 minutes, or until the vegetables are beginning to brown. Transfer the veggies to a food processor or blender and puree. Pour in a little of the broth and continue to process until the mixture is smooth. Transfer the mixture back to the pan and add the remaining broth and the half-and-half. Bring to a boil, lower the heat, and simmer for about 10 minutes. Season with the peppers and salt.

Meanwhile, stir together the sour cream and chili powder. Place this mixture in a ketchup dispenser and pipe the soup in wild squiggles just before serving.

Serve soup hot in wide-rimmed soup bowls.

Carrots Vichy

¹/₂ cup water

1 cup baby carrots, sliced ¹/₂ inch thick

1 cup peeled and sliced parsnips, ¹/₂ inch thick
(you may use all carrots or all parsnips)

4 tablespoons butter

3 tablespoons sugar

3 tablespoons freshly squeezed lemon juice

PREPARATION TIME: 1 0 MINUTES

COOKING TIME: 1 2 TO 1 5 MINUTES

MAKES 4 SERVINGS

May be made 1 day in advance.

Combine the water, carrots, parsnips, butter, sugar, and lemon juice in a saucepan. Cook over high heat, covered, for 5 minutes. Remove cover and continue cooking until the water evaporates, about 3 to 4 minutes. Brown the carrots in the pan, for 3 minutes, to caramelize the sugar. Serve at once, or refrigerate covered and reheat in the microwave, or on the stove-top to boiling.

Individual Beef Wellingtons

4 (5-ounce) tournedos or fillets mignons of beef

Freshly ground black pepper

2 tablespoons peanut oil

¹/₄ pound pâté (goose liver, country, or whatever you like)

1 (14-ounce) package frozen puff pastry, completely thawed

1 egg

1 tablespoon milk

PREPARATION TIME: 5 MINUTES

SEARING TIME: 3 MINUTES

BAKING TIME: 20 MINUTES

MAKES 4 SERVINGS

May be made up to point of baking 1 day in advance.

Thoroughly pat dry the fillets and pepper them generously. Preheat a black cast-iron skillet for 1 or 2 minutes. Add the peanut oil and place the fillets in the skillet. Sear the fillets over high heat without moving them for 1 minute. Then turn and sear the other side for 1 minute. Do not overcook, as they will finish cooking in the oven. Remove from the heat and set aside to cool. When the fillets are cool to the touch, place them on a cookie sheet.

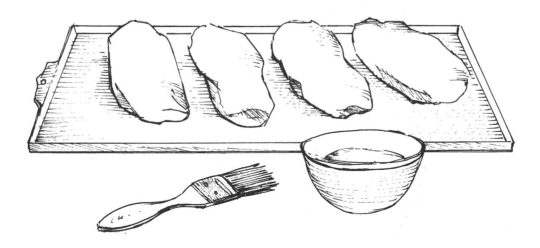

Top each fillet with a $^1/_2$-inch-thick slice of pâté. Cut the puff pastry into squares large enough to drape over the fillets, completely covering the top and sides of the meat. The bottom will not be covered but will be directly on the cookie sheet. Pinch the pastry together at the corners. At this point, the uncooked Wellingtons can be stored, covered, in the refrigerator for 24 hours. When ready to continue cooking them, preheat the oven to 400°. In a small bowl, beat the egg and milk together to make an egg wash. Brush the wash generously over the pastry just before baking. Bake for 20 minutes. If the Wellingtons have been in the refrigerator, you may want to bake them for 25 minutes. Serve hot golden Wellies to grateful guests.

Imported Beer and Nosh Bash

After our trip to Alsace, home of choucroute, we added this traditional menu to our list of party favorites. Our version is easy, and we do not even pretend to serve our guests the volume of sauerkraut, meats, and sausages the Alsatians offer in restaurants. Good heavens! There, every person is presented with a platter that holds a mountain of sauerkraut buttressed by enough meat to feed a family of four for a week.

When Gordon mentioned to Simon, a Parisian on his neighborhood soccer team, that we were serving choucroute for our party, he insisted that the authentic version must be served with beer. He was preaching to the choir. We already had the beer on ice. We added applesauce as a side dish, the way the Alsatians do, to complement the flavors, and Katherine's grandmother's favorite Bundt cake for dessert.

We've found that this buffet is also great for a Sunday of sports with friends. After a morning soccer game, Gordon's team, in the over-thirty league, wolfed it down. We made the cake the day in advance. On the day of the game, we simply put it together then laid it out.

The Menu

PRETZELS AND MIXED NUTS

DELI SOUR AND HALF-SOUR PICKLES

CHEESE COURSE (SEE PAGE 287)

BLACK PUMPERNICKEL BREAD

CHOUCROUTE GARNI À L'ALSACIENNE

ROASTED RED POTATOES

APPLESAUCE

GRANDNONNIE'S SPICE BUNDT CAKE

IMPORTED BEER OR WINE

Wine Suggestions

Main Course—As an alternative to beer, this Alsatian meal begs for an Alsatian Riesling, dry or semidry, or a Tokay or gewürztraminer. Watch the alcohol content on all Alsatian wines—12.5 percent or below is best with food. Too much alcohol in the wine overwhelms the food.

Cooking Tip

Buy only the highest-quality sausage, sauerkraut, pickles, bread, and other ingredients. If you are worried about cost, just imagine what a dinner for a crowd would be if you ordered in or ate out in a first-rate restaurant. If good food costs a few dollars more, it is worth it.

All the Trimmings

Serve the choucroute garni on a very large platter with a ring of potatoes around the dish. The sheer size and variety of the sausages are dramatic. Serve the beer from a large ice chest. Put the cheeses out on a board with a toothpick flag identifying each one.

Choucroute Garni à l'Alsacienne

4 thick slices smoked bacon, cut into 1-inch slices

2 large onions, chopped

2 cloves garlic, peeled and thinly sliced

10 juniper berries

1 teaspoon dried thyme

1 teaspoon caraway seeds

4 pounds highest-quality sauerkraut, rinsed in a colander and squeezed dry (the best is found in the deli section at most grocery stores)

1 (1-pound) ham steak, sliced

$1/2$ litre bottle dry white wine, or more as needed

1 cup chicken broth, to be added as needed

6 to 8 thinly sliced pork chops

1 pound kielbasa

1 pound bratwurst

1 pound knockwurst

2 tablespoons kirsch

We know that good cooking begins in the market. But in Alsace, it actually begins on the farm. Drive through cabbage fields at harvesttime and you're likely to see giant shredders right there. A farm worker with a huge knife hacks the outside leaves off the cabbage head, then tosses it into the shredder. The sauerkraut is salted before it ever leaves the field. The Alsatians do not fool around. As the famous French Alsatian chef André Soltner of Lutèce says, "If you have good ingredients, it is hard to spoil them, hard to make bad food from them. But to make good food from bad ingredients, that is impossible."

PREPARATION TIME: 20 MINUTES

COOKING TIME: 2 HOURS

MAKES 12 SERVINGS

The choucroute can be made up to 2 days in advance and, with a little extra broth, reheated in the oven just before serving.

Preheat the oven to 325°. Place the oven rack in the lower third of the oven. In a large skillet, cook the bacon until limp, add the chopped onions and sauté until limp, about 5 minutes total. Add the garlic, juniper berries, thyme, caraway, and cook 1 minute more. Transfer the mixture to a large roasting pan and spread it over the bottom. Do not wash the skillet. Layer the sauerkraut on top of the onion mixture and add the ham and the wine. Lay a sheet of waxed paper directly on top of the ham and bake for $1^1/2$ hours. Check periodically to make sure the kraut does not dry out. Add broth and wine as needed. In the same large skillet that you used to cook the onions, prick the sausage with a fork and brown

on all sides with the pork chops, and frankfurters, about 6 to 8 minutes. The cooking process will be completed in the oven. Slice the sausages into 3-inch chunks and set the meats aside. After the sauerkraut has cooked for $1^{1}/_{2}$ hours, bury the browned chops and sausages in the sauerkraut and cook for $^{1}/_{2}$ hour more. Add enough chicken broth to just moisten, cover again, to cook for 30 more minutes. Check at least once to make sure the choucroute does not dry out. Add extra chicken broth, if necessary, to keep it moist, being careful not to add too much, as most of the liquid should be soaked up by the time it comes out of the oven. The final dish should be moist but not runny. Toss with the kirsch and serve on a large platter.

ROASTED RED POTATOES

36 small red new potatoes (about 3 pounds), washed and dried

2 tablespoons extra virgin olive oil

1 teaspoon salt

Freshly ground black pepper, to taste

PREPARATION TIME: 5 MINUTES

COOKING TIME: 45 MINUTES TO 1 HOUR

MAKES 12 SERVINGS

Toss the washed and dried potatoes with the olive oil, salt, and pepper. Spread them on a four-sided cookie sheet or in a roasting pan in a single layer. Bake at 325° for 45 minutes to an hour, or until a fork can easily pierce the potato.

GRANDNONNIE'S SPICE BUNDT CAKE

2 cups dark brown sugar

1 cup water

1 cup raisins

$^1/_4$ cup vegetable oil

$1^1/_2$ teaspoons ground cinnamon

$^1/_2$ teaspoon ground nutmeg

$^1/_4$ teaspoon ground cloves

3 cups cake (or all-purpose) flour

$^1/_4$ teaspoon salt

1 teaspoon baking powder

1 teaspoon baking soda

$^1/_2$ cup chopped walnuts

Ginger Drizzle Frosting (recipe follows)

1 quart vanilla ice cream (optional)

PREPARATION TIME: 15 MINUTES

COOKING TIME: 50 MINUTES

COOLING TIME: 30 MINUTES

MAKES 12 SERVINGS

The cake can be made and frosted 1 day in advance and held in a domed cake dish until serving time.

A favorite in our house, this cake is dense and intense with spices, and never hints that it is so easy to put together. Grandnonnie cut this recipe out of a newspaper during the Great Depression, when eggs, milk, and but-

ter were hard to come by. We like it because it can be made easily, with no special equipment but a good old wooden spoon, and it goes with this hearty menu quite well. A scoop of vanilla ice cream is always welcome.

In a heavy saucepan, combine the brown sugar, water, raisins, oil, cinnamon, nutmeg, and cloves, and bring to a boil. Reduce the heat and simmer for 3 minutes, then remove from the heat and cool until you can put your finger into the mixture without burning it, about 5 minutes.

Place the oven rack in the lower third of the oven. Preheat the oven to 350°. Coat a nonstick 12-cup Bundt pan with cooking spray and set it inside.

In a large mixing bowl, combine the flour with the salt, baking powder, and baking soda. Whisk thoroughly, then add the walnuts.

Use a wooden spoon to combine the flour and brown sugar mixtures. Don't use an electric mixer because it will overmix the batter. Simply stir until there are no more flour bits showing. Pour the batter into the prepared pan. Using the back of the wooden spoon, smooth the top of the batter, then bake for 50 minutes, or until a toothpick comes out clean. Cool in the pan on a rack 5 minutes, then turn out of the pan onto the rack and cool at least 30 minutes before frosting. Cut thin slices and serve with a scoop of vanilla ice cream if you wish.

GINGER DRIZZLE FROSTING

½ cup confectioners' sugar	2 teaspoons milk
1 teaspoon powdered ginger	

Stir together the confectioners' sugar, ginger, and milk until smooth.

Brunch for a Cool Autumn Sunday

Brunch on Sunday is simply an expanded breakfast without the time constraints. Gather together your friends, offer mimosas, champagne, and hot drinks of their choice. There is something so relaxing about the sun streaming in on a cool autumn day.

If you want to expand the guest list to accommodate fifteen or twenty, don't double the recipes, just add other items—Oven-Roasted Pepper Bacon (see page 186), clafouti (see page 86), Walnut Bread with Toasted Gruyère (see page 338), and a toaster with an assortment of muffins, breads, and bagels with cream cheese, butter, jams, and a station of cold cereal. Brunch is a truly American meal. This menu uses great American flavors and will be bright and colorful on the sideboard.

The Menu

MIMOSAS AND CHAMPAGNE

CRANBERRY PECAN QUICK BREAD

CEREALS AND YOGURT

CHILI CORN CUSTARD PIE WITH GORGONZOLA STREUSEL

BLACK BEAN AND CORN SALAD

SLICED TOMATOES WITH LEMON JUICE AND CILANTRO

LOX AND CAPER ROSES

BUNCHES OF GRAPES

HOT COFFEE AND TEA

Cooking Tip

Making mimosas is one of those too simple ideas that simply combines equal parts icy-cold champagne and fresh orange juice in a footed glass. Make them by the pitcherful or—if you're ambidextrous and love drama—pour individual drinks into a glass from two sides. Practice a little and you can hold the bubbly and juice as high as a resort waiter can and still hit the glass from 3 feet up. Make a mistake and you've probably splashed your guest with the sticky combination.

All the Trimmings

All these dishes are colorful, minimizing the need for extra table decorations. A pitcher of daisies will suffice. Serve the meal buffet-style. Cut the Chili Corn Custard Pie into diamond, square, or wedge shapes, then arrange them on a platter or tray with bunches of cilantro on one side. Add a platter of red tomatoes, a bowl of Black Bean and Corn Salad, and a tray of rosy lox flowers. Serve the red-flecked cranberry breads in a basket next to a bowl of grapes. Be sure to cut the grapes into little serving-size bunches for proper grape service! Your guests' plates will be beautiful. Group the forks, plates, and napkins at one end, and the cream, sugar, and coffee and tea at the other. We like to serve a carafe of decaf as well as one of regular, since many folks these days avoid caffeine. You can provide a selection of cold cereals and fruit yogurts for those silly guests who want their usual breakfast, no matter what. Do what the hotels do—nestle the yogurt and pitchers of milk and cream in a big bowl of ice, then arrange serving bowls of assorted cereals with individual bowls and spoons nearby.

CRANBERRY PECAN QUICK BREAD

3 cups pastry flour* (can substitute all-purpose flour)

1 tablespoon baking powder

1½ teaspoons baking soda

1½ teaspoons salt

1 cup sugar

2 large eggs

2 cups whole cranberry sauce, homemade or 1 (16-ounce) can

½ cup milk

½ cup melted butter

½ cup pecan pieces

Sliced and fanned onto a tray, this red-flecked, sweet brown bread is festive and tastes so good you may wish to save a loaf to give to a special friend as a holiday gift.

PREPARATION TIME: 10 MINUTES

BAKING TIME: 50 TO 55 MINUTES

MAKES 2 (8½ x 2½-INCH) LOAVES

May be made the day before, cooled, and wrapped in plastic wrap until slicing and serving time.

Preheat the oven to 375°. Spray two 8½ × 2½-inch loaf pans with cooking spray and set aside.

In a large bowl, stir together with a wooden spoon the flour, baking powder, baking soda, salt, and sugar. Make a well in the center and add the eggs, cranberry sauce, milk, melted butter, and pecans. Stir just until the flour is completely moistened.

Divide the batter equally between the pans and bake on the middle rack of the oven for 50 to 55 minutes, or until a skewer or toothpick inserted into the center of the loaf comes out clean. Cool in the pans on a rack for 5 minutes, then turn out onto the rack and cool completely. Wrap in plastic wrap to store. To serve, cut into thin slices and fan onto a tray.

* Pastry flour is a secret weapon for muffins, cakes, cookies, or other quick breads. The flour is softer, has more starch and less protein than all-purpose, and yields more tender baked goods. We think White Lily is the best.

CHILI CORN CUSTARD PIE WITH GORGONZOLA STREUSEL

2 cups yellow cornmeal

1 cup all-purpose flour

2 tablespoons sugar

2 teaspoons baking soda

2 teaspoons salt

2 cups buttermilk

4 large eggs

2 cups whole milk

1½ cups fresh or frozen corn kernels (about 2 medium ears)

1 (4-ounce) can chopped green chilies

¼ cup melted butter

1 cup crumbled Gorgonzola or other cheese (feta, goat, Danish blue, Vermont white Cheddar)

This recipe makes its own corn bread crust on the bottom with a layer of silky chili corn custard in the middle, finished with a sharp, crusty cheese top. Stir it all together in one big bowl, pour it into the baking dish or two deep-dish pie tins, and let gravity and heat work the magic.

PREPARATION TIME:	15 MINUTES
BAKING TIME:	30 MINUTES
COOLING TIME:	10 MINUTES

MAKES 10 SERVINGS

Combine the dry ingredients in a Ziploc bag 1 day in advance, then make and bake the pie an hour before the party is scheduled to begin.

Preheat the oven to 375°. Spritz a 9 × 13 × 2½-inch baking dish (or two 9-inch deep-dish pie pans) with cooking spray and set aside.

In a large bowl, stir together the cornmeal, flour, sugar, baking soda, and salt. Whisk in the buttermilk, eggs, and half the whole milk. Stir in the corn, chilies, and melted butter. Pour the batter into the prepared pan and pour the remaining whole milk on top.

Bake for 20 minutes, then sprinkle the top with the crumbled cheese and continue baking 8 to 10 minutes more, or until the top is brown and crusty and the center still jiggles when shaken. Cool on a rack for 10 minutes. Cut into squares, diamonds, or wedges, and serve warm or at room temperature.

Black Bean and Corn Salad

2 (15-ounce) cans black beans, rinsed and drained

2 (15-ounce) cans corn kernels, rinsed and drained

1 red onion, chopped

1 red bell pepper, chopped

2 stalks celery, chopped

1 cup coarsely chopped cilantro leaves

$1/2$ cup freshly squeezed lemon juice

$1/2$ cup extra virgin olive oil

1 teaspoon cumin

Salt and freshly ground black pepper, to taste

PREPARATION TIME: 15 MINUTES

MARINATING TIME: 30 MINUTES

MAKES 10 SERVINGS

May be made 2 days in advance.

In a serving bowl, combine the black beans, corn, red onion, bell pepper, celery, cilantro, lemon juice, olive oil, cumin, and salt and pepper. Stir, cover, and refrigerate 30 minutes to marinate or until serving time.

Sliced Tomatoes with Lemon Juice and Cilantro

4 large beefsteak tomatoes, sliced

$1/2$ cup coarsely chopped cilantro

$1/4$ cup freshly squeezed lemon juice and zest from 1 lemon

$1/4$ cup extra virgin olive oil

Salt and freshly ground black pepper, to taste

Best if made just before serving.

Arrange the tomato slices on a platter, in one layer, fanned out and slightly overlapping. Sprinkle the chopped cilantro on top and drizzle with the lemon juice, zest, and olive oil. Season with salt and pepper. Cover and refrigerate until serving time. Just before serving, spoon some of the liquid from the bottom of the plate on top of the tomatoes.

Lox and Caper Roses

20 slices lox (¹/₂ to ³/₄ pound, depending on   20 capers
how thinly it is sliced)

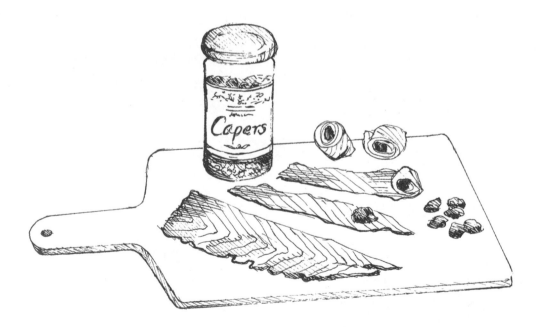

Best if made no more than 1 hour before serving.

Making lox roses with capers couldn't be simpler. Figure 1 to 2 slices of lox per person. Roll a slice of lox, then turn it on end and press out the "petals," placing a caper in the center for the flower bud. Cover and refrigerate until ready to serve.

Autumn Hors d'Oeuvre

Autumn on the Oregon coast means excellent crabbing. We know you won't be starting your party by dropping crab pots over the side of a dinghy, but let us tell you that nothing can be finer than taking live crabs to the steam cooker on the dock, having them cooked and cleaned, then calling together an impromptu party to celebrate the catch.

We didn't really want to take the time to do much beyond making the incredible crab cakes, so we simply set out a feast for our friends, then stood on the porch and watched the sun set over the Pacific. Most of the items were finger food, more assembled than cooked, but the highlight of that stand-up party was the mini-crab cakes, piping hot and sweet, as only fresh-caught crab can be.

The Menu

CRUDITÉS Y OLIO (RAW VEGETABLES AND FLAVORED OLIVE OIL)

MIXED OLIVES AND PEPPERONCINI

BROCCOLI FLORETS, RED ONION, AND BACON

SPICY CRAB CAKES

PESTO TORTA AND ITALIAN RUSTIC BREAD

FIGS AND MELON WITH PROSCIUTTO

ASSORTED COOKIES AND COFFEE

Wine Suggestions

Hors d'oeuvre—This meal, with its West Coast flavors, wants a spicy California Zinfandel or an Oregon Pinot Noir. Again, with West Coast wines, try to buy those with alcohol contents at 12.5 percent or lower. The higher alcohol wines are out of balance and don't taste good with food. If you smell a wine and you get a burning alcohol smell before the grape smell, the wine is out of balance.

Cooking Tip

If you have a source for crabmeat that's been cooked and picked from the shell and sold by the pint, by all means buy it. If you have several spare hours and plenty of extra hands, cooking, cleaning, and picking the meat isn't difficult. It just takes time and the fine-motor coordination of a surgeon. Bring a big pot of water to a boil on the stove and salt it generously. Drop the live crabs into the water and cook only until the shells turn a bright coral color, 3 or 4 minutes is all it will take. Lift them from the water, let them cool, and then prepare to clean them.

Gather two or three friends around the kitchen table, which you've covered with layers of newspaper. Ask the volunteers to pull up a chair, and use nutcrackers, tiny forks, and skewers to remove the meat from the shells. Prepare to spend an hour or so at this traditional cooking task, still performed by people all over the world who still really do make their food from scratch. You'll soon get into the rhythm of it. You'll not worry about that briny juice running back to your elbow, or the hair that drifts in your face. Just sit back and relax. Gossip, tell funny stories, and enjoy the unhurried company of friends as you step into the traditional river of food preparation, which offers a pleasure that far exceeds the rewards of that big bowl of picked crabmeat you'll have when you're done.

All the Trimmings

The food is really the star of this show: platters of colorful raw vegetables; bowls of mixed olives; an assortment of rustic European breads with spreads you pick up from the deli; the brilliant green broccoli and the rich brown crab cakes at the center. Serve this from a table or sideboard, with a stack of small plates and forks at one end, masses of candles in the middle, and autumn flower petals strewn across the table. At another station, serve wines in stemmed glasses. Have a stack of cocktail napkins and you're ready to serve as many as forty people with very little trouble at all.

If you have access to a first-class deli, purchase prosciutto sliced to order. This prevents leathery dried-out prosciutto slices that are hard to eat with any grace at all.

Then, to make the classic Italian offering, simply drape a thin slice of prosciutto over

a whole fig or a wedge of melon. We bought two melons because they looked so good we couldn't choose: a honeydew and a cantaloupe. The rosy salty prosciutto tasted as good over that sweet brilliant chartreuse honeydew as it did over the pale orange cantaloupe. And it makes it easy to create a dazzling tray, massing the chartreuse wedges on one side and the cantaloupe on the other, tying the whole thing together with freshly sliced prosciutto.

CRUDITÉS Y OLIO
(RAW VEGETABLES AND FLAVORED OLIVE OIL)

½ pound ready-to-eat baby carrots

1 bulb fennel, trimmed and separated into pieces

10 celery stalks, cut into 2-inch pieces

1 bunch green onions with tops, trimmed

4 bell peppers (red, yellow, orange, and green) seeded and cut into chunks

1 pint cherry tomatoes

1 cup extra virgin olive oil, flavored with lemon (or chopped garlic, chili, rosemary, or porcini)

Salt and freshly ground black pepper, to taste

With the harvest upon us, and the farmer's markets bursting with fully ripe produce, what could be more glamorous than a platter of fresh raw vegetables, cut into bite-size pieces, with nothing more than a first-quality flavored olive oil for a dip. Even plain old extra virgin olive oil—seasoned with black pepper and sea salt—is heaven. What could be easier?

PREPARATION TIME: 10 MINUTES

MAKES 40 BITE-SIZE SERVINGS

May be made several hours in advance.

Wash, cut, and arrange the platter of vegetables. Cover with plastic wrap and refrigerate. At serving time, nestle a bowl of seasoned oil with salt and pepper in the middle and you're ready to go. If time is really tight, begin with packages of prepared crudités from the supermarket.

Broccoli Florets, Red Onion, and Bacon

1¹/₂ pounds broccoli

1 medium red onion, thinly sliced

²/₃ cup currants

¹/₄ pound pancetta or smoked bacon, diced

¹/₃ cup pine nuts

¹/₃ cup red wine vinegar

2 teaspoons Dijon mustard

2 tablespoons clover honey

2 tablespoons water

Serve these brilliant green and red bites to be eaten with a fork.

PREPARATION TIME: 10 MINUTES

COOKING TIME: 4 MINUTES

CHILLING TIME: FROM 30 MINUTES TO 8 HOURS

MAKES HORS D'OEUVRE SERVINGS FOR 20 OR DINNER FOR 8

Make and refrigerate this early in the day. The broccoli stays bright green and mouthwatering after hours of chilling.

Cut the broccoli into bite-size florets, then peel the stems and cut them into bite-size pieces. Combine them in a large bowl with the sliced onion and currants.

In a large skillet, brown the pancetta or bacon over medium heat until crisp, about 5 minutes, stirring, then lift the meat from the pan and add it to the broccoli bowl. Add the pine nuts to the skillet and cook a moment or two until they begin to color up. Pour the vinegar, mustard, and honey into the hot skillet, along with 2 tablespoons of water and stir. Pour the boiling dressing over the broccoli and toss to mix. Cover and refrigerate at least 30 minutes or until serving time.

SPICY CRAB CAKES

$^1/_2$ cup dry Italian bread crumbs

$^1/_2$ cup mayonnaise

2 large eggs

6 green onions with tops, minced

$^1/_4$ cup each: diced red bell pepper and celery

2 tablespoons Dijon mustard

$^1/_2$ teaspoon hot red pepper flakes

$1^1/_2$ pounds (4 cups) cooked crabmeat (from 1 [3-pound] Dungeness crab)

2 tablespoons butter and 2 tablespoons canola oil, or more as necessary, for frying

Cocktail sauce, for serving

We use Dungeness crabmeat in our cakes, but you can substitute whatever crabmeat is available in your area. Fresh is best, so for the sweetest flavor, don't buy it until the day you plan to serve the cakes.

PREPARATION TIME:	15 MINUTES
CHILLING TIME:	30 MINUTES TO 2 HOURS
COOKING TIME:	5 MINUTES

MAKES 40 HORS D'OEUVRE OR 20 DINNER-SIZE CAKES

Stir together the crab cake mixture, cover, and refrigerate it for up to 2 hours. Cook the cakes up to an hour before serving and keep them warm in a 200° oven.

In a large bowl, combine the bread crumbs, mayonnaise, eggs, green onions, bell pepper, celery, mustard, red pepper flakes, and crabmeat. Stir to mix. Cover and refrigerate at least 30 minutes or up to 2 hours.

To fry the crab cakes, preheat a nonstick skillet over medium-high heat, melting the butter and heating the cooking oil in the pan until hot. Use 2 tablespoons to form small mounds of the crabmeat mixture. Place the cakes in the hot fat, then flatten them slightly with the back of the spoon. Cook until the bottoms are lightly browned, about 2 to 3 minutes, then turn only once and cook on the second side. Transfer them to a covered warm platter lined with paper towels as they are done. Continue cooking—adding oil and butter to the pan as necessary—until all the cakes are cooked. Hold the cakes, covered, in a warm 200° oven for up to 1 hour before serving.

To serve, place the crab cakes on a sideboard with a side dish of cocktail sauce.

Pesto Torta

³/₄ cup minced dried tomatoes in olive oil

³/₄ cup freshly grated Parmesan cheese

¹/₂ cup soft unsalted butter

1 pound cream cheese (use low-fat, if desired)

¹/₂ cup sour cream (use low-fat, if desired)

³/₄ cup prepared pesto

Fresh basil leaves, for garnish

You will love the luscious red and green ribbons running through this rich spread . . . it makes European breads sing. Not only does the torta look good, it tastes terrific. Form it into a dome mold and chill it in the refrigerator from 30 minutes to 2 weeks, or freeze it for up to a month. Serve it on a platter, chilled, alongside a selection of sliced European breads.

PREPARATION TIME: 10 MINUTES

CHILLING TIME: 3 HOURS TO 2 WEEKS

MAKES 40 HORS D'OEUVRE SERVINGS

Make and freeze this up to a month in advance, then simply defrost and serve it at party time. Divide the ingredients into two molds and hold one back for reserve. This makes a great emergency hors d'oeuvre.

Spritz a 6-cup mold (or two or three smaller molds) with cooking spray. Line the entire inner surface with plastic wrap and spray again. Layer the minced tomatoes on the bottom.

Place the Parmesan cheese, butter, cream cheese, and sour cream in the bowl of a food processor fitted with the steel blade, and process until thoroughly blended, about 1 minute. Scrape down the sides and pulse again.

Spoon half the cheese mixture into the mold over the tomatoes. Spread half the pesto atop the cheese, then spoon the remaining cheese mixture into the mold. Top with the remaining pesto. Cover loosely with plastic wrap and refrigerate for at least 3 hours.

To unmold, remove the plastic wrap from the top, turn the mold upside down onto a serving plate, then carefully pull the mold away and remove the wrap. Garnish with fresh basil leaves.

A Farmer's Market Harvest Dinner

Here's a menu to please your vegetarian or sometime-vegetarian friends. When you set out the glorious-looking, main-dish vegetarian pie, no one will ask, "Where's the beef?" It smells so rich and good, your mouth will water. Yet a generous serving has just under 300 calories, and only 19 percent of those calories are from fat.

Making dinner in the oven, with two or three items roasting at the same time, turns your kitchen into a warm, aromatic, and cozy haven for friends and family. When we serve this dinner to our closest friends, we gather around the kitchen table and serve from the pots we cooked in. Provided we shopped the farmer's markets for the best of the fall produce, we can serve this dinner to friends with no more than a couple of hours lead time. And part of that time, while the dishes are in the oven, we can use to prop our feet up.

The flavors of autumn are what make this dinner. Begin with harvest tomatoes and molten sautéed mozzarella towers, followed by rich root vegetables served with rustic European bread and a hearty red wine. Finish with an easy French version of an apple and pear pie—the famous tarte Tatin. Where you live will determine the varieties of apples and pears you select to make the tart. All we can say is, go to the farmer's market and ask for the best produce available in your area. It will make your reputation.

Menu

SAUTÉED MOZZARELLA AND TOMATO TOWERS ON A BED OF MESCLUN

ROASTED ROOT GRATIN WITH MASHED POTATOES

RUSTIC EUROPEAN BREAD

APPLE AND PEAR TARTE TATIN

COFFEE

All the Trimmings

Gather autumn leaves, nuts, gourds, and garnet- and golden-colored flowers and strew them across your bare dining table. Light candles everywhere. Tonight's the night to light the first fire in the fireplace. Since this meal is oven-to-table casual, use pottery or antique dinner plates. Who cares if they match? Mix and match your best old stuff for a homey, comfortable table.

The mozzarella and tomato towers are a good living room hors d'oeuvre. Put little plates and forks on a tray, then make a composition of tomato towers on mesclun and let your guests help themselves. When serving the roasted root gratin, garnish the plate with feathery fennel tops and place the gratin dish in the center of the dinner table for people to help themselves. The tart is best presented on a large flat plate. Sprinkle edible flower petals on top of the fruit for added color.

SAUTÉED MOZZARELLA AND TOMATO TOWERS ON A BED OF MESCLUN

³/₄ pound fresh mozzarella cheese, cut into ¹/₂-inch-thick by 2-inch-wide squares

1 cup Italian bread crumbs

¹/₂ cup freshly grated Parmesan cheese

¹/₂ teaspoon Italian seasoning (available in grocery stores—oregano, chives, parsley, and/or basil)—or 1 tablespoon fresh herbs

Salt and freshly ground black pepper, to taste

2 large eggs beaten with ¹/₄ cup extra virgin olive oil

4 cups torn mixed baby greens (mesclun)

4 large ripe beefsteak tomatoes, cut into thick slices

¹/₄ cup olive oil

¹/₂ stick (¹/₄ cup) butter

Make your own Leaning Tower of Pisa with alternating layers of molten, slightly salty, sautéed mozzarella and thick slices of big blood-red beefsteak tomatoes on a bed of mixed salad greens for an opener that's everything at once: hors d'oeuvre, cheese course, and salad.

PREPARATION TIME: 1 0 MINUTES

CHILLING TIME: UP TO 2 HOURS

MAKES 8 SERVINGS

Slice the tomatoes, dredge the cheese in the crumbs, and refrigerate up to 2 hours before serving time. Sauté and stack the towers just before your guests walk in the door.

Place the mozzarella cheese on paper towels and pat it dry. Stir together the crumbs, Parmesan, and herbs, along with a dusting of salt and pepper. Dip the mozzarella slices into the egg mixture, then pat the crumb mixture around each slice. Place them on a plate, cover, and refrigerate (up to 2 hours) until serving time.

Just before serving, divide the mixed baby greens among eight salad plates, or arrange them on a large serving platter. Arrange half the tomato slices in a single layer on top of the greens. Heat the oil and butter in a large skillet over medium-high heat and sauté the mozzarella slices until golden—turning them only once—no more than 2 minutes per side. Use a spatula to transfer the cooked cheese slices to a waiting tomato slice. Cover with a second tomato slice, then a second cheese slice, and serve.

Roasted Root Gratin with Mashed Potatoes

2 cups chicken broth

2 cups water

1 teaspoon salt, plus additional to taste

8 medium russet potatoes, peeled

2 tablespoons extra virgin olive oil

2 small rutabagas, peeled and cut into uniform bite-size pieces

2 small turnips, peeled and cut into uniform bite-size pieces

1 small red onion, diced

2 medium carrots, peeled and cut into uniform bite-size pieces

2 medium parsnips, peeled and cut into uniform bite-size pieces

3 ribs fennel, green and white part, chopped

6 medium brown Cremini mushrooms, sliced

1 teaspoon dried oregano

Freshly ground black pepper, to taste

1 cup Marsala wine

2 tablespoons low-fat sour cream

$1/2$ cup 2 percent milk, or more as needed

$1/4$ cup freshly grated low-fat Parmesan cheese

Feathery fennel tops for garnish

The process called for in this recipe, which infuses the vegetables with other flavors, then finishes them in a blast furnace, makes for a meal of maximum flavor and minimum fat. We adore it. We believe you will, too. Don't be daunted by the long list of ingredients. And if you can't find everything on the list, just double up on the items you can find.

PREPARATION TIME: 20 MINUTES

COOKING TIME: 50 MINUTES

MAKES 8 SERVINGS

May be made as much as half a day ahead, then reheated at the last minute by popping it back into the oven at 350° for about 10 to 15 minutes or until warmed through.

Preheat the oven to 500°. Heat the broth, water, and 1 teaspoon salt in a large pot over high heat. Place the potatoes in the boiling liquid and cook until tender, about 20 to 30 minutes.

Coat the inside of a 14-inch oval ovenproof gratin dish (preferably Le Creuset) with the olive oil and fill it with the prepared vegetables. Season the vegetables generously with oregano, salt, and pepper, then pour in the Marsala. Roast in the hot oven until tender, about 40 minutes, stirring from time to time.

Once the potatoes are tender, remove them to a bowl and mash with a potato masher, along with the sour cream, milk, and Parmesan cheese. Taste and adjust seasonings with salt and pepper. Add more milk, if necessary, to maintain a soft mashed texture.

After the roasted vegetables are tender, remove the gratin dish to the stovetop. Spoon heaping tablespoonfuls of the mashed potatoes around the edge of the dish, leaving the roasted roots showing in the middle. Return to the oven and brown the potatoes slightly, about 10 more minutes.

There are several secrets to the success of this dish. First is the method. Cut the vegetables into uniform small pieces, so they'll cook evenly. We find that the quickest way to do this is to cut the roundish ones in half, then line the two halves up, flat side down, end to end, and, using a chef's knife, make long cuts through both halves, about half an inch wide. Then cut them crosswise in uniform pieces. This is a chef's method and a proven fast technique.

Roasting vegetables in a very hot oven guarantees that they will caramelize and develop the best flavor possible. Adding Marsala to the roasting dish plus a generous seasoning of oregano, salt, and pepper, further improves the flavor.

Finally, cooking potatoes in part chicken broth instead of all water enriches the flavor so you don't have to use any butter at all to get a rich-tasting finished product.

And for roasting, we turn once again to our all-time favorite French ovenware, the 14-inch Le Creuset gratin dish. For maximum flavor, this is the one. It heats evenly, maintaining a radiant heat that promotes caramelization. And it's easy to clean. Soak the dish after dinner, then a quick wipe with a plastic scrubber will clean it right up.

Apple and Pear Tarte Tatin

Pastry:

1 cup all-purpose flour or pastry flour (see page 357), plus additional for rolling the dough

½ teaspoon salt

½ cup (1 stick) chilled unsalted butter, cut into bits

1 tablespoon egg yolk

1½ tablespoons cold water

Filling:

3 large ripe apples, peeled, cored, and cut into thick wedges

3 large nearly ripe pears, peeled, cored, and cut into thick wedges

Juice and zest of ½ lemon (about 2 tablespoons juice)

¾ cup sugar

¼ cup (½ stick) unsalted butter

Vanilla ice cream, for serving

Edible flowers, for garnish

Instead of buying all-purpose flour, get in the habit of buying pastry or cake flour for pastries and bread flour for bread. Long a baker's secret, it does make a difference. We like White Lily flour. This soft white winter wheat flour from Tennessee is well named and makes the tenderest pastry on the planet. Call 1-800-264-5459 to order your own private stash. Order at least 10 pounds at a time and store it in a cool, dark place.

Master the upside-down tart, as the Tatin sisters did, and your reputation as Dessert Queen will be made. Choose the best fruits, caramelize them in a cast-iron-clad skillet, top with pastry, and bake. Flip it over, and you'll have a dessert that your guests won't soon forget. If you're in a total time crunch, use premade pastry from the refrigerated section at the market and zoom straight to the directions for cooking the fruit. Don't worry too much about how the fruit looks as you cut it. Once the tart is made, baked, flipped, and served, the aroma of apples and pears, along with the rich homemade caramel from the sugar and butter, will be so overwhelming, no one will notice if your knife technique is less than perfect.

Preparation time:	20 minutes
Chilling time:	10 to 15 minutes
Baking time:	25 to 30 minutes
Cooling time:	10 minutes on a rack before serving
Makes 8 servings	

Best if made and eaten within 2 hours.

Position the rack in the bottom third of the oven. Preheat the oven to 375°.

To make the pastry, combine the flour and salt in a food processor fitted with the plastic blade. Add the butter and pulse five or six times until the butter is incorporated and the mixture resembles coarse meal. Combine the egg yolk and water and, with the motor running, pour the mixture through the feed tube and process just until the dough begins to mass around the blade, no more than 10 seconds. Remove the dough from the bowl and press it into an 8-inch disk. Cover with plastic wrap and chill in the refrigerator for 10 to 15 minutes while you start the fruit.

If you own one of those apple cutters that both cores and cuts the fruit into wedges, haul it out. Now's the time to use it. Place peeled and wedge-cut fruit into a bowl as you cut and toss it with the lemon juice and zest to prevent browning.

In a dry 10-inch cast-iron-clad ovenproof skillet, melt the sugar over medium-low heat, stirring, until it turns a pale straw color. Immediately remove the skillet from the heat and arrange the fruit artfully around the pan, making concentric circles, alternating pears and apples, going round and round until you've used all the fruit. Add any juice remaining in the bowl to the skillet. Cut the butter into bits and scatter it over the fruit. Place the pan over medium heat and cook, without stirring, until the sugar turns a deep caramel color and the fruit juices have nearly evaporated, 15 or 20 minutes.

Meanwhile, using a heavy rolling pin coated with flour, roll the dough out onto a lightly floured surface to a $1/4$-inch-thick circle, at least 11 to 12 inches across. Carefully lift the pastry over the rolling pin and transfer it to the fruit in the skillet. Roll the dough over the top of the skillet. Trim the dough with a sharp knife to overhang the skillet by half an inch all around. Tuck the overhanging dough in and around the fruit.

Bake until the crust is golden brown, about 25 to 30 minutes. Cool on a rack for 10 minutes, then run a knife around the edge of the tart to loosen the edges. Now, using your best 12-inch or bigger flat plate, place it on top of the skillet and, carefully and quickly, flip the tart over onto the plate. Let it stand a few minutes, then use a rubber spatula to loosen any remaining fruit or sauce and smooth the top. Serve warm, cut in wedges, with a scoop of vanilla ice cream.

Apples and Pears for Tarting

Mouthwatering, puckery flavor and a slice that will maintain its shape when cooked are the characteristics you're looking for when choosing apples and pears for pies and tarts. Now that both fruits are available almost year round, it makes sense to choose the best variety for your purpose. Leave the common Delicious apple—both Red and Golden—as well as the Bartlett pear for eating out of hand. They turn to mush in a pie.

In the East, look for shiny red York apples, or tangy Jonathans, Cortland, or the rarer Northern Spies. Also good and readily available are crisp McIntoshes, Macouns, or Empires. Devoe pears are lovely. In the West, look for Gravenstein apples from California, Granny Smiths, or pippins from San Diego to Seattle. Other good apple choices for tarts include Greening, Stayman Winesap, Akane, and Idared.

The Cadillac of cooking pears are the Boscs with their long slender necks, but barely ripe Comice, Anjous, or Packham pears work admirably.

The Basic 101 Pantry

Do you need an expensive "set" of good pots and pans to begin entertaining? Not at all. Let's cut to the chase here. All you need are a few good pots and some time-saving tools. In fact, four of the six pans we think you cannot live without are never included in the sets. Those four are a 10-inch black skillet, a 12-inch nonreactive skillet with a lid (vital for pasta sauces), a 6-quart Dutch oven, and a 6-quart stockpot. The only useful part of a set is the 3- or 4-quart saucepan, which you can buy separately. So we think the sets are useless. Save your money and buy really good versions of the above listed pots and pans. And remember they are tools, they do not have to match. We get Le Creuset on sale and have every color. We swear by them. The weight of the pot just helps you tone your biceps so you can look better in the sleeveless black dress for your formal dinner party. Who needs to pump iron when you have Le Creuset!

The same goes for knives. The sets are useless. Save your money and buy a really good 10-inch or 12-inch chef's knife, a paring knife, a serrated bread knife, and some kitchen shears. Also more important than a set is a carbon steel to sharpen your knives. You should really sharpen them at the very least twice a month, preferably each time you cook. If you must get fancy, buy a fillet knife and a cleaver. Don't bother with the set!

A trip to the local Goodwill or Salvation Army will turn up a number of these items. Think of all the ungrateful relatives who turned in Grandmama's best kitchen tools. You can pick them up for a pittance and give them another life. Grandmama will smile on you from heaven. We also have to say, for many hand tools, you can't beat Williams-Sonoma. The potato and apple corers are always sharper, tougher, and built to last. You *will* pay more, but the item will work better and last longer than the supermarket model, which is, surprisingly, not that much less expensive. And we can't say enough good things about restaurant supply stores for pots, knives, glassware, serving pieces, and other tools. These stores offer reasonably priced items that are designed to take a beating and will last forever. And, professional quality utensils produce better results.

If you live in an apartment and have limited storage space, some tools can double up. A large Le Creuset Dutch oven can be used as a soup pot on top of the stove, an open roasting pan, or a covered casserole dish in the oven.

We are the first to admit we love our kitchen toys. Good heavy pots and pans, sharp knives, labor-saving whisks, and a zester can enhance the cooking chores as much as a great pair of inline skates or skis can make your other sports more fun. But you don't need a pasta machine, juicer, deep frying machine, and sandwich grill. They take up room, collect dust (which is also greasy in the kitchen), and are a waste of money.

Here's Our 101 "Must Have" List

- *1 or 2 (10-inch) black skillets—Good for in the oven or on the stovetop, an absolute must!*

- *1 (12-inch) nonreactive skillet with a lid—A must for most pasta sauces—we'll love our Le Creuset till death do us part.*

- *1 (6-quart) Dutch oven/soup pot with lid. Ditto on Le Creuset!*

- *1 large roasting pan with rack, the heavier the better the finish on the roast.*

- *1 (3- to 4-quart) medium saucepan with lid. Again we take the vows with Le Creuset.*

- *2 each (8- and 9-inch) aluminum cake and pie pans.*

- *2 large heavy aluminum baking (cookie) sheets with sides.*

- *1 (13 × 9 × 2-inch) utility pan (Pyrex lasts longer than most marriages).*

- *2 (8^1/$_2$ × 2^1/$_2$-inch) Pyrex or aluminum loaf pans.*

- *1 each (2-cup and 4-cup) glass measures for liquids.*

- *^{1}/$_4$ to 1 cup metal or plastic nesting measuring cups.*

- *3 nested glass mixing bowls, small, medium, and large.*

- *1 or 2 (12 × 2-inch) oval gratin or (1^1/$_2$-quart) baking dishes (Le Creuset). Great for roasting garlic, potatoes, onions, and for most gratin and casserole dishes.*

- *2 thermos coffee carafes with a cone drip* (one for decaf and one for regular).*

- *1 salad spinner.*

- *1 (12-cup) Bundt pan (nonstick if possible).*

* We are always complimented on our coffee. The secret is freshly ground beans, and boiling hot water poured through a cone drip into a carafe. The home coffee machines just never get the water hot enough— you know, product liability and all. Boil your own water for the best results!

Must-Have Tools

- best-quality chef's knife
- good paring knife
- serrated bread knife
- kitchen shears
- pepper mill
- lemon zester
- lemon reamer and/or juicer with strainer
- potato peeler and corer
- rubber spatula
- wooden spoons
- cutting board
- rolling pin (can use a straight-sided glass in a pinch)
- graters
- balloon whisk(s) from large to small

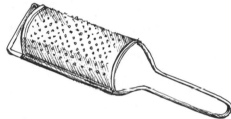

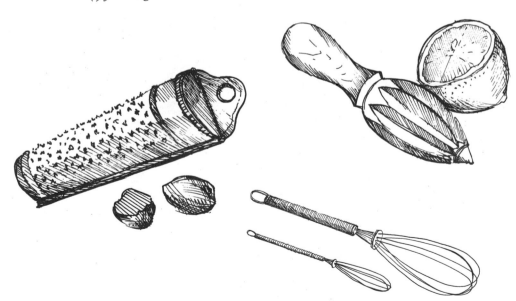

Nice to Have

- electric rice cooker

- blender or KitchenAid mixer

- coffee grinder

- waffle iron

- microwave oven

- food processor

- bread machine

- indoor or outdoor grill

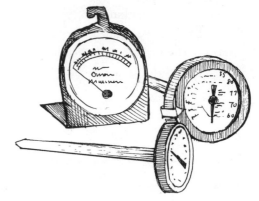

- 12-inch pizza pan or tart pan with removable bottom

- cupcake pans and paper liners (regular and/or large Texas size)

- plastic ketchup/mustard dispenser (to add ruffles and flourishes to serving platters)

- 12-inch square piece of marble from the tile store to serve desserts or cheeses

- instant-read meat thermometer

Time-Savers

- Ziploc bags (can be used instead of bowls for mixing and marinating)

- parchment paper (to bake on)

- a second pepper grinder (for other spices)

- bamboo skewers

- Pam or other cooking spray

Entertaining Items That Are Really Useful

In line with our anti-set mantra, you do not need a matched set of dishes to entertain in style. In our houses nothing matches but everything goes. We pick up platters, bowls, and dishes from tag sales, antique stores, and the Goodwill. We prefer balloon-style wineglasses. They are good for all wines, dessert, and cold soups. They also look great on the table. And if you or a guest drops one, it can be replaced for $10, not $60! We all feel better about that.

- *24 balloon glass wine goblets*

- *a variety of cake stands*

- *collection of baskets*

- *several large platters*

- *several large serving bowls*

- *lots of candleholders and no drip candles (IKEA and Pottery Barn are great sources)*

- *several vases, large and small*

- *a good ice chest*

- *picnic set*

- *chafing dish*

- *ramekins*

- *a variety of table linens*

- *fun, brightly colored paper cocktail napkins*

Well-Stocked Pantry Items You Can't Live Without

One of the most important aspects of being able to entertain on the fly is to minimize shopping time. We suggest having these basics on hand at all times. Then, just before having friends over, you only have to pick up the fresh ingredients:

- red wine, balsamic, rice wine, white wine, sherry wine, and tarragon vinegar (don't buy plain white vinegar unless you're planning to clean the floors)
- extra virgin olive oil
- flavored oils
- seeded mustard
- roasted red peppers
- saffron threads
- herbes de Provence
- all basic spices
- pastry and bread flour
- sugar
- cornmeal
- cornstarch
- dry flavored and plain bread crumbs
- frozen spinach
- frozen peas
- frozen pearl onions
- frozen blackberries or raspberries
- good commercial red spaghetti sauce (we prefer Barilla)
- yellow cake mix

- sun-dried tomatoes

- dried cranberries

- raisins

- a piece of Parmesan cheese (to grate as needed)

- tube of tomato paste

- several types of dried pasta

- anchovies

- capers

- cans and jars of olives

- canned chickpeas

- canned white beans

- canned black beans

- canned chicken and beef broth

- canned tomatoes

- bacon, kept frozen

Index